Contents

Part Three—Punch and Counter-punch

Part Four—Order of the Day: Survival

A TREASURY OF
CIVIL WAR
TALES

Also by Webb Garrison

Atlanta and the War
Civil War Curiosities
Civil War Trivia and Fact Book
Great Stories of the American Revolution
More Civil War Curiosities
A Treasury of White House Tales
The Amazing Civil War
Creative Minds in Desperate Times
Friendly Fire in the Civil War
Lincoln's Little War
The Lincoln No One Knows
A Treasury of *Titanic* Tales
White House Ladies
Amazing Women of the Civil War

A TREASURY
—OF—
Civil War Tales

Webb Garrison

RUTLEDGE HILL PRESS®
Nashville, Tennessee
A Thomas Nelson Company

Published by Rutledge Hill Press, a Thomas Nelson Company, P.O. Box 141000, Nashville, Tennessee 37214.

Typography by Compass Communications, Inc., Nashville, Tennessee. Design by Harriette Bateman.

Library of Congress Cataloging-in-Publication Data

Garrison, Webb B.
    A treasury of Civil War tales.
    Includes index.
    ISBN 1-55853-716-3
    1. United States—History—Civil War, 1861–1865—Anecdotes. I. Title. II. Title: Civil War tales.
E655.G37   1988   973.7   88–23826

Printed in the United States of America

3 4 5 6 7 8 9 — 03 02

Part Five—The Devil Take the Hindermost

Part Six—Every Fire Eventually Burns Itself Out

Part Seven—Bittersweet Aftermath

Every Man, Woman, and Child Had a Tale to Tell

Pushed by winds of hurricane force, the engulfing conflagration that was the Civil War left no part of the nation unscorched. No soldiers or civilians, no men or women, no blacks or whites or Indians were wholly uninvolved spectators. All were participants at some level, in one way or another.

Hence there are tales galore about every major participant and each well-publicized event, plus a myriad of vivid stories that revolve about persons who played bit roles in the all-consuming drama.

From this immense body of tales, some of the most compelling and revealing have been woven together to form a comprehensive account. Each story is self-contained, yet all are interconnected in a series that proceeds from threats of a coming storm, through four unforgettable years of war April 1861 to April 1865, to the bittersweet aftermath.

Because stories are less formal and more fluid than are straight narrative accounts, they are better able to convey moods and emotions. Most of the tales included here rest upon widely accessible documents, but oral traditions have not been neglected. Letters, dispatches, telegrams, proclamations, and diaries are quoted—with much extraneous matter omitted. For ease in reading, punctuation has been added to telegrams, and other quoted material has been divided into paragraphs. Some of the dialogue that appears in this volume comes from written sources of the Civil War era; much represents what persons involved might reasonably have been expected to have said under the circumstances.

Illustrations are credited to newspapers, magazines, and books in which they first appeared; to artists and photographers who produced them; and to institutions holding originals. Because it is cited frequently, *Frank Leslie's Illustrated Newspaper* is abbreviated to *Leslie's Weekly* to distinguish it from his magazine and other periodicals.

In spite of the decades that have passed, documentation of stories is not complete and, indeed, may never be completed. Especially among northern scholars, the Dahlgren papers (chapter 37) were long regarded with skepticism, if not openly derided as having been fabricated by southern interests. Virgil C. Jones effectively laid that controversy to rest by means of elaborate tests made in the laboratory of the National Archives; Ulric Dahlgren really did sign those damning documents. But precisely what happened at Fort Pillow, and why (chapter 38), remains an unsolved mystery, placing it in the same category as the incident at Ebenezer Creek (chapter 45).

This volume does not begin to exhaust the rich lode of Civil War material available. Hopefully, though, it may provide some insight into the fashion in which ordinary persons—not simply soldiers dashing about on large horses—were caught up in the conflict and contributed, perhaps by a quirk of fate, to its ultimate outcome.

Part One

Thunder, Lightning, and Hail

Harriet Beecher Stowe. [LIBRARY OF CONGRESS]

CHAPTER

1

A Little Woman's Book
Made a Great War

"Speak!" demanded Simon Legree, beating Tom over the head. "What do you know?"
"I know, Mas'r; but I can't tell anything. I can die!"

Tom did die under the blows of his master, and as he breathed his last, tears welled from eyes of readers of *Uncle Tom's Cabin* and of those who viewed one of the many stage versions.

Later, Abraham Lincoln, who never said he had read Harriet Beecher Stowe's book or watched its performance by a traveling "Tom company," invited Mrs. Stowe to the White House. He is said to have greeted her, "So *you* are the little woman who wrote the book that made this great war!"

At age forty Harriet could have passed for a student at her father's seminary in Maine. Married for fifteen years to one of the school's teachers, she was a rarity in the early 1850s, a woman activist.

Partly because money was scarce, she took one of the few career paths open to a respectable woman. By writing elegant sketches and loosely plotted tales, she hoped to win a degree of financial independence. The health of her husband, Calvin Stowe, was so precarious that she could be forced to become the family breadwinner any day.

An early collection of short pieces, *The Mayflower*, didn't earn enough to pay medical bills for three months. Daughter of clergyman-educator-writer Lyman Beecher, she wasn't stopped by literary failure. From the campus of Bowdoin College she surveyed the American scene and came up with a great idea. When her novel was completed, she insisted that it wasn't really hers. "The Lord himself wrote it," she said. "I was but an instrument of His hand."

Whether from God Almighty, Harriet Beecher Stowe, or both, *Uncle Tom's Cabin* was written largely as an emotional response to the Fugitive Slave Law of 1850.

Senator James M. Mason of Virginia, proud author of the law, saw the gains the abolitionists were making in working for control of the House of Representatives and the U.S. Senate. Seeing that the balance of power was moving away from them, Mason and his fellow slaveholders fashioned this hated law that gave an owner of a fugitive slave the right to seek runaway human property in any state or territory. If unable to pursue a fugitive himself, the owner could use a hired agent. No warrant was necessary in order to seize a slave even in Boston, cradle of American independence.

Like others, Harriet Beecher Stowe was powerless to prevent implementation of the Fugitive Slave Law, but at least she could protest it. However, her firsthand knowledge was skimpy and she had never lived in the South.

Maybe that was just as well, she realized. Instead of depending upon interviews, she could—with the help of the Almighty—allow her imagination free rein. Even if her novel was never published, it would give her great personal satisfaction to write it.

Editors of the antislavery *National Era* magazine in Washingon, D.C., expressed interest. If she cared to try her story in serial form it would bring her a readership, even if only minimal income.

Launched in 1851 and eventually completed in the magazine, Harriet's story got little attention at first. Then the John P. Jewett Company of Boston decided to bring it out as a two-volume novel, *Uncle Tom's Cabin, or Life Among the Lowly.*

Shifts in public sentiment, linked with fast-increasing tension over the slavery issue, produced a publishing miracle. A so-so serial became a sensationally popular book. Within five years it was in 500,000 American homes.

Advertising flier for Uncle Tom's Cabin. [NEW YORK HISTORICAL SOCIETY]

Few people would claim that *Uncle Tom's Cabin* was great literature. It had no well-structured plot and was entirely too long. Much of the "lowly life" it claimed to depict was completely inaccurate.

But the novel was rich in pathos. Dramatic incidents—however unbelievable—abounded. Characters were depicted so vividly that their names became household words: Uncle Tom, Simon Legree, Topsy.

Most of all, the book had a message. People who plowed through its two volumes could no longer be neutral about slavery, the plantation system, or the rights of the oppressed. More than any other single factor, a housewife's novel transformed the long-simmering North/ South feud from a political contest into a great moral battle.

Today it makes little difference that few plantation owners were so evil as Simon Legree or that beneath stolid faces few blacks were so ready to take whatever the white man gave as was Uncle Tom.

Impact of the novel was greatly accentuated by dozens, and then by scores, of traveling theatrical companies who performed before enthralled audiences. Many such companies used genuine bloodhounds on stage; some settled for whatever vicious-looking dogs that were available.

Translated into a dozen languages, the book became an international sensation. It also exercised a subtle, but powerful, influence on leaders of nations considered likely to aid the South, who could not ignore public opinion. Hence the book that Lincoln credited with having started the war was also influential in preventing the seceded states from receiving desperately needed, eagerly expected help from Europe.

Theatrical poster showed Little Eva fleeing from "bloodhounds." [MASSACHUSETTS HISTORICAL SOCIETY]

CHAPTER
2

"The Little Giant" Set the Stage for "Bleeding Kansas"

"**H**onorable men of the North must come to terms with those of the South! Honorable men of the South must come to terms with those of the North!"

Diminutive Stephen Arnold Douglas, "the little giant" of nineteenth-century American politics, paused for emphasis. With a dramatic gesture he continued, "North and South can and must be joined in Kansas. So joined, their citizens will be neither Northerners nor Southerners. All will simply be red-blooded Americans!"

Vermont-born Douglas threatened and pleaded, challenged and cajoled for seventy-four minutes. Few present in the U.S. Senate chamber on that fateful day in January 1854 listened attentively. All knew how they would vote. Each was aware of Douglas's presidential ambitions, boosted mightily, he hoped, by his everlasting emphasis upon compromise.

Densely populated industrial states of the North—increasingly abolitionist in sentiment—dominated the House of Representatives. But since each state was entitled to two U.S. senators, regardless of population, the rival factions were nearly equally represented there. So long as that delicate balance could be preserved, it would be impossible for advocates of abolition or die-hard supporters of slavery to dominate the legislative process.

From the day on which he entered the Senate from his adopted state of Illinois, Douglas had frankly and openly advocated compromise at any cost. He had shuddered on the February 1850 day that saw Henry Clay of Kentucky warn fellow senators that "this Union is threatened with subversion."

In a long and tension-filled speech, Clay said that the Union faced destruction. Himself strongly opposed to the idea of secession, he saw it as inevitable unless warring factions made peace. Nothing in the

U.S. Constitution provided for an orderly secession by a dissatisfied member state, but nothing in that document prohibited secession.

Without compromise by all, Clay said, there would soon be at least three confederacies instead of the existing United States of America. There would be a confederacy of the North and abolition; there would be a confederacy of the southern Atlantic slave-holding states; and there would be a confederacy of the valley of the Mississippi.

In the spirit of Clay's oration, Stephen A. Douglas strongly supported the Compromise of 1850. Actually a complicated series of separate acts, the famous "compromise" rested solidly upon Douglas's platform of "popular sovereignty" for U.S. territories. Under this doctrine, citizens of territories could come from the North and from the South, and they could bring their strongly held views with them. Once a territory became a state, however, voters would decide whether or not slavery would be lawful within its boundaries.

Northerners assailed the 1850 package of acts as entirely too vague and clearly shaped to foster the expansion of slavery. Southerners denounced it as the work of abolitionists and demanded extension of the Missouri Compromise line to the Pacific Ocean, thereby opening the Southwest and much of California to slavery. Small wonder that by 1854 it was far harder to reach compromise than in 1850.

It was Douglas of Illinois who introduced into the Senate a bill calling for the erection of two vast new territories to be known as Kansas and Nebraska. He shaped the passage which stressed that slavery should neither be legislated into any territory nor excluded therefrom by law.

Felix Darley's interpretation of border ruffians invading Kansas. [YALE UNIVERSITY ART GALLERY]

Topeka, seat of free government in Kansas, was protected by a gun crew. [KANSAS HISTORICAL SOCIETY]

"Leave the people [of the territories] perfectly free to form and regulate their domestic institutions in their own way," Douglas insisted. Popular sovereignty should be applied to the issue of slavery in the new territories.

After long and bitter debate, the Kansas–Nebraska Act was passed and became law when signed by President Franklin Pierce. In theory, it opened both Kansas and Nebraska to slaveholders. In practice, the struggle was confined to Kansas; Nebraska was too cold to support a slave-based agricultural system.

As soon as the territory of Kansas was officially established, it became the new focal point of North/South tensions. At Weston, Missouri, a citizens' meeting brought forth a resolution designed "to remove any and all emigrants coming to Kansas under auspices of the Northern emigrant aid societies." Most slave-holding states selected Kansas counties as targets, then tried to persuade and sometimes to bribe citizens to go there as emigrants. Pulled by horses, mules, and oxen, wagon trains from Virginia and Mississippi, South Carolina and Georgia snaked their way toward Kansas in a bid to help win it for slavery.

Abolitionists responded by doubling, and then redoubling, their financial aid to Kansas-bound emigrants from the North. The Reverend Henry Ward Beecher helped to recruit a party of Connecticut citizens as Kansas emigrants; and in a grand parting gesture, he presented them with twenty-five Bibles and twenty-five Sharp's rifles.

In practice, Stephen Douglas's "compromise act" simply caused Kansas to become the site of civil war long before the nation as a whole was plunged into conflict. Pro-slavery forces attacked Lawrence in May 1856; two days later, abolitionists led by John Brown and his sons killed five settlers at Pottawatomie because Brown believed them to be proslavery. No one then anticipated Brown's later raid at Harpers Ferry, Virginia.

Although the antislavery capital was protected by artillery, President Pierce was forced to send federal troops to the territory. Their dual mission was to calm the civil strife and to oversee elections.

Four separate constitutions for the proposed State of Kansas were rejected by citizens. Partly due to the influence of federal troops, a fifth draft—aimed at making the territory into a free or antislavery state—was adopted. By then, "bleeding Kansas" had seen over fifty men die in border warfare over the slavery issue.

Was Stephen A. Douglas persuaded to change his stance? Not at all. He continued to insist that popular sovereignty, and only popular sovereignty, could guarantee peace and stability in each new territory.

Denounced in the North and burned in effigy in the South at least once, Douglas was courted by many aspiring politicians, North and South. So great was his personal influence that (though they are given a transposed title today) his oratorical contests with Abraham Lincoln were popularly known as the *Douglas–Lincoln Debates* in 1858.

These debates became a springboard to national prominence on the part of Abraham Lincoln. They also became the foundation from which Douglas launched his 1860 bid for the presidency on a platform of compromise and popular sovereignty.

John Brown, soon after his Kansas raid. [KANSAS HISTORICAL SOCIETY]

3

Dred Scott Was Hammered Between North and South

"**Y**essir, I sure did want to be free. Did all I could, I did. Even asked my missus to let me buy my freedom. She just laughed at me." Dred Scott coughed convulsively, swallowed hard, and continued, "It would have made a heap of difference then. Now it don't seem to matter much.

"Not to me, anyway. Might make things a little better for Harriet, though."

There are no formal documents concerning the single brief interview held in 1854 between attorney Montgomery Blair and his new client, a slave of about sixty years who was sure he would soon die of tuberculosis. Oral tradition, preserved in East St. Louis, Illinois, insists that Dred Scott had only the foggiest idea of what was meant by taking his case to the U.S. Supreme Court. That same tradition stresses, though, that Scott had one bright, burning hope. While freedom would mean little or nothing to him or his wife, it would make a difference for their two daughters.

"Yessir, I could die a happy man," he told the Kentucky-born attorney, "if'n only I could know that 'Liza and Lizzie would go free."

Montgomery Blair, a long-time resident of St. Louis, had known of the Dred Scott case for years. Ardent abolitionist Henry Blow, a son of one of Scott's early owners, had dreamed of a sweeping legal victory that would set precedents and make lasting changes. Blow had hired attorneys to represent Scott in lower courts; now he was willing to pay court costs in order to get a definitive verdict from the U.S. Supreme Court.

Blair agreed to represent Scott without fee. He already had substantial friends in Washington, and a Supreme Court victory on a key national issue would almost guarantee him a top appointment in the next administration.

"Besides," Blair told his friends and family who questioned his judgment in providing free service, "it is practically an open-and-shut case. Henry Blow has helped me to assemble army records which show that Dred was a resident in free territory for maybe five years. That is enough to convince the high court to set him free."

Earlier, Blow had provided a capsule account of the illiterate slave's life. "Dred was born somewhere in Virginia, a few years before or after the turn of the century," Blow said. "He belonged to my father and went to Alabama with him. After nearly twenty years, they came here to St. Louis.

"At my father's death in 1832, Dred was sold to Dr. John Emerson, an army surgeon. I never have been able to find out how he became tagged with the name Scott. Most slaves with surnames take them from their masters, and Dred was the property of my father the minute he was born.

"Anyway, he had become Dred Scott by the time he was taken to Illinois by Dr. Emerson. Later, the doctor spent quite a bit of time in Wisconsin. Old army records prove that Emerson and his slave had lived in a free state and in a free territory for quite a while. It should be easy to get him freed," Henry Blow said.

Blair agreed.

"Precedents are clear on this point, if no other," he said. "I remember that when George Washington lived in Philadelphia as president, he brought some of his slaves with him. Because Philadelphia was free territory, Washington was afraid he might lose his favorite slave if he kept him there. So after he'd been in Philadelphia for about five and one-half months, he sent the slave back to Mount Vernon for two or three weeks to prevent him from claiming his freedom. That

Dred Scott. [Missouri Historical Society]

cycle—Philadelphia to Mount Vernon and then back to Philadelphia—continued as long as Washington lived in that city."

Blair had read all of the arguments and rulings in the legal contests that had revolved around Dred Scott's freedom since Henry Blow first took action on his behalf in 1846. Missouri law had refused to consider residence in free territory in its decision, and the refusal of the U.S. Circuit Court in St. Louis to overrule had seemed to end the matter, until Blair decided to appeal to the U.S. Supreme Court eight years later.

Despite George Washington's slave and dozens of other precedents, the arguments before the high court would have to be carefully prepared. High-powered advocates of the extension of slavery had almost unlimited funds, and they had retained two noted attorneys for John Sanford, the recent owner of Dred Scott. One was Henry S. Geyer, newly elected U.S. senator from Missouri; the other, Reverdy Johnson, was former U.S. attorney general and former senator from Maryland.

Partisan leaders—North and South—believed the Dred Scott case could be used to strengthen their own positions. Both sides were sure of a victory. Proslavery forces counted on the southern majority sitting on the high court. Antislavery forces were confident that precedent, the U.S. Constitution, and the law were on their side.

Arguments began in Washington on February 11, 1856, and continued for four days. Justices conferred twice, reaching no decision, then adjourned for the month of March.

When Horace Greeley's New York *Tribune* charged that the delay was part of a southern plot, the Dred Scott case quickly became national news. Greeley was positive that the plot involved the upcoming presidential election in which the infant Republican party was emerging as a power.

Outspoken John McLean of Ohio, the only clear-cut abolitionist on the Supreme Court, hoped to be the Republican nominee. Should he be a lone dissenter in what was fast becoming the nation's most celebrated legal case concerning a slave, McLean and his Republicans would have a fighting chance to win the White House. Thus it was in the interest of Democrats, and proslavery forces in general, to stall, Greeley charged. Anything that could give McLean a big national forum would boost his chances for the presidency.

No one knows positively whether Greeley was right in his beliefs, but it is clear that Supreme Court justices were subjected to intense pressure. When they met in May, they voted, five to four, not to decide the case until after hearing new arguments in December, following the election. By the time those new arguments were presented, Democrat James Buchanan was the president-elect.

Buchanan's rambling inaugural address touched upon the divisive issue of slavery in the territories. Claiming it was a legal, not a political, issue, he declared that the pending case would settle the issue once and for all.

In Buchanan's veiled allusions to the Dred Scott case, Republicans saw official confirmation of their worst fears. Already it had been rumored that the southern majority on the high court would strike down the territorial limitations of slavery embodied in the Missouri Compromise, thus opening the expanding West to the "most abominable of institutions."

Two days after Buchanan's address, Chief Justice Roger B. Taney issued the majority decision. An Andrew Jackson appointee, the eighty-year-old Taney, who had held the nation's top judicial post for twenty-one years, issued a ruling that was even more sweeping than abolitionists had feared.

Dred Scott could not be freed, Taney said, because there was no basis for the suit brought by others on his behalf. Scott was a slave—property, pure and simple—who could not be a citizen of any state. Hence, he could not sue anyone. The fate of the gray-haired slave who was dying of tuberculosis was settled, once and for all.

Then Taney added a series of additional rulings that, while not directly related to the case before the court, held that the act by which Congress had forbade slavery in northern territories was unconstitutional. A slave is property, the argument ran. Under the U.S. Constitution, no right is more clearly protected than a man's right to his property. Congress could not deprive any man of that right; therefore, it was legal to take slaves anywhere in the expanding nation.

Clearly, anti- and proslavery forces had tried to use Dred Scott for their own purposes. In the end their efforts had driven the warring factions farther apart, rather than reconciling them.

Nationally, the Democrats were moving toward an open split. Senator Jefferson Davis publicly hoped that the Dred Scott decision would help persuade Southerners to dump "the namby-pamby advocate of futile compromise," Stephen A. Douglas. The Republicans, some of whom were dedicated to the eradication of slavery, listened with new understanding to a lanky lawyer from Illinois and swore that despite his defeat in a bid for the U.S. Senate, Abraham Lincoln would be heard from again.

Barely two years after having been a pawn in a national power struggle, still-enslaved Dred Scott died of tuberculosis at his St. Louis home. Henry Blow paid the bills for his simple funeral.

By then, Scott's wife and children had been free Americans for twelve months, not through judicial process but as a result of private manumission.

4

James H. Hammond Called upon Americans to Acknowledge Cotton as King

Unwritten rules of the U.S. Senate required a newly elected member of the body to keep silent, no matter how strongly he might wish to speak.

That is why friends of freshman Senator James H. Hammond of South Carolina nudged one another and shook their heads in despair. Hammond had somehow managed to gain the attention of the presiding officer. Taking a nod to mean assent, he strode toward the podium "as though he were behind a pair of fine hunting dogs in a forest filled with 'coons."

Hastily reciting the virtues of cotton and of the region that produced it, the ex-governor of South Carolina turned to his principal theme. Far away in Newberry, South Carolina, he said, he had heard talk that disturbed him. Apparently some Americans—perhaps including at least one U.S. senator—wanted sectional strife.

That would be suicidal to the nation, he warned. It would cut the great cotton-producing belt away from the industrial northeast in which much of the cotton was made into finished goods.

"Would any sane nation make war on cotton?" he demanded. Then he answered his own rhetorical question.

"Without firing a gun, without drawing a sword, when anyone, anywhere makes war on the South we can bring the whole world to our feet. If no cotton were furnished for three years, old England would topple headlong and carry the whole civilized world with her.

"No, sir, you dare not make war on cotton. Cotton is king!"

Speaking to fellow senators on March 4, 1858, the freshman senator became noted as the man who had put into the *Congressional Record* the declaration that "Cotton is king!"

Hammond's idea was not new.

Writing in the *National Intelligencer* in 1854 and addressing mostly northern readers, R. E. Scott gave an emotion-packed plea for national unity in order to preserve the cotton trade. "Deprive Great Britain of the fruits of her commerce in our great staple, and she would be almost stricken from the list of independent states," Scott insisted. "Without our staple, Britain could not clothe and give employment to her thronging masses, nor long stagger under the impressive weight of her accumulating debt."

Scott then turned to his second major theme. "Deprive the great cities of Boston, New York, and Philadelphia of the fruits of the South, and their huge proportions would fall to decay. Scenes of wretchedness more absolute than words would depict and mark their ruin."

There was no need to publish such sentiments in the South. Most people in the cotton kingdom, literate as well as illiterate, already held the same general opinions.

Much evidence supported the doctrine that cotton really was king of the American marketplace. New York financial expert T. M. Kett compiled data leading to an explosive volume, *Southern Wealth and Northern Profits*. The United States' exports come almost entirely from the South, he reported. "Unmanufactured cotton" plus leaf tobacco and wheat were the only commodities about which export statistics were available. Not until 1881 would analysts add a column to report annual shipment abroad of manufactured goods—"engines, parts, etc."

No doubt about it, cotton did dominate the nation's external flow of money-producing commodities. In 1860 Great Britain and Europe bought $191 million worth of southern cotton. Tobacco, the closest rival, accounted for $16 million and exported wheat brought only $4 million.

Savannah's booming cotton exchange was challenging London's for recognition as the world's largest. Warehouses and docks at Savannah, Charleston, New Orleans, and many smaller ports bulged with 400-pound bales headed overseas.

Relatively few openly admitted that King Cotton remained on the throne only by virtue of slavery, but everyone knew it. There were no machines with which to plant, cultivate, and harvest the crop, and producers couldn't afford to hire poor white folk to work in fields at the prevailing wage of eighty cents a day.

Dependent as they were upon slave labor, most Southerners remained confident to the point of exuberance. In the 1840s Senator Dixon Lewis of Alabama proclaimed, "Give us six cents a pound for cotton, and we will grow rich!"

By 1857, the year before Hammond spoke in the Senate, cotton was bringing sixteen cents per pound. No wonder that men such as Colonel Joseph Bond of Macon, Georgia, whose 1859 crop reached 2,100 bales, began to yearn openly for an excuse to cut ties with the North.

Political differences aside, Bond pointed out that northern vessels transported southern cotton at high rates. Northern banks lent money and handled international transactions for high profits. Northern manufactured goods flooded the South, hauled there by railroads operating under a rigged tariff system that discriminated against "the land of cotton."

According to James H. Hammond, Augustus Longstreet, Joseph Bond, and hosts of other influential southern spokesmen, when—not if—the South could cut loose and become independent, it would be a time for rejoicing like never before. Southern cotton would go abroad in southern ships; southern banks and import-export houses would flourish; and the money trickling down from the top would lead to a higher standard of living for all Southerners.

This line of reasoning—perfectly logical in many respects—ignored the incredibly high hidden cost of cotton production. One-crop farming often depleted land in six or eight years. When that happened, a plantation owner moved west, where there was plenty of land.

Most southern states made it a crime to teach a slave to read and write; slaves didn't need such skills. Only the most perceptive saw that this system also fostered low-level education for whites.

Shutting their eyes to the evils and hidden costs of the cotton-plus-slavery culture, many educated Southerners—perhaps a majority—believed that southern independence would foster prosperity such as no part of the youthful United States had ever seen. By adopting this point of view without quite realizing what they were doing, Southerners readied themselves to seek independence.

Southerners continued to seek independence in the halls of Congress and at the ballot box. But if these methods failed, they'd win it by whatever means necessary—even on the battlefield.

5

Both North and South Embraced the Song "Dixie"

Daniel Decatur Emmett had noticed that his employer, the man who had organized Bryant's Minstrels, was prone to snap judgments and unreasonable requirements. Thus he was not surprised when he demanded of Emmett, "Dan, I want a walkaround for Monday."

"No use to write a song unless it will catch on enough to be sung in the streets," the composer mused. "Rome wasn't built in a day. . . ."

Bryant interrupted abruptly. "That's exactly the reason I'm giving you two days, Dan. It's a new walkaround for Mechanic's Hall on Monday night, or else!"

According to the account given by Emmett himself, heavy rain kept him in the house the following day. His wife tried to help him find a starting point for a new composition, but he made no progress.

Emmett, son of an Ohio blacksmith, was a veteran performer and composer. Already popular for his "Old Dan Tucker," he had joined a circus company in 1835 at age twenty.

Seven years of circus life were enough, so Dan cut loose and organized the Virginia Minstrels, one of the earliest blackface performing groups. They played for weeks at the Bowery Amphitheatre in New York. Then they went on to Boston, and from that port sailed to England, playing to standing room only crowds. Only the big guarantees offered by Bryant's Minstrels persuaded the Ohio native to quit the road and go to work for someone else.

Emmett was never sure where he got the idea for "Dixie." Perhaps the talk of "King Cotton" may have had some influence, but he later recalled telling his wife that the bad weather made him wish he was in Dixie.

Questioned years later, he admitted that he "wasn't exactly sure" where he first heard of Dixie. According to him, he may have heard slaves singing about their happy life on "Dixie's land" without realizing they were referring to the New York plantation of Dutch slave owner Johann Dix.

"On the other hand," Emmett once said, "lots of our performers came from the South, especially New Orleans. Most of these fellows liked to carry around a lucky piece, one of those French-language ten-dollar bills marked in big block letters DIX. I saw lots of these, and always wished I had one myself."

Regardless of where he had picked up the word *Dixie*, the Buckeye composer later admitted, "Saying I wished I was in Dixie on a dreary day when it didn't seem a bit like spring sort of lighted a candle in my mind.

"Suddenly, I jumped up and sat down at the table to work. For the first time I had an idea for Monday night. In less than an hour, I had the first verse and chorus.

"After that, it was easy. When my wife got back home, I sang it to her and explained, 'It's all finished now, except the name. What should I call it?'"

Mrs. Emmett didn't hesitate. "Why, call it 'I Wish I Was in Dixie Land,'" she suggested. And so it was.

First sung on April 4, 1859, "Dixie" was an instant hit. Other minstrel shows quickly stole the melody, and portions of the words appeared in newspapers. In New Orleans, where "DIX" bank notes were still treasured as good luck pieces, P. P. Werlein issued a complete edition, pirated, of course. Then New York's Firth Pond & Company brought out an authorized edition of words plus music, which Emmett had sold for $500.

Even ardent abolitionists were often fond of blackface minstrel shows, so they became familiar with words and music almost as quickly as did slaveowners. Visitors to New York, Philadelphia, Washington, or Richmond, were likely to hear the tune sung and played.

Charleston, South Carolina, hosted the first southern performance in December 1860. Three months later it was used as march music for forty ladies dressed as Zouaves in a production of *Pocahontas* at New Orleans's Variety Theatre. Enthusiastic residents of the port city gave "Dixie" seven encores that night.

In a climate of growing hostility that threatened to lead to establishment of a rebellious southern nation, "Dixie" became what historian Vera B. Lawrence called "a curious musical sidebar." Both North and South sang the tune and wrote sets of highly partisan words.

Meanwhile, Daniel Decatur Emmett watched the phenomenon with astonishment. "I couldn't believe it when I first heard the version that came out of the Republican convention," he confessed.

Barely a year old, his spur-of-the-moment tune was given entirely

Title page for the "Lincoln Quick Step" ("Dixie"). [NEW YORK PUBLIC LIBRARY]

LINCOLN QUICK STEP.

DEDICATED TO
ABRAHAM LINCOLN
PRESIDENT OF THE UNITED STATES.

new meaning by a fresh set of words. At Chicago they selected:

> Lincoln, who will be elected,
>   Abraham, Abraham,
>   Abraham, Abraham,
> As Honest Abe the people know him,
> And all his actions go to show him
>   A true man, a true man,
>   A true man, a true man.

No one knows how greatly the melody written for blackface minstrels affected the election of 1860—if at all—but it clearly was regarded as important by Abraham Lincoln and his advisors. At the March 4, 1861, inauguration of the nation's sixteenth president, Dan Emmett's tune was set to the words of the "Lincoln Quick Step," especially written for the occasion.

Seceded Southerners had already snatched up the melody composed in New York City. Adapted for use in "The Confederacy March," sheet music was on sale to the public when Jefferson Davis was inaugurated President of the Confederate States of America on February 18, 1861.

Having been played at the inaugurations of two heads of state within a thirty-day period, "Dixie" became musical ammunition for abolitionists and slaveholders alike. Before the end of 1861, hosts of Northerners were using "Dixie for the Union" to urge the faint-hearted:

> On! ye patriots to the battle,
> Hear Fort Moultrie's cannon rattle;
> Then away, away, then away to the fight!

Another northern version began:

> Away down South in the land of traitors,
> Rebel hearts and Union haters,
> Look away, look away, look away to the traitor's land.

On the southern side, General Albert Pike—chiefly remembered for recruiting Cherokee Indians for Confederate military service—borrowed the same melody in order to sound his version of the alarm:

> Southrons! hear your country call you!
> Up lest worse than death befall you!
> To arms! To arms! To arms in Dixie!

Widely sung in much of the North until at least as late as the 1863 siege of Vicksburg, Mississippi, "Dixie" had by then already become the unofficial battle song of the Confederacy.

All adapted and pirated versions lost their vitality long ago. Daniel Decatur Emmett's 1859 original is almost universally familiar to Americans after nearly one hundred and fifty years. Strangely, the 1980s saw a rekindling of emotions about the song written for blackface minstrels. Once more a fighting song, it is used defiantly by many die-hard believers in causes that produced the Confederacy and is vigorously condemned by many who view the song born in New York City as a symbol of the Lost Cause.

Title page for the "Confederacy March" ("Dixie"). [NEW YORK PUBLIC LIBRARY]

Fiery Abolitionist John Brown Set Out to do God's Work

I *have been whipped. But I am sure that I can recover all the lost capital occasioned by the late disaster.*
I'll do it by only hanging a few minutes by the neck.

Written as the day of his execution approached, these lines were sent by John Brown to his wife, Mary Anne, who had borne thirteen of his twenty children.

Brown's brief letter does not sound like the ravings of a lunatic. Were his life story as clear as his death-row message, it would be easy to decide just who and what he was.

Born in Connecticut in 1800, young Brown drifted from place to place and job to job. He failed at nearly everything he tried, except at helping fugitive slaves escape to freedom in Canada.

When Kansas began to emerge as crucial in the North/South political conflict, prominent abolitionists of Massachusetts organized a Kansas State Committee. Some of the earliest money they raised was used to send John Brown and some of his sons to Kansas.

Already he was sure that he was acting under direct orders of Almighty God. "Politicians in Washington ain't gonna do anything about slavery," he told anyone who would listen. "That sorta leaves it up to me. Guess I'll have to recruit me an army for the Lord."

With barely a squad of his military force organized, Brown led his first raid. Followed by four sons and a few other males, he moved toward Potawatomie Creek on May 24, 1856. It was rumored that Southerners had settled there and planned to bring slaves with them. Near Dutch Henry's Crossing, Brown's band brutally murdered five men without bothering to ask any of them how they felt about slavery.

The outpouring of outrage drove the slavery-hater to Ohio and then to Canada. Still largely financed from Massachusetts, he received a fresh message "from the Lord."

It was the U.S. military arsenal that caused John Brown to choose Harper's Ferry, in present-day West Virginia, as his objective. [VIRGINIA STATE LIBRARY]

"He told me to set up a stronghold in the southern mountains," Brown announced to his followers. "Slaves can come there and be safe. It will be our army base, from which we will launch our campaigns."

In Chatham, Ontario, Brown presided over a May 1858 convention he himself had called. Fifty or so "delegates," thirty-five of whom were black, adopted a constitution for a new free state that would be carved out of Virginia and Maryland. They wanted to name Brown their president on the spot, but he modestly declined the post. For the present, he said, he had been instructed by God Almighty to serve as commander-in-chief of the new nation's army.

Brown was surprised that ex-slaves didn't flock to him. "Very well," he reasoned, "if they are afraid to come to me, I will go to them."

Having grown a long beard to disguise the face that had appeared on "wanted" posters in Kansas, Brown moved slowly toward a carefully chosen objective. October 16, 1859, found him riding into an obscure Virginia village about fifty miles northwest of Washington, D.C.

Harpers Ferry, Virginia, at the confluence of the Potomac and Shenandoah rivers, had a splendid covered bridge with lanes for both rail and highway traffic. The village had been chosen as the site of a U.S. armory, which elevated it to importance in the eyes of John Brown. Stockpiles of guns and ammunition from the armory would serve to arm the military forces of the nation he was about to form.

Brown's 1859 "army of attack" was made up of about twenty-one men whose chief weapons were pikes. Guns being scarce, the Lord's commander-in-chief had conceived the idea of lashing Bowie knives to long poles.

Brandishing these crude, but lethal, weapons, Brown's soldiers won an easy victory. They took over Harpers Ferry and the all-important arsenal, then herded many residents together as hostages. It was the first—but far from the last—instance of deliberate use of hostages in the increasingly militant North/South strife.

All he had to do, Brown reasoned, was to wait for word about his exploit to be spread. Slaves would run away from their masters in droves. They'd flock to enlist in his army and—thanks to Uncle Sam—lots of them would get guns, instead of pikes. With his army behind him, Brown would seek a mountainous site at which he would establish the nation whose constitution had been prepared in Canada.

Within hours, Brown's reasoning was proved to be wrong. Harpers Ferry residents who escaped capture fled to the hills. Church bells quickly tolled the fearful message, "Slave insurrection! Slave insurrection!" Fast-moving companies of Virginia militia captured bridges and effectively isolated Brown and his army.

Worried not a bit, the intrepid commander-in-chief sent to the Wager House Hotel for breakfast for his men and approximately thirty hostages.

Instead of runaway slaves flocking to his banner, the band of new arrivals at the tiny settlement was a company of U.S. Marines led by Colonel Robert E. Lee and Lieutenant J. E. B. Stuart.

On October 18, Lee formally offered to accept Brown's surrender without bloodshed. When Brown laughed at the idea, Lee signaled his men, and they stormed the fire engine house in which Brown's soldiers and their hostages were barricaded. In the assault, half of Brown's fighting men were cut down. He was wounded, then beaten to the floor with a sword.

John Brown got a quick trial. While waiting for his execution at Charles Town, Virginia, he gloated that "by only hanging a few minutes by the neck" he'd more than recover from the disaster at Harpers Ferry.

His death-row vision was prophetic, indeed. Abolitionists quickly elevated him to the role of a folk hero. They borrowed the tune of an old hymn popular in Charleston, South Carolina, and set new words to it. Wherever it was sung, "John Brown's Body" had dynamic impact; initially at antislavery rallies and later at military recruitment stations, men and women who heard the song often broke into tears.

"Was John Brown a traitor to the State of Virginia, whose actions properly brought him to the gallows?" many a northern orator thundered. "Not at all! He was a martyr for the cause of freedom!"

Revered in the North and hated in the South, it made little difference whether John Brown was legally and morally a traitor or a martyr. Having died gloriously for a cause that totally engulfed him, "Old Brown of Osawatomie, Kansas," became one more symbol of the insoluble differences between the North and the South.

7

John C. Breckinridge Played the Role of Spoiler in the Election of 1860

Delegates to the Illinois state Republican convention were jolted upright on the evening of June 16, 1858. Speaking at Springfield, the attorney whom they'd just nominated as a candidate for the U.S. Senate startled supporters and opponents alike by his acceptance speech.

Part of his preparation had involved re-reading the voluminous papers related to the Dred Scott case. Arguments for and against the Kansas–Nebraska bill of Stephen A. Douglas had been pondered with great care. Douglas would be his opponent in the upcoming political contest; it was important to go on record very early as an opponent of the doctrine of popular sovereignty that Douglas advocated.

Nominee Abraham Lincoln was noted for having made only one public statement about religion, in which he denied membership in any church. Yet on that humid June night he deliberately quoted scripture in the first paragraph of his acceptance speech. Stressing the nation's critical need to put an end to "slavery agitation," Lincoln said that it would not cease "until a crisis shall have been reached and passed." He then pulled out a biblical quotation he had used earlier: "A house divided against itself cannot stand."

Many who had voted for the Springfield attorney cringed. Such talk was more than radical. It was downright dangerous—dangerous to the upcoming race for the Senate, and dangerous to the image of the youthful Republican party.

When the tumult that followed his quotation from scripture ceased, Lincoln continued. "I believe this government cannot endure permanently, half slave and half free. I do not expect the Union to be dissolved: I do not expect the house to fall; but I do expect that it will

Stephen A. Douglas

cease to be divided. It will become all one thing, or all the other."

Antedating his now-famous series of public debates with Douglas by more than sixty days, Lincoln's Springfield address became widely known as the "House Divided Speech." Cartoonists rushed to depict the beardless candidate as a workman busy applying "union glue" to a North/South house nearly in ruins.

Inevitably, the personal views of Abraham Lincoln were debated everywhere. Many ardent abolitionists considered him soft on the slavery issue; after all, he had never given an unqualified statement of condemnation. Many proslavery leaders admitted that his Kentucky background should make him lean a bit toward the South but publicly worried that he was sounding as though he put the preservation of the Union above every other issue.

Democrats convened in Charleston, South Carolina, to choose their nominee for president on April 16, 1860. They had been squabbling publicly for weeks; now they tried to find a way to come to agreement. During fifty-seven ballots, no candidate received a majority of votes. Stephen A. Douglas of Illinois was far ahead of the pack, but his top vote was 151½ out of a required 202. Angrier than when they came together, they decided to call off the futile exercise and try again in Baltimore after a cooling off period of sixty days.

Republicans convened in Chicago on May 16. Backers of William Henry Seward of New York filled The Wigwam with noise and smoke but never got more than 180 of the required 233 votes for their man.

Supporters of Abraham Lincoln gave him only 102 votes on the first ballot. By the time the third ballot was taken, the tide had begun to move swiftly; Lincoln received 231½ votes. A sudden shift boosted his total to 364 votes before the ballot was formally closed. The nominee remained at his Illinois home and kept very quiet.

Many of the Democrats re-convened in Baltimore one month after Lincoln's nomination. Since most southern delegates refused to take part in the parley, it was easy to reach a decision concerning their nominee for the White House.

Stephen A. Douglas—always a giant but suddenly no longer "little" —carried the day on the second ballot. He quickly let it be known that he would campaign on a platform warning that election of Lincoln would lead to the secession of some or many southern states.

To balance their ticket, the regular, or Northern, Democrats wanted a Southerner as a vice-presidential nominee. When ballots put Benjamin Fitzpatrick of Alabama in the crucial slot, he flatly refused to accept. Delegates then turned to Herschel V. Johnson of Georgia, who accepted the nomination.

That didn't end the convention season, however.

Independent Democrats, also meeting in Baltimore, decided to transact no business until their northern counterparts had gone home. Many urged that they swallow their pride and back the Douglas–Johnson slate. Others resisted such a move. After all, they pointed out, a splinter group of Southern Democrats may have provided them with a candidate.

The famous "House Divided" cartoon derided Lincoln. [NEW YORK PUBLIC LIBRARY]

Meeting in Baltimore's Market Hall on June 28, these Southern Democrats had selected a nominee on the first ballot. Their man was President James Buchanan's running mate, the former vice president of the United States, John C. Breckinridge of Kentucky.

It was a good omen, said his backers, that he and Lincoln had been born in the same state. What's more, the Princeton education of their candidate gave him "a nice touch of the North." To balance their ticket, these Southerners chose Joseph Lane of Oregon as their vice-presidential nominee.

Did Breckinridge—and Lane—think for even one minute that they had the slightest chance to defeat their Republican rivals? Probably not. Most of the big northern states with large numbers of electoral votes were already regarded as likely to go to Lincoln. California was in doubt. Most or all southern states would reject him. But if he was to be barred from the White House, it would be Stephen A. Douglas who would have to stand in the door.

At this point in the political process, Breckinridge may have wished simply to make a public stand. He heartily endorsed the platform by which Southern Democrats held that it was both the right and the duty of Congress to protect slavery in the territories, anywhere and everywhere that their masters should choose to take slaves along as part of their personal belongings. By running on that platform and picking up perhaps 200,000 votes, Breckinridge could dramatize to the nation the danger that it faced.

Matters changed when the Independent Democrats decided that they, too, would back Breckinridge. Their platform called for a transcontinental railroad, the acquisition of Cuba, and Stephen Douglas's formula of popular sovereignty for territories in the process of becoming states.

Veteran of the House of Representatives and the U.S. Senate, as well as former vice president, Breckinridge was too astute not to have been aware of what he was doing. He had no chance whatever of winning the White House; he was playing the role of spoiler, pulling votes from Douglas and, it was hoped, from Lincoln as well.

Stephen Douglas thundered warnings, but few Republicans listened. Lincoln, he said, had never put himself clearly on record concerning the burning issue of the day: slavery. But as his "House Divided" speech clearly indicated, the Republican nominee would stop at nothing in an attempt to hold the Union together. Douglas repeatedly went on record as personally wanting nothing to do with secession movements, but as being sure that the Union would dissolve if voters chose Abraham Lincoln.

November 6, 1860, saw the Republican nominee win a guaranteed victory in the electoral college. The popular vote was another matter.

Many states were so close that the outcome was in doubt for days. California went into the Lincoln column by less than one thousand votes, and a call for a recount was skilfully evaded.

Lincoln took only 40 percent of the votes cast nationwide. Opponents split the remaining 60 percent, with Douglas trailing the winner by less than 500,000 votes, just over half the number siphoned from him by Breckinridge.

As late as April 1859, the lawyer from Springfield who became president with less than half the votes cast had discounted his own fitness for the role. Writing to the editor of the Rock Island, Illinois, *Register*, Lincoln confessed, "I must, in candor, say I do not think I am fit for the Presidency."

Fit or unfit, the mood of the North, plus the campaign of Breckinridge, put Lincoln in the driver's seat. That position produced exactly the result predicted by Stephen A. Douglas.

On December 21, six weeks after the election, South Carolina seceded. Mississippi, Florida, Alabama, Georgia, and Louisiana followed in quick succession. Sharecroppers joined with plantation owners in rushing to form companies of "Lincoln Killers." Virginia wavered, but decided to secede when President Lincoln issued a call for troops. Hardly having adjusted to the schedule of life in the White House, the chief executive found himself presiding over a fraction of the former nation.

John Cabell Breckinridge never forgot that he had won seventy-two electoral votes from eleven states. For a time he continued to preside over the Senate, and for a full year he advocated seeking a compromise solution to sectional problems.

When military rule was established in Kentucky, Breckinridge returned home and put on a Confederate uniform. He became a brigadier general and fought at Shiloh, Vicksburg, Stone's River, Chickamauga, and Cold Harbor.

At war's end the man who did at least as much as any other American to put Abraham Lincoln in the White House was serving as Jefferson Davis's secretary of war. Following Lee's surrender, Breckinridge escaped to Cuba on his way to England, where he was beyond the reach of U.S. marshals carrying orders for his arrest.

Part Two

No Shelter from the Storm

Brigadier General Thomas L. Crittenden. [NATIONAL ARCHIVES]

C.S.A. Major General George B. Crittenden. [VALENTINE MUSEUM]

8

George and Thomas Crittenden Mirrored the Sundered Nation

BIG PEACE RALLY

7:00 SUNDAY NIGHT
COME!

IT'S TIME TO BIND UP WOUNDS

Hand-lettered signs scattered about Russellville, Kentucky, urged residents to come to the Baptist Church four nights after the election of Abraham Lincoln.

No explanation was needed; everyone in Logan County knew that the seat of justice was a hotbed of Confederate sympathizers and also the old home place of the author of the last bold attempt at sectional reconciliation.

"Won't catch me at the peace rally," George Crittenden informed his wife at breakfast on the day after the invitations were posted. "George, you're forty-eight years old," his wife scolded. "Ought to be ashamed of yourself. A grown man putting down his father."

Not simply locally, but throughout the nation George's father was noted as perhaps the most eloquent advocate of compromise other than Stephen A. Douglas, whose ideas about compromise were entirely different.

John J. Crittenden had been a U.S. senator, governor of Kentucky, U.S. attorney-general. As a devoted follower of Henry Clay, he put his influence behind sectional compromise as soon as he entered the political arena.

"That fellow born up in Hardin County is going to make it to the White House," he told intimates a month before the election of Lincoln. "Someone will have to work mighty hard to prevent bloodshed; guess I'd better get busy."

By November 6, Crittenden was half through drafting a series of resolutions he proposed to present to the Senate. With luck and persistence, maybe he could get them on the calendar as early as December.

Senator Crittenden planned to ask fellow lawmakers on both sides of the slavery issue to make concessions. He'd propose that the lines of the Missouri Compromise, setting a boundary between free and slave states, be made permanent. In return, he'd try to persuade abolitionists to agree to put the full power of the federal government behind the support of slavery wherever it existed.

It called for a lot of give and take. It would take some arm twisting. But it had a chance . . . maybe.

On Sunday evening, forty-one-year-old Thomas Crittenden walked to the Baptist church, arm-in-arm with his father. George sat on the front porch with his feet propped up "where everybody in Russellville could see him" and watched his relatives and neighbors trickle into the house of worship.

George's defiant gesture, publicly repudiating his father's famous compromise effort, was a silent way of saying that he'd already made up his mind.

Soon he acted. Back at the base, after having gotten leave in order to go home to vote, Lieutenant Colonel George Bibb Crittenden, U.S. Army, took off his uniform and folded it for the last time. He turned in his uniform, along with his resignation, and accepted appointment as a brigadier general in the Confederate army.

His younger brother took an opposite course. From his law office in Louisville, which he had left to return home to support his father, he sent out notices advising clients to seek other attorneys. He intended to join the state militia immediately, he said, and would deal only with cases already before the courts.

Thomas Leonidas Crittenden was soon named a major general of militia. He had hardly grown accustomed to his uniform before General Simon B. Buckner resigned to join the Confederacy. Thrust into the vacancy created by Buckner's resignation, Crittenden became head of the state militia. Soon he was named brigadier general of volunteers in federal service.

Hot-headed George Crittenden, who became a Confederate major general before the end of 1861, led 4,000 troops to defeat in the battle of Mill Springs. Censured for a rash and unauthorized strike at Federal forces, he was placed under arrest. That led to his resignation, but that did not end his loyalty to the C.S.A. For the duration of the war, the son of the Crittenden Compromise author was a civilian volunteer on the staff of General John S. Williams.

His younger brother, loyal to the Union from start to finish, fought valiantly at Shiloh and at Murfreesboro (Stone's River). Advanced to the rank of major general in the state guard, Thomas Crittenden commanded the Twenty-first Corps, Army of the Cumberland, at Chickamauga.

Senator John J. Crittenden's sons were far from unique. Outbreak of civil war literally ripped states, counties, towns, and families—especially families—in two. It was a genuine war of brother against brother.

Four of the brothers-in-law of the commander-in-chief of Federal forces wore Confederate uniforms. Washington gossip spoke mournfully of the fact that the president's own household was split down the middle, with Mary Todd Lincoln termed "two-thirds proslavery and the other third Secesh."

Members of the Senate's special Committee on the Conduct of the War seem to have considered bringing formal charges of treason against the First Lady. A surprise appearance by Lincoln and a formal statement from him declaring that no member of his family had ever treated with the enemy ended this *cause celèbre*.

In dozens, if not hundreds, of other instances, brother versus brother meant combat participation on different sides. At Bull Run, Frederick Hubbard of New Orleans's Washington Artillery saw his brother for the first time in at least six, maybe seven, years. Henry, who wore blue as a member of the First Minnesota infantry, had been

Senator John J. Crittenden. [NATIONAL ARCHIVES]

wounded and was carried to a field hospital. Soon the empty bed next to him was filled—by Frederick in gray, also wounded.

Virginia-born General William B. Terrill was disowned by his father when the West Pointer decided to stick with the Union. Still, his mother-in-law managed to persuade an aide to General Winfield Scott to transfer Terrill to the far West as a safety measure, not for his personal safety but to prevent the possibility that he'd meet his brother, C.S.A. General James B. Terrill, on the battlefield.

Four of Henry Clay's grandsons fought for the South; three spent the war years in blue.

At Chickamauga, the death of C.S.A. General Ben Hardin Helm brought mourning to the White House. Helm's widow was a sister of Mary Todd Lincoln.

Culp's Hill, Pennsylvania, named for owner John Culp, saw a homecoming during the Battle of Gettysburg. Sharp action around the hill involved both of Culp's sons, one wearing gray and the other wearing blue.

Robert J. Breckinridge of Kentucky remained fiercely loyal to the Union. His nephew, for whom he was guardian, became vice president of the C.S.A.

Commodore Franklin Buchanan of the Confederate navy was the first commander of the ironclad *Virginia* (or *Merrimac*). In one of its early engagements, the ship that helped to transform naval warfare shattered the U.S.S. *Congress*, on which Buchanan's brother was an officer.

Vicksburg, Mississippi, was defended by Confederates under Pennsylvania-born General John C. Pemberton. He was defeated by Federal gunboats, one of which was commanded by his brother-in-law.

At Hilton Head, South Carolina, Confederates at the strategic site had full confidence in their commanding officer, Brigadier General Thomas F. Drayton. Even news that a powerful Federal squadron had reached Port Royal did little to change the mood of men in gray.

But Thursday, November 7, 1861, saw big naval guns pound the earthworks of Hilton Head's Fort Walker. Outgunned Confederates were forced into hasty retreat and abandonment of their vital position. Much of the damage inflicted by Union guns came as the result of an officer's familiarity with the region. Commander Percival Drayton of the U.S.S. *Pocahontas*, a native of South Carolina, was in the forefront of those attacking the fortress over which his Confederate brother had charge.

No mere figure of speech, "brother against brother" is a verbal reminder that in the war called "civil," no one really won. Family, sectional, and political rifts were so wide and so deep that it is small wonder that some wounds still have not fully healed.

CHAPTER

9

The President-elect Moves Toward His Inauguration Incognito

Abraham Lincoln was in the offices of the Springfield, Illinois, *Journal* when word came that a sudden switch by many delegates had made him the Republican nominee for the presidency. A few hours later he received a long telegram from his campaign manager in Chicago: "Do not come here, for God's sake. You will be telegraphed by others to come. It is the united advice of your friends not to come. This is important."

Judge David Davis, with whom Lincoln had ridden the circuit in his early days, had used his suite in Chicago's Tremont House as a lookout post. "Seward's men broke down and cried like little children," he later recalled. "They were in a frenzy, beside themselves with fury at their loss. It would have been disastrous for Mr. Lincoln to have come to the convention. That would have required them to face him in person."

Accepting the advice of his long-time friend, nominee Lincoln remained in Springfield. Soon he agreed to a new set of suggestions. He was to go nowhere on anything that might seem to be a political mission. He was to write nothing and say nothing on any doctrinal issue. He was to stay away from rallies held on his behalf, even in Springfield.

When German-born Carl Schurz came to Springfield to make a speech in midsummer, it was the only time the candidate disobeyed instructions. Wearing his customary linen duster, Lincoln put on his stovepipe hat and walked to the capitol in order to applaud Carl Schurz.

His followers were not so careful.

Republican "Wide-awakes" staged parades in New York City.

Boston created a rail-splitters' battalion, whose sole requirement for membership was that a man had to be at least six feet, four inches tall—Lincoln's own height and a full twelve inches taller than his rival, Stephen A. Douglas. Boston's rail-splitters, and the voters of the nation, believed that they were backing "a man of the people who split rails for a living when he was young."

"Mr. Lincoln really was born somewhere in Kentucky," Judge Davis once told a group of intimates. "He really is almost entirely self-educated, and he may have split a few rails some time in his boyhood.

"But the public figure and the private man are not the same. Everybody is calling him 'Honest Abe.' Never dare call him 'Abe' to his face," the judge warned. "He despises that nickname."

Most of those listening intently to Lincoln's campaign manager knew that the candidate's wife, the former Mary Todd of Lexington, Kentucky, came from an aristocratic family. They also knew, as did everyone in and around Springfield, that Abraham Lincoln was no run-of-the-mill backwoods lawyer.

Prodded on this topic, Judge Davis became expansive. He explained:

Mr. Lincoln is an all-purpose attorney. He has always stood ready to accept any client. He has argued cases on murder, disputed wills, maritime law, foreclosures, and debt. He has defended horse thieves, land grabbers, and accused rapists.

Most of you men here know that Mr. Lincoln defended several accused murderers, but how many of you remember that he also acted as court-appointed prosecutor in several murder cases?

During twenty-three years of legal practice, Mr. Lincoln was involved in several thousand cases. He was always "a lawyer's lawyer" who handled a great many appeals. Some of them went all the way to the Illinois Supreme Court. He argued the Sand Bar case, involving ownership of shore land at the mouth of the Chicago river, before the U.S. Supreme Court, and won!

No matter what the professional politicians say, Mr. Lincoln has come about as far from a log cabin as a man can get. Remember the Illinois Central Railroad case? He was representing the railroad and won. When he gave them his bill for $20,000, railroad executives laughed and handed him a check for $200.

What did our Mr. Lincoln do then? He took the case to a jury and asked for the $18,800 he figured that the Illinois Central still owed him. He got a judgment, but the railroad refused to pay. So the man the country calls a rail-splitter got a sheriff's order for seizure of the property of the biggest corporation in Illinois. You can bet that they paid him in a hurry!

Long before the tall man in the stovepipe hat was ready to take up residence in the White House, the outcome envisioned by Stephen A. Douglas had become reality. Some militant southern states had already seceded; others appeared poised to follow.

By February 1861, Lincoln had disposed of much of his personal property. Springfield druggist S. H. Melvin responded to an advertisement in the *State Journal* and became the owner of "parlor and chamber sets, carpets, sofas, chairs, and glass." His handwritten bill of sale, presented to him by the president-elect, included acknowledgement of receipt of $4.75 for nine and one-half yards of stair carpet.

As Lincoln prepared to take the long and circuitous railroad journey to the nation's capital, his intimates became alarmed. They retained Allan Pinkerton, a pioneer private detective, to arrange for the security of the president-elect on the trip.

Pinkerton was especially bothered by the climate of opinion in Baltimore, half of whose citizens openly supported the seceded states. A change of trains there would require a ride through streets that could be filled with rioters. Anything could happen in such a situation.

That is the reason why Pinkerton persuaded the reluctant president-elect to leave off his now-familiar hat and to dress as inconspicuously as possible in mufti for the Baltimore leg of his journey to Washington. Although he was never actually disguised, once his foes learned of the Baltimore transfer carefully timed to occur late at night, they bragged that he had traveled incognito.

Secessionist newspapers crowed that "the man who wants to be the head of a nation crept through Baltimore in disguise, like a thief in the night." Cartoonist Thomas Nast sketched a version of the incident, depicting Lincoln clad in plaid with a Scottish cap. At the *Illustrated*

Baltimore dentist's version of "President-elect passing through the city in disguise."

London News artists showed him sneaking through Baltimore wearing a slouched hat that concealed his face.

But the most widely circulated lampoon of the cautious transfer in Baltimore came from the pen of an amateur artist. Dentist Adalbert J. Volck portrayed a frightened Lincoln peering from a railroad box car at a snarling cat.

Disguise or no disguise in Baltimore, Washington was in a state of near frenzy. Fresh rumors circulated every day: A contingent of South Carolina militia, wearing civilian clothing, was on the way to the capital with rifles and plenty of ammunition; Edmund Ruffin, a notoriously outspoken Virginia advocate of slavery, had hired an outlaw to assassinate the president during the inaugural parade.

Lincoln reached Washington ahead of schedule—about 6:00 A.M. —February 23, 1861. In drizzling rain, he stepped off the train "without fanfare, without reception—a solitary figure in the early morning mist."

At Richmond on the previous day, Jefferson Davis, who had been inaugurated in Alabama on February 18, had taken over the reins of the permanent government of the Confederate States of America.

For Lincoln's inauguration, squads of soldiers were stationed on roofs of houses along Pennsylvania Avenue. Their commander, General Stone, had given specific orders: "Watch all of the windows on the opposite side of the street. Keep your rifles at the ready. If there is any attempt to fire upon the presidential carriage from a window, you are ordered to direct a volley at the source of the attempted assassination."

Accompanied by outgoing President James Buchanan, Lincoln rode to the ceremonies in an open carriage. But squadrons of cavalry formed a moving protective barrier on the right and on the left of the carriage.

Abraham Lincoln took the oath of office from trembling Chief Justice Roger B. Taney, who had shaped the Dred Scott decision. In his inaugural address he pleaded with the already-formed Confederate States of America: "We are not enemies, but friends. We must not be enemies. Though passion may have strained, it must not break our bonds of affection. The mystic chords of memory . . . will yet swell the chorus of the Union when again touched, as surely they will be by the better angels of our nature."

Few who listened that day and hardly any who later read Lincoln's words in print took them seriously. Southerners and their sympathizers did not believe that the new president meant what he said when he promised that "the government will not assail you."

"Abe Lincoln may have managed to slip through Baltimore in disguise," said an aide to Jefferson Davis, "but when the shooting starts he'll have no place to hide."

10

The Free and Independent Republic of Georgia Never Fully Yielded Sovereignty

The secession of South Carolina just before Christmas, 1860, triggered wild excitement in adjoining Georgia. Savannah secessionists held parades and burned bonfires.

Already, South Carolina native Joseph E. Brown had requested the Georgia legislature to convene a special convention. Elected at age thirty-six as a compromise candidate when the Georgia state Democratic convention deadlocked, Brown was an ardent and an articulate proponent of states' rights in the full sense. Even his mentor, John C. Calhoun, had not been so insistent upon the right of each state to have the final word concerning implementation or rejection of any and all federal legislation.

Along with his call for a convention at which to put the matter of secession to a vote, Governor Brown asked lawmakers of Georgia to establish a new military fund of one million dollars "to be used in order to put the state in a posture of defense."

With the special fund voted and the secession convention scheduled to convene at Milledgeville on January 16, 1861, the youthful governor acted swiftly. He sent Colonel A. R. Lawton and the First Georgia regiment to Fort Pulaski, a federal installation at the mouth of the Savannah River. Rated as one of the strongest in the South, it had been built by the U.S. Army's corps of engineers, for a time under the direction of Robert E. Lee.

Following the directive of the governor, Lawton seized the fort. Almost simultaneously, other units of Georgia's military force converged upon the huge arsenal at Augusta and took possession of it. Federal forces made no resistance.

January 18 saw a fiery resolution introduced into the special con-

Georgia's Clinch Rifles review before the seized Federal arsenal in Augusta.
[*LESLIE'S ILLUSTRATED*]

vention. It repudiated Georgia's ratification of the U.S. Constitution before declaring and ordaining that "the Union now subsisting between the State of Georgia and other States, under the name of the United States of America, is hereby dissolved . . . making the State of Georgia in full possession and exercise of all those rights of Sovereignty which belong and appertain to a free and independent State."

In spite of spirited opposition, the resolution carried by a vote of 208 to 89; eventually all but seven delegates to the convention signed the ordinance of secession. Georgia was a free and independent republic!

Official documents were hastily printed for the Republic of Georgia. Plans were made to send envoys to England and to major European countries. Bankers were consulted concerning the need for an immediate issue of the new republic's currency.

These grandiose plans collapsed when delegates to a South-wide convention held in Montgomery, Alabama, decided to pool their manpower and other resources instead of going their separate ways. Reluctantly, Governor Brown and his allies yielded to pressure and agreed to join the Confederate States of America. The Republic of Georgia had survived for less than six weeks.

But the ideas that led to its formation were alive and well. Jefferson Davis had not reached Richmond when Brown issued an order that all

Georgia military units were to remain in the state, under his personal command.

Brown launched a recruitment drive and began establishing new regiments. He placed orders for rifles, artillery, and ammunition. Though Georgia owed token allegiance to the C.S.A., Brown intended to continue to run the state as an independent entity with its own army and even its own navy.

Bickering, squabbling, and downright defiance of orders from Richmond continued throughout the war. North Carolina's governor approached, but did not quite reach, Brown's level of defiance. Neither of these executives ever conceded that Richmond had any more right to tell them and their citizens what to do than did the old federal government in Washington.

Consequences of this stance were sweeping. Long before it was formally promulgated, most states had gone their independent ways in important respects. Nearly all had a special gauge, or width, for railroad tracks. South Carolina's locomotives could not run on Georgia's tracks without elaborate adaptation. That might add to the pride of both the Palmetto and the Peach states, but when military materiel was being shipped from Charleston to Savannah it had to be unloaded at the state line, then clumsily reloaded in boxcars built to Georgia's specifications.

Georgia Governor Joseph E. Brown. [GEORGIA STATE DEPARTMENT OF ARCHIVES AND HISTORY]

Continually at war with Jefferson Davis, Brown is believed by some analysts to have contributed to the fall of Atlanta and to the collapse of the Confederacy. Pushing southward from Chattanooga, General William T. Sherman and his men relied entirely upon the single-track Western & Atlantic Railroad as their supply line. State owned, the line was built from Chattanooga southward to Atlanta in prewar days.

As Sherman moved farther and farther from other Federal forces, the railroad that was the lifeline of his campaign became increasingly vulnerable. To many, it seemed obvious that Jefferson Davis could have sent guerrilla units to cut the railroad, not just once, but over and over and over again. Such a delaying tactic might have meant an entirely different end to the Atlanta campaign.

For reasons wholly unaccountable to ordinary citizens, Davis never sent sappers in gray to wreck the Federal supply line. Was this a way of retaliating for Joseph E. Brown's stubborn refusal to concede that his government was subordinate to that in Richmond? No one knows positively, but the weight of evidence suggests that Brown, Georgia, and the Confederacy paid heavily, indeed, for the governor's rigid insistence that the rights of states came first, last, and always.

Likewise, during at least one period of crisis, Abraham Lincoln had his own hands full with northern governors who, perhaps for the first time, wanted to claim states' rights as a way of evading increasingly stringent draft laws. But the crux of the long struggle over the extent of central power of a united or confederated government, as opposed to the rights of member states, always lay in the region whose states had claimed the right to secede.

After the fall of Atlanta, Georgia's governor pulled from the Confederate Army of Tennessee the troops he had reluctantly lent to that army. Brown is believed to have seriously considered the possibility of negotiating a separate peace with Union forces, without consulting Richmond.

At one astonishing point in 1864, Brown simultaneously led legal fights against the rights of the Confederate government and sent Georgia troops to contest with Confederate troops led by General John B. Hood.

Viewed from the perspective of over a century, it is astonishing that the C.S.A. managed to function at all. Georgia, North Carolina, and other member states were almost as angry with Richmond as they had been with prewar Washington.

Seldom told in the North and virtually unknown in the South, this story of internal strife within the C.S.A. yields fresh understanding of some of the difficulties faced by those who decided to fight it out in the name of states' rights and for the preservation of the plantation/slavery system.

11

The World's First
War Correspondent
Barely Managed to Last
One Year in America

March 27, 1861, saw the Honorable William Howard Russell of London, England, arrive at a Washington train station. Quite unlike the president-elect, who had slipped quietly into the capital less than a month earlier, Russell shouted "Bravo! Bravo!" to crowds who had come to greet him in the early afternoon.

He took up quarters at the Willard Hotel and beamed broadly when handed copies of local newspapers. One and all lauded him for his recent St. Patrick's Day speech in New York City. Speaking as though with a single voice, editors praised the decision of the London *Times* to send its famous war correspondent to cover what some called "the looming unpleasantness" between Unionist and seceded states.

Russell had been in the city only nineteen hours when he was ushered into the White House to meet the president. Lincoln expressed gratitude for his coming. "The London *Times* is one of the greatest powers in the world—in fact, I don't know anything that has more power, except the Mississippi. I am glad to know you as the minister of the *Times*."

News stories of the day applauded Russell for his urbane dress, which consisted of a khaki suit plus a battered brown felt hat and a pair of deeply scarred boots.

"We must do everything in our power to please this gentleman," one editor confessed in private. "His powerful pen can be the most potent of all weapons in the war that is sure to come."

Listeners needed no explanation. Americans everywhere doubted that Britain could remain neutral if and when armed conflict erupted among her former colonies. Southerners counted on the power of King Cotton to bring the English to the aid of the Confederacy. Northerners, rejoicing that Russell had elected to arrive by way of New York rather than Charleston, hoped that his dispatches would attract the interested attention of a different monarch—Queen Victoria.

Most members of Lincoln's cabinet knew something about the background of their distinguished guest. Widely acclaimed as the world's first war correspondent, at age thirty-three he had sent stirring accounts of the Crimean War. So impressive were his firsthand reports of incompetence, they were credited with causing the fall of a British government. His vivid accounts of desperately wounded men with little or no medical aid had inspired Florence Nightingale to become England's "angel of mercy."

It was hoped that Russell's dispatches from North America could persuade Queen Victoria and her ministers to put their weight behind the move to subdue the rebellious states quickly and restore the glorious Union!

Clearly, these considerations were in mind when plans were made for a White House dinner party on March 28. Although it was the first state dinner of the Lincoln administration and was to honor cabinet members and their ladies, the portly visitor from London was among the invited guests.

Russell found the food tolerable, but the conversation dull. "Mrs. Lincoln, in a bright-colored dress, looked and talked as though she belonged in Kentucky still," he wrote. "Yet she made every effort to be agreeable."

Two days later Mary Todd Lincoln sent Russell a bouquet of flowers. It was one of the last bouquets he received from any American source.

To cover the impending military engagements properly, he said, it was essential that he visit the South. He may have had instructions to do that before leaving London because the *Times* had already taken a decidedly pro-Southern stance in its editorial columns.

The world's first war correspondent expressed surprise at the size and strength of Fort Pulaski. He cheerfully posed near the touchhole of a 10-inch gun so that an artist might depict him in action. He rushed to Montgomery, Alabama, to interview Jefferson Davis and members of the Confederate cabinet. And he was in Charleston less than forty-eight hours after the fall of Fort Sumter.

Few of his long dispatches made him popular in the South. "He sounds as though he were ready to fight this war—on the Union side," one newspaper editor grumbled.

When he got wind of a plan for a preemptive strike by Federal forces and left to cover the action, Confederates, who at first had welcomed him even more enthusiastically than had official Washington, were glad to see him depart.

Brigadier General Irvin McDowell personally met him at the station on his second arrival in Washington. That said a great deal, for McDowell had just been promoted and ordered to fashion a fighting army from 75,000 motley members of state militia units.

"Yes, we plan to make a decisive move very soon. We believe that a smashing victory will bring an end to this unwelcome conflict before it becomes a genuine war," the Federal commander confessed to the *Times* correspondent.

"Beauregard, the Creole who led the assault upon Sumter, has a rebel force of perhaps 25,000 men. They're encamped within easy striking distance, not more than thirty miles away."

Russell eyed his host doubtfully. "When in the South, I learned a great deal about Beauregard," he said. "He was your classmate at your West Point military academy. How can you make plans to descend suddenly upon him in order to humiliate him?"

McDowell did not answer the question, simply shaking his head silently. "We have the approval of the president," he said. "Soon he will get the support of his cabinet. Once he has that, we'll head for Manassas Junction on the double."

Except for cabinet officers, few civilians other than Russell had accurate advance word of Federal plans. Following a suggestion from McDowell, the war correspondent put on a white uniform and moved out with Federal forces in order to cover the smashing blow they expected to deliver.

William Russell, falsely depicted as a boozer, watching the battle of First Bill Run from a safe distance. [NEW YORK ILLUSTRATED NEWS]

His first dispatch from First Bull Run, which took up an incredible seven columns in the London *Times,* was devoted to a detailed account of Federal fumbling and failure. Conduct of many troops was labeled disgraceful.

Russell didn't hesitate to use hard words: "a miserable, causeless panic"; "scandalous behavior by men calling themselves soldiers"; "officers conducting themselves as though they were camp followers."

Northern leaders were, if possible, even more furious with Russell than with McDowell. In New York, a lead editorial branded the correspondent as a Confederate agent in disguise. According to the Chicago *Tribune,* his dispatches about First Bull Run were the products of his imagination. Charged the staunchly Lincoln paper, "Russell has described what he dares to call a rout; actually, he was never anywhere near Bull Run Creek during three days of action."

No longer courted by the highest Federal officials and despised by many ordinary folk in the North, the war correspondent began receiving anonymous letters and threats. Matters grew worse when a naval officer stopped the British mail steamer *Trent* and seized Confederate officers aboard it. With Britain openly growling at the North, William Howard Russell's capacity to cover the escalating war was severely limited.

One year after having been greeted as "minister of the *Times,*" he managed to get permission to go with the Army of the Potomac to Fortress Monroe. Just as his steamer was about to sail, U.S. Secretary of War Edwin Stanton—Lincoln's old rival who now dominated the cabinet—ordered him off the vessel.

Livid with anger, Russell remained in Washington less than two days. He was on a steamer headed for England as soon as he could book passage. Though no formal statements were issued from Washington or Richmond, fighting Americans of both North and South wanted no more of foreign correspondents incapable of understanding what Russell had termed "a nasty little domestic dispute."

CHAPTER

12

James B. Eads Put Together an Ironclad Inland Navy

When Indiana-born James Buchanan Eads arrived in St. Louis at age thirteen, his first job was selling apples on the streets. After a term as clerk in a dry goods store, he became a purser on a Mississippi River steamer.

During his four years on the river, Eads became convinced that it held the key to development of the growing West, while remaining vital to the entire East. He conceived the notion of getting the federal government to clear the river of wrecks and snags, but Washington did not listen to his proposal.

"When he couldn't get action here," a war office clerk explained to General Winfield Scott, "Mr. Eads took things into his own hands. He invented a contraption he called a diving bell, enabling workmen to stay under water without wearing pressurized suits. Using his patented bell, he began hauling up wrecks himself. He made a fortune in a hurry. He's no man to take lightly."

General Scott, head of the entire U.S. Army, had demanded a briefing as preparation for acting on a request from President Abraham Lincoln. According to the president's instructions, Scott was to listen patiently to the salvage master. He was not to dismiss any of his ideas out of hand. Once the two of them came to a working agreement of some sort, they were to come together to the White House.

Receiving his visitors on a crisp evening in February 1861, the lanky chief executive was thrilled by their joint report. Scott had consented to the idea of having Eads build for the army a fleet of armored steamers designed to give Federal forces complete and permanent control of the Mississippi and its major tributaries. Like his commander-in-chief, General Scott was convinced that the coming war would have to be won in the West.

Shrewdly, Lincoln had bypassed top naval officials. He knew they never would consent to plans for an armored vessel designed by a self-taught salvage master, not a veteran shipbuilder.

James B. Eads was so enthusiastic that he almost danced when Lincoln indicated his approval of the tentative plans developed in conversation with General Scott.

"Mr. President," he cried, "you'll have your turtle-backs in one hundred working days, and that's a solemn promise!"

On the long journey back to St. Louis, the successful inventor, whose schooling had ended at age thirteen, made a series of sketches. They became the basis for working drawings that called for production of eight armor-plated steam-powered gunboats.

Each vessel was to be 175 feet long and just over 50 feet at the beam. Plates of armor bolted to the bows were to overlap enough to hold against head-on fire. In order to deflect enemy broadsides, the sides of the queer ships were to be sloped at thirty-five degrees. Since they were designed specifically for river use, it was hoped that they would draw no more than six feet of water. Their bizarre appearance produced the nickname "turtle-back."

Two weeks after returning to his home base in St. Louis, Eads had 4,000 men at work. Forty-five days after her keel was laid, the armored *St. Louis* was floated. Her boilers and engines were already in place, but the thirteen guns she was to carry were not yet finished.

In just under 100 days the salvage master managed to build seven of his strange gunboats and to convert one of his wrecking boats into an eighth.

By the time the "inland navy" was ready for action, Confederates had made good use of Island #10 about sixty miles below Columbus, Kentucky. Batteries constructed there, augmented by guns mounted on bluffs, were designed to block the lower Mississippi to Federal traffic.

James B. Eads. [ALEXANDER RITCHIE ENGRAVING, *DICTIONARY OF AMERICAN PORTRAITS*]

The Eads-built Carondelet. [KENNEDY GALLERY]

Gunboats of the Eads-built navy were manned chiefly by volunteers from the U.S. Army. But once it was seen that the vessels were going to be put into use, the navy assigned veteran officers for their quarter-decks. That is how Virginia-born Henry Walke, who'd started his naval career as a midshipman in 1827, came to be put in charge of Eads's *Carondelet*.

To an extent that few army leaders liked to admit, the *Carondelet* contributed to Union victory at forts Henry and Donelson before returning to the Mississippi River for patrol duty. It was the Eads vessel that ran the Confederate gauntlet on April 4, 1862, and showed heavily armored Island #10 to be vulnerable. Three nights later her sister ship, the *Pittsburg*, also got through the narrow passage and was little damaged by heavy Confederate fire. Consequently, April 8 saw C.S.A. General William W. Mackall surrender Island #10, along with 3,500 men and huge quantities of ordnance.

That meant the Mississippi River was open as far south as Fort Pillow, Tennessee. Within a few months, the "inland navy" had won victories that put Federal forces in control as far as Vicksburg. For practical purposes, Eads's strange boats had cut the Confederacy in two.

Their early engagements at forts Henry and Donelson had taken place before foot-dragging officials in Washington had paid Eads for his vessels. The early and important battle on inland waters took place between Confederate forces and turtle-backs manned by Federal soldiers, but still owned by James B. Eads of St. Louis.

13

West Pointers Sparred Bloodlessly at Fort Sumter

Major Robert Anderson:
All proper facilities will be afforded for removal of yourself and com-
mand, together with company arms and property, and all private prop-
erty to any post in the United States which you may select.

The flag which you have upheld so long and with so much fortitude,
under the most trying circumstances, may be saluted by you on taking it
down.

> *Respectfully yours,*
> *P.G.T. BEAUREGARD*
> *Brigadier General, Confederate States of America Army*
> *West Point, Class of 1838.*

Fifty-six-year-old Robert Anderson needed no introduction to the Creole who had been named superintendent of the U.S. Military Academy on January 1, 1861. He had held the post only a few days before being dismissed for outspoken southern views. Earlier, Beauregard had been Anderson's artillery instructor. As commander of Illinois volunteers during the Black Hawk Indian war, Anderson had briefly in his service a raw recruit named Abraham Lincoln.

Kentucky-born Anderson, married to the former Eliza Clinch of Georgia and a one-time slave owner himself, had been sent to Fort Moultrie in Charleston harbor because he was viewed as unlikely to antagonize Southerners. From Moultrie he had moved his men—without authorization—to stronger and larger Fort Sumter, which was entirely surrounded by water.

From Sumter he regretfully responded to the invitation to surrender peaceably. That invitation, he wrote, constituted "a demand with which I regret that my sense of honor, and my obligations to my government, prevent my compliance."

Delivering his memorandum to Beauregard's emissaries, the West Point graduate of the class of 1825 remarked to the Rebel messengers, "Gentlemen, if you do not batter us to pieces, we shall be starved out in a few days."

By early April 1861, virtually all Federal installations in the South had been seized: forts, arsenals, customhouses, and even lighthouses. Only four remained under direct control of Washington authorities: Fort Pickens, off Pensacola Bay; Fort Taylor, at Key West; Fort Jefferson, in the Dry Tortugas; and Fort Sumter, in Charleston harbor.

Sumter was of little military significance. Until Anderson abandoned Moultrie to Confederates and took over the larger base in the dead of night, Sumter had had no permanent garrison. If, as many believed, the North/South schism would be healed only in battle, Sumter would play an insignificant role at best.

But the grim little bastion perched on a tiny island was the most important Federal installation in the South not yet seized by military forces of seceded states. All three Florida bases combined were less significant than was Sumter.

Secession had begun in Charleston less than four months before Beauregard invited Anderson to surrender the installation. Loss of Sumter would do immense psychological damage to the Washington government. Like Uncle Tom, Dred Scott, and John Brown, Fort Sumter was a symbol that could serve to rally thousands to fight for a cause.

General Pierre Gustave Toutant Beauregard. [HARPER'S WEEKLY]

Major Robert Anderson. [LESLIE'S ILLUSTRATED]

C.S.A. President Jefferson Davis, who had graduated from West Point in the Class of 1828, three years after Anderson, had not yet transferred his government to Richmond. In Montgomery, Alabama, he read a telegram reporting that Anderson refused to give up Fort Sumter. From South Carolina Governor Francis W. Pickens he had learned that high officials in Washington had promised to give up Sumter. Days later, though, the same persons regretfully informed the governor that a naval relief expedition was under way.

Beauregard was instructed from Montgomery to demand from Anderson a specific time of surrender. If no such time was indicated, he was told to "reduce the fort" with big guns that already ringed much of Charleston harbor.

It was already April 12, 1861—a few minutes past midnight—when that ultimatum was received from Jefferson Davis. Hoisting a white flag over a small boat, four Rebels rowed hastily to Sumter and told Anderson what had taken place. He offered to evacuate at noon on the fifteenth, barring receipt of "controlling instructions from my government, or additional supplies."

Following Beauregard's instructions, aides regretfully told Anderson that his terms were unacceptable. Relief ships, they knew, were already close to Charleston.

"Our batteries will open fire in one hour," they told the Federal commander before climbing back into their white-flagged boat for a return to the shore.

Anderson carefully noted the time: 3:20 A.M. Before taking leave of the messengers, he had shaken the hand of each man. "If we do not meet again in this world," he told them, "I hope we may meet in a better one."

Roger Pryor of Virginia, who headed the band of messengers, ordered his tiny vessel toward Cummings Point. There he gave the order to fire, without reporting to Beauregard. Gunners offered him the honor of touching off the first shot; he shook his head and refused with obvious deep emotion.

Close by was Edmund Ruffin, age sixty-seven, editor of a farm paper and a longtime hard-line secessionist. Standing very close to the Richmond Grays at the execution of John Brown, Ruffin had chatted with an aspiring actor in the ranks. Congratulating him on having taken part in the capture of Brown, the older man said to John Wilkes Booth, "My hair may be white, but my blood is red. I am ready to spill it for the South."

When Roger Pryor refused the honor of firing the first shot at Fort Sumter, Edmund Ruffin eagerly asked for the privilege. At 4:30 he pulled a lanyard and a "tracer" shell arched across the sky, illuminating the pentagonal structure that Anderson had refused to yield.

Charleston ladies watched the bombardment from rooftoops. [HAR-PER'S WEEKLY]

Howitzers and mortars—at least forty-seven in number—were fired leisurely during hours of darkness but began a furious bombardment as dawn approached. Anderson held his fire until dawn, then gave Captain Abner Doubleday the honor of firing the first shot at heavily fortified Charleston.

Ladies and gentlemen of the city gathered on rooftops and other observation points to watch the show. At first they cheered every Confederate move, even applauding the arrival of Beauregard's Spanish barber and valet.

As the day wore on and spectators grew hoarse, the rate of fire became even faster. Although Anderson had forty big guns, he was short of ammunition; and so he ordered his men to aim precisely and to fire leisurely.

The supply ships expected by the Federal commander arrived on the afternoon of the twelfth, but they were kept out of the harbor by Confederate gunners. By the time the ships were visible, Anderson had nearly exhausted his supply of powder-bag cartridges. A band of civilians who were employed at the base sewed furiously, making bags from burlap, scraps of linen, and even from socks. Even so, the effective Federal fire was reduced to six guns.

Beauregard began using hot shot late in the afternoon. As a result, Sumter's defenders had to extinguish at least three separate fires by nightfall.

Confederates shelled only periodically throughout the night, and Federal guns were silent. At dawn on the thirteenth, Beauregard's men resumed the furious pace that had marked the heat of the previous day's exchange. Sumter's casemates were so filled with smoke that cannoneers held wet handkerchiefs over their faces and crawled along the ground to their stations.

A Confederate shell ripped the U.S. flag from its staff. A sergeant hastily nailed it back in place, and Anderson's men continued to fire an occasional symbolic shell.

Having seen the flag disappear, Beauregard's aide-de-camp, Louis T. Wigfall, commandeered a rowboat and—unauthorized—set out for Sumter. He offered to accept the surrender of the installation. Anderson stalled but did not refuse outright.

At 12:48 P.M. the flag was again shot from its staff. Anderson managed to signal to the shore that he was ready to give up. Beauregard immediately sent official messengers to accept the surrender.

During the thirty-four-hour artillery duel, Confederates had launched more than 4,000 shells. Federal guns had fired infrequently but had managed to take off part of the roof of the Moultrie Hotel. Several soldiers had been wounded, as had a few civilians; but not a person had died.

While Charlestonians staged a glorious celebration, Confederate soldiers prepared to hoist South Carolina's Palmetto flag over the captured installation. Anderson, who had been promised the privilege of a final salute to his own flag, insisted upon giving it. At first he planned to fire 100 guns, but was forced to settle for just 50.

Wind carried a burning ember to a stack of cartridges during the final salute to the U.S. flag. A great explosion injured five men and killed gunner Daniel Hough, the first casualty of the war that was now three days old.

Jubilant Southerners danced in the streets of cities. Louis Wigfall taunted the North, "Your flag has been insulted; redress it if you dare!" In eight states where sentiment was divided, leaders begged for action "appropriate to events that have taken place at Fort Sumter."

Eventually four more states joined the C.S.A.: Virginia, North Carolina, Tennessee, and Arkansas. Maryland, Delaware, Kentucky and Missouri voted to remain in the Union. All eight had both Unionist and secessionist parties that created wide and lasting division internally.

Word of the fall of Sumter reached Washington on Sunday, only an hour or two after Daniel Hough had died. Newspaper editors hurriedly opened their offices to write their stories. Abraham Lincoln called his cabinet together in emergency session, demanded, and got assent to a presidential proclamation calling on states to provide 75,000 militia for ninety days of service against "combinations too powerful to be suppressed by ordinary judicial proceedings."

It was not a declaration of war; only Congress could make such a declaration, and lawmakers were not in session. But the military draft was issued on Monday, April 15, with quotas assigned to each state and territory except the seven that had already seceded.

His voice trembling, staunch abolitionist Horace Greeley of New York solemnly informed employees of his newspaper and Northerners in general, "Sumter is lost, but freedom is saved!"

CHAPTER

14

Baltimore Saw the First
Deliberate Shedding of Blood

At the same time that President Lincoln issued his call for 75,000 militia, he made plans for a special session of Congress. That proclamation, also issued on Monday, April 15, set the day for the conclave as July 4.

"Why wait ninety days in a state of national emergency?" some angry lawmakers demanded. They received no official explanation from the White House.

A few governors wired their acceptance of troop quotas within hours. But almost as promptly, North Carolina and Kentucky notified the chief executive that his order would not be obeyed. Virginia took the same course on Tuesday, during the hours when North Carolina troops seized two unmanned Federal installations. Protesting what he termed plans to subjugate the southern states, Governor John Letcher of Virginia solemnly warned that his state would never provide fighting men "for any such use or purpose as envisioned."

Wednesday saw refusals from Missouri and Tennessee; the same day a special Virginia convention voted to present the secession issue to the people in a May referendum. Jefferson Davis publicly invited applications for letters of marque, which would permit privateering on the high seas.

On Thursday, members of the Sixth Massachusetts staged a triumphal march in New York City, and five companies of Pennsylvania troops reached Baltimore on their way to Washington. Mayor George W. Brown of Baltimore protested the use of his city as "a staging ground for war," while secessionists, who had held a series of public rallies, boasted that they were in control of the city.

Friday, April 19, brought a presidential proclamation declaring a Federal blockade of ports in seceded states. Soon it was extended to Virginia and North Carolina, still in the Union.

The arrival from New York of the Sixth Massachusetts into Baltimore that afternoon—a full week after the first shots were fired at Fort Sumter—brought out angry citizens *en masse*. "Welcome to Southern graves!" they shouted to men who had responded to Lincoln's call. Along Pratt Street, which carried the only railroad linking Philadelphia with Washington, cobblestones had been dug up during the night and placed in neat piles.

Two thousand men of the Sixth Massachusetts piled out of their train at the President Street Station and tried to crowd into horse-drawn cars for the four-block transfer to Washington Station. Five hundred jeering men surrounded the horse cars; before they were filled, the crowd had swelled to 2,000.

Eight cars made the trip to Washington Station with no incident more serious than the throwing of a few stones and bricks by civilians who shouted, "Jeff Davis and the Confederacy forever!" But as the ninth horse car set out for Washington Station, a hail of stones smashed every window. Someone shouted, "Tear up the track!" Not having tools for this job, members of the mob seized heavy anchors and used them to block the track.

Massachusetts men left their cars, formed ranks on the sidewalk, and prepared to march to their station. Civilians hit several men with stones, seized their muskets, and fired them into the air.

Captain A. S. Follansbee of Lowell, Massachusetts, ordered his men, "Cap your pieces!" Already loaded, the weapons thus were ready to be fired. By now, the mob had grown to 10,000. A section of iron girder thrown from an upper window knocked the breath from a soldier.

"Self-preservation called for action," a member of the Sixth Massachusetts later said. "Our men turned and began firing at random on the mob. For a moment, it looked as though that would end the affair.

"Regrouping, though, the mob surged toward us. Soon the streets became a battle ground. Stones rattled and muskets cracked. Bullets whistled and women screamed.

"Finally most of us made it to our station, surrounded by another mob. We managed to get into our cars and the locomotive began moving. Members of the mob ran alongside our cars for more than a mile. They shouted, threw stones, and fired on us with some of our own muskets."

Chaplain John W. Hanson, who doubled as regimental historian, gave a slightly different account of the clash. "Pistols and guns were fired from windows and doors of stores and houses as we passed along Pratt Street," he wrote.

"Getting a little accustomed to these strange circumstances, our boys loaded their guns as they marched. Whenever they saw a hostile

Men of the Sixth Massachusetts took careful aim, then fired. [*HARPER'S WEEKLY*]

demonstration, they took as good aim as they could and fired.

"Some of the rioters fought like madmen. One of our boys took dead aim at a rioter, but his musket did not fire. Rioters then rushed forward, seized his musket, and plunged the bayonet through his shoulder. Marching on the double, our men fired again and again, as rapidly as they could reload their pieces."

As best the casualty list could be put together, it appeared that three soldiers were dead and at least nine were injured. Baltimore merchant Robert T. Davis was dead; so were at least eight other civilians. Several dozen civilians were seriously wounded; many of them were not expected to live.

At Fort Sumter, the only bloodshed had been the result of an accidental explosion during surrender ceremonies. In Baltimore, the deliberate attack upon Federal forces, followed by their retaliation, brought bloodshed in soldier/civilian combat.

America had tasted civil war. Now it was clear that no person would be sheltered from its effects, whether in uniform or out of it.

In Richmond, editors of the *Enquirer* newspaper lauded actions of that bloody Friday. Speaking in Atlanta ten days later, C.S.A. Vice President Alexander H. Stephens said of the Baltimore battle, "Lincoln may bring his 75,000 soldiers against us, but seven times 75,000 men can never conquer us!"

Governor Andrew of Massachusetts telegraphed Mayor Brown of Baltimore, asking that bodies of dead fighting men "be immediately laid out, preserved in ice, and tenderly sent forward by express to me." Luther C. Ladd of Lowell, age seventeen, was termed by Andrew "the first martyr of the war." Graves of Ladd and Addison O. Whitney, also of Lowell, were later marked by a monument of Concord granite, 27½ feet high. "Nothing is here for tears, nothing to wail or knock the breast," the inscription reads. "Nothing but well and fair, and what may quiet us in a death so noble."

At least two artists sketched their interpretations of the soldier/civilian clash, and the Massachusetts legislature published detailed accounts of funerals held for their dead soldiers. There is no record of what happened to bodies of slain civilians.

Washington's response to bloodless Fort Sumter clearly meant war, whether declared by Congress or not. Blood in the streets of Baltimore four days later served clear-cut notice that, for abolitionists and secessionists alike, the coming conflict would offer anything but "well and fair"—plus unlimited opportunities for death far from noble.

CHAPTER
15

Clara Barton Made Bandages of Red Tape

"Thanks to the wonders of the magnetic telegraph, we in the capital had word of the Baltimore clash long before its survivors reached the city.

"Rumors sprang up everywhere: A Confederate force is marching toward us! President Lincoln has dispatched bands of militia to avenge the slaughter in Baltimore! A state of emergency will be declared, and you must have a pass to walk the streets!"

Recounting events of April 18, 1861, Theodore Winthrop of the Sixth New York regiment remembered, "As five o'clock approached, it seemed that all Washington had gathered at the station to pay homage to survivors from the Baltimore massacre."

On the train headed for the city, Captain John Pickering of the Sixth Massachusetts had heard, and had dismissed, rumors that troops from Maryland and Virginia were marching toward it. Pickering had his hands full trying to make the wounded comfortable.

Pickering's careful count showed that four dead had been left behind in the streets. Not counting bruises that did not break the skin, thirty-one men were wounded. Some were barely scratched, but others had serious bullet wounds.

Acting under instructions from Pickering, unscathed men held back when the train stopped. Those wounded who could walk emerged to deafening cheers. Then the seriously wounded were borne out on improvised stretchers and laid on the cobblestones while officers inquired directions to the nearest hospital.

Almost as one, assembled masses of civilian spectators gasped when the first stretcher emerged from the car. A few persons began screaming curses at the Confederates. Most persons stood as though frozen.

Suddenly a woman barely five feet, three inches tall pushed through the front ranks. She darted to the side of the man whose stretcher had been unceremoniously deposited in the street. With her own hand-kerchiefs, Clara Barton tried clumsily to staunch the blood still seeping from a shattered leg.

"A hush fell over the crowd of spectators," according to Theodore Winthrop. "Then, one by one, other women stepped forward. Pulling out handkerchiefs of their own, they followed the lead of the little clerk from the U.S. Patent Office." A native of Oxford, Massachusetts, Clara Barton later said that she "simply couldn't bear the sight of a man from my own state, bleeding to death before my eyes."

Youngest of five children and described as "spoiled and willful," she became a teacher at age fifteen. After years of classroom experience, she launched her own free school in Bordentown, New Jersey. Soon it became so large that she had her first run-in with bureaucracy. Town fathers dusted off old ordinances and forced her to leave; the school supposedly was too big for a woman to manage.

Not long afterward, at age thirty-three, she went to Washington and applied for a government job. Shuffled from one department to another by clerks who didn't want to tell her that the government didn't employ women in white collar jobs, she landed at the Patent Office.

"Someone pretended to give me a test," she said. "When I produced copperplate script as splendid as that from the hand of any male, he was astonished. I got the job and became the first white-collar female government worker in the nation's capital."

At the Patent Office, the young woman from Massachusetts worked as a clerk. Hour after hour, she meticulously produced copies of official documents. Each completed document was carefully rolled, then tied with a piece of standard-issue red tape. By 1861 she was drawing $1,400 a year, a salary high even by male standards.

Within days after having rushed forward to bandage a wounded man whom persons in authority seemed to be neglecting, Clara Barton was reprimanded. She was spending entirely too much time in the Senate

Clara Barton. [DICTIONARY OF AMERICAN PORTRAITS]

chamber, a supervisor told her. When she ignored the warning, she was terminated.

Her dismissal made no difference to her. For the present, her heart was in the Senate chamber, where the men of the Sixth Massachusetts were quartered. Other units camped in the hall of the House of Representatives. A few squads were temporarily housed in the White House.

"Once in the Representatives' chamber," said Theodore Winthrop of the Sixth New York, "we washed. Some of our companies were marched upstairs into the galleries. The sofas were to be their beds. Most of us were bestowed in the amphitheatre.

"Some three thousand of us were quartered within the Capitol. The Massachusetts Eighth were under the dome. No fear of want of air for them. The Massachusetts Sixth were eloquent in their state in the Senate chamber."

These and other men belonging to militia units temporarily assigned to Federal service took their oath of allegiance to the fighting forces of the United States on the afternoon of April 26. Until then, the North had had no soldiers other than the 16,367 officers and men who made up the entire United States Army.

By the time militia members came under the formal authority of the U.S. government, Clara Barton was reveling in her self-discovered role. On April 19 she brought dainty food to the men of the Sixth Massachusetts. Soon she came back with towels, handkerchiefs, and salves. Needles and thread followed, along with buttons.

Incredibly, she managed to get her hands on a copy of the Worcester, Massachusetts, *Spy* that was only two days old. Brandishing it triumphantly, Clara Barton strode to the vice president's desk and signaled for silence. Then she read column after column of the newspaper to the boys from her home state.

Soon she began placing her personal advertisements in the *Spy*. She called on all patriotic readers to send food, provisions, and medical supplies. When medical supplies began to accumulate, the prim little brown-eyed woman, whose friends said privately that she was subject to nervous breakdowns, began badgering the office of the surgeon general. Colonel Daniel H. Rucker managed to arrange for her to transport her supplies through army lines, directly to fighting fronts.

At first she rode in a big army wagon, complete with a black driver. Soon she was handling the reins of four horses herself.

Clara Barton's medical training, if it could be called that, consisted of two years' experience nursing an invalid relative. Yet she insisted upon taking to the front not only bandages and salves and lotions, but also lanterns, so that surgeons could see to use scalpels and saws at night.

Two well-funded volunteer organizations for the aid of soldiers had already sprung up, both in New York City. Because of their influential supporters and contributors, both the Christian Commission and the Sanitary Commission soon had virtually official status.

With no organization except her volunteers personally recruited, and with no financial backing except what she managed to drum up herself, Clara Barton was very much a presence on the battlefield. By the time the Army of the Potomac began moving into Virginia, she had become attached to the Ninth Corps. She had accumulated four big wagons—all heavily loaded—plus an ambulance.

So far as she was concerned, military red tape did not exist. When she could not persuade officials to relax or to bend regulations, she blithely went her own way and ignored them. Always following the troops, she went as far south as Charleston, South Carolina.

However, in Edwin McMasters Stanton of Ohio, she met her match. Fully as stubborn as the little woman who had badgered him for weeks and himself destined to be the focus of impeachment charges against a president, the U.S. secretary of war knew all about Clara Barton's valiant performance on the battlefield. He also thought that she was an infernal nuisance, competing with and frequently challenging the work of the Sanitary Commission and the Christian Commission. So Stanton refused to give her passes to move "at her own discretion among the troops," as she demanded. Only when news of the casualties in the Wilderness reached Washington did he relent temporarily.

Unable to topple the male establishment that controlled not only the war but also the care of sick and wounded, Clara Barton found a new focus for her effort. She turned to the neglected cases of men who had once been members of Federal units, but who had simply disappeared. Long before the label M.I.A. was fashioned, she was busy trying to locate and identify the missing. In postwar years her bureau of records closed the cases of thousands of men, including many who died at Andersonville prison.

Once she and her workers had found as many graves as possible and had identified men buried in them, Clara Barton turned her energy overseas. While active in relief work during the Franco–Prussian War, she learned about activities of the fledgling International Red Cross organization. Her enduring monument, the fruit of the spontaneous wielding of a handkerchief in an effort to help a wounded man, is the American Red Cross.

16

"Boy Drummer of Chickamauga" Refused to Be Refused

"Can't use you, son. We're not enlisting infants. You will have to wait till you grow up."

John Lincoln Clem, age nine, continued to stand at attention before the commander of the Third Ohio Regiment. He snapped a clumsy salute, turned without a word, and headed toward the nearest other Federal unit. At headquarters of the Twenty-second Michigan, he got another prompt refusal of his offer to "help fight the rebels."

Since there was no other fighting force within miles, the boy took his second refusal calmly, but refused to go home. He persuaded members of a squad to let him bunk and eat with them. Holding an imaginary drum and beating it with precision, Johnny tagged along after the Twenty-second Michigan.

Many men of the unit were delighted with their human mascot. Gradually the resistance of the commander was worn down, and he participated when officers began passing the hat each month to collect thirteen dollars for Johnny's pay. Someone found for him a real drum, battered but functional, and he became a Union drummer boy in every respect except official enrollment.

"Johnny showed us something," said a member of his regiment long afterward. "He showed us that this was a war in which everybody was involved; there were no onlookers."

Once the real fighting began, most barriers toppled. By the time the battle of Shiloh saw the forests and swamps run red with blood, Johnny was regularly enrolled. National newspapers featured him as "Johnny Shiloh."

In North and South alike, small boys by the hundreds, and then by the thousands, eagerly enlisted and marched off to war like veterans.

Federal recruitment officers, always pressed to meet their quotas, stopped asking meddlesome questions. If a candidate for uniform looked as though he might be somewhere near eighteen, had two eyes and more than half of his teeth, he got only a perfunctory physical examination before being assigned to a unit.

Southern recruitment officers were few and far between. They were not needed. Sectional loyalty plus ever-expanding draft calls eventually put nearly all C.S.A. white males from sixteen to sixty into uniform.

Brigadier General Charles King of the U.S. Volunteers searched Union records. Although he found no precise statistics, he did uncover abundant evidence that each of more than two thousand blue-clad regiments nearly always had two drummers.

"No officer willingly assigned any man to a drum if that man was strong enough to carry a rifle," King noted. "So the field musicians to whose beat our men marched were usually boys of about fourteen, plus or minus."

Compared with Johnny Clem, Newton Peters was an oldster. When he was mustered out after four full years of service, on June 29, 1865, Newton was nearly nineteen. No drummer, he carried a rifle throughout the conflict.

"Uniforms were expensive and often scarce," said a clerk in the Federal quartermaster's corps. "That's why our men would outfit drummer boys in whatever gear was available." Some of the sketches made by artists show boys of the Eighth New York National Guard wearing uniforms from the Mexican War.

With total Confederate strength somewhere near 50 percent of all Union forces, about 20,000 small boys, more or less, ate, slept, marched, and fought with Johnny Reb.

Individual records are scarce, but it is known that Charles F. Mosby

Johnny Clem. [*HARPER'S WEEKLY*]

Unidentified drummers.

enlisted in 1861 when the Elliott Grays of the Sixth Virginia Infantry went into Confederate service. After two years of combat experience, at age thirteen, Charlie was transferred to the Henderson heavy artillery.

Not all juvenile musicians were drummers. Many were buglers. Strangely, though, few photographs show these young buglers, while several dozen portray their contemporaries who served as drummers.

Union army regulations stipulated that a man had to be eighteen years old before he could be given a musket, but they said nothing about the age at which a fellow could bear a sword. That resulted in a remarkably large number of sword-wielding cavalrymen of fifteen, sixteen, even thirteen or fourteen, years of age.

Most boys marched, camped, and fought on land; but a few lucky ones made it to sea, usually recruited for such duty in defiance of regulations. Young boys were priceless on warships. Black powder plus shot, stored below in bulk, had to be brought to magazines in powder buckets that were actually canvas bags. Twisting stairways and narrow walkways made it hard for a fully grown man to achieve any speed with a powder bucket. So the rule of thumb came to be, "when it comes to powder monkeys, the smaller they are, the better they perform."

Nearly every Federal warship had a few powder monkeys age fifteen or under, who were selected not in spite of their small stature but because of it. Whether a vessel flew Old Glory or the Stars and Bars, a boy past fourteen had to be a bit stunted in his growth if he was to have any luck in getting a berth.

C.S.A. statistics are even less reliable than those of Union forces. But, like their enemies from the North, most large bands of southern fighting men included small boys. At least half of them were fifteen or younger.

No other western nation of modern times has experienced anything even close to the trauma of the American Civil War. Total national involvement in the four-year struggle was so complete that at least 60,000 small boys were called to the colors. While most remained anonymous, a few were sketched or photographed. Johnny Clem came to be admired throughout the North and hated everywhere in the South.

"At Chickamauga, Johnny was a sight to see," said an aide to Major General George H. Thomas. "When we decided to move in and break the Confederate siege, Johnny rode a caisson to the battle line. He waved a musket that someone had trimmed down to size for him.

"Our men had hard going that day. We seesawed back and forth. During one of our retreats, a Rebel chased the piece of artillery on which Johnny rode. By then, everybody on both sides knew who Johnny was. So when the Rebel got close, he shouted out, 'Surrender, you damned little Yankee!'

"Johnny Clem didn't say a word. He just raised his sawed-off musket and took the fellow down."

That exploit made the twelve-year-old more famous than ever and earned him the epithet, "drummer boy of Chickamauga."

For reasons unknown, he put his drum aside a few months later and became a courier for the rest of the war. When peace came, Johnny tried to enroll at West Point but couldn't qualify because his education had ended during the third grade.

"I have been turned down in my dream of going to West Point and becoming an officer," he reported in a letter that was actually an appeal. "But I am sure that my battle experience that began at Shiloh qualifies me to command. Please do all you can to help me!"

General U. S. Grant, who had been Johnny's commander at Shiloh, was starting his second year in the White House when he learned that his drummer boy had been turned down at West Point.

Grant personally intervened in the case and managed to bypass the U.S. Military Academy. As a result, the young veteran with limited education was named a second lieutenant in the U.S. Army in December 1871.

Except for brief intervals, the boy who had managed to talk his way into military service spent fifty-five years in uniform. The one-time drummer boy retired in 1916 as a major general.

Part Three

Punch and Counter-punch

Major General George B. McClellan. [LIBRARY OF CONGRESS]

17

At Bull Run Creek,
a Sunday Picnic
Got Out of Hand

"**I**'m going to pack a splendid picnic lunch on Sunday," Kady Brownell told her husband. "When the show is over, will you let me bring the company colors home in my gig?"

"You're lucky to have transportation," her husband responded. "Everybody in Washington wants to get a look at Rebels on the run. Sure, it will be fine for you to display the colors—we won't be needing them until the victory parade."

Official Washington had been eager since the big July 4 parade and was buzzing with excitement on July 16, 1861. Troops under Major General George B. McClellan began pouring into the city that day. They brought with them a captured Rebel flag, perhaps planting the idea in the mind of Kady Brownell.

Ambulances and wagon trains began leaving the city in droves. Everyone knew they were headed toward Manassas Junction, roughly thirty miles to the southwest, where they'd meet and quickly humiliate troops under the leadership of "that vile Creole, Beauregard."

Brigadier General Irvin McDowell was the lucky man selected to head Federal forces. Gossip said the choice had been influenced by his having been Beauregard's classmate at West Point.

McDowell was delighted to have the honor of leading the army that would bring the rebellion to a quick end, but he had many nuisances to face. On the morning that he had met Russell of the London *Times* at the depot, the commander was vexed that he was personally having to seek artillery units that were unaccountably lost.

"Practically all of my troops are green," the West Pointer confided to the war correspondent. "Their officers hardly know how to bring them up into a decent formation. It has become a major undertaking to get meals cooked."

McDowell waited for Russell to speak. When he did not, the Federal leader continued. "Truth of the matter is, we have no choice. We must fight very soon, or not at all. Most enlistments are for ninety days, and they'll be running out in a matter of days."

Russell had already reported to his editors that officers of the regular army had a very low opinion of McDowell's "horde of battalion companies—clad in all kinds of different uniforms, diversely equipped, and perfectly ignorant of the principles of concerted action."

Ammunition seemed to be plentiful, but field artillery varied widely in caliber. Few if any units would be capable of using ammunition borrowed from another unit's supply.

"There is considerable bravado," Russell reported to England. "Only time will tell whether or not it is warranted."

That observation grew out of his having noticed the departure of the Garibaldi Guard for what everyone knew to be the fighting front. They trudged out of the city bearing rations of bread on their bayonets, in the style of French regulars.

Frederick Law Olmsted, later to gain fame as a city planner and designer, had just returned from a long journey to the South. He surveyed the capital and confessed himself to be dismayed at finding it to be running over with "a most woe-begone rabble."

Word trickled back to the capital that McDowell's forces had reached Centreville. That meant he was within easy striking distance of Beauregard's eight-mile line, drawn up along the steep banks of Bull Run Creek.

General Winfield Scott, who headed the U.S. Army, objected to fighting at this time, as did most veteran military commanders and many political leaders. Knowing that if they did not fight soon, men whose enlistments were about to expire would not fight at all, Lincoln had insisted upon a showdown. Without it, his ninety-day army would have disbanded and Confederate forces would have greatly outnumbered units of the regular Federal army.

Clearly, the action was set for Sunday, as rumored several days earlier. What a great day for an outing, to be followed by celebrations! More expansive than he had been since the fall of Fort Sumter, powerful Senator Charles Sumner of Massachusetts was confident that the Rebel capital, Richmond, would be an occupied city "some time early next week."

Sumner's boundless confidence affected some of his colleagues. Congressman Albert Riddle of Ohio announced his plans to "meet our grays on the field in order to rejoice with them." Alfred Ely of New York let it be known he felt an obligation to be on hand personally to

Allen C. Redwood's sketch of Rebels en route to First Bull Run. [BATTLES AND LEADERS OF THE CIVIL WAR]

congratulate the men of the Thirteenth New York upon their part in the victory. Zach Chandler, Henry Wilson, Ben Wade, and other prominent Republican leaders joined the fast-growing number of men and women who planned to watch the battle.

Early Sunday morning, so many carriages had reached Centreville—by then nearly empty of soldiers who had left their bivouacs behind—that the village "gave the appearance of being ready for a monster military picnic."

Transportation was so scarce that when Russell of the *Times* tried to hire a gig, he found the owner reluctant to turn it over to him at any price. At least one senator paid the incredible price of twenty-five dollars to hire a trap for a single day's outing.

Accompanied by a sprinkling of ladies, the gentlemen of Washington took along plenty of good food: sherry, roast chicken, and crisp cornbread or sweet biscuits. More than one female excursionist took her opera glass. Annie Etheridge, whose father was in the Second Michigan, decided at the last minute to carry a brace of pistols. "Not that I'm likely to need them," she confided to friends. "It simply seems the sensible thing for a daughter of the regiment to do."

McDowell roused his men very early on Sunday, July 21, and had them en route to a site just east of Manassas by 2:30 A.M. Federal artillery, already stationed at strategic points near Bull Run Creek, began lobbing shells toward Confederate lines at precisely 5:00 A.M., as planned. But a rivulet fed by Sudley Springs proved much bigger than expected; units ordered to flank the Rebels didn't reach assigned positions until three hours late.

Ragged and late though the assault was, Confederates were not well prepared to meet it. After seesaw fighting that lasted until nearly noon, brevet Brigadier General Francis Bartow chose a desperate plan. He told his men that he'd personally lead an assault down Henry Hill.

Bartow's Georgians, along with many other units in Beauregard's army, knew that they were led by a graduate of Yale Law School. Francis Bartow, they told new friends with great pride, had defied orders of Georgia Governor Joseph E. Brown. Instead of remaining in the state with his volunteers, Bartow had defiantly marched off to join the Confederate army, taking state-owned weapons with him. "To reduce confusion," Bartow suggested very early, "our brave men should be uniformly dressed in gray."

Leading his men in a charge against Federal forces, Bartow took a direct hit by a rifle ball. He dropped from his horse and managed to mumble to subordinates, "They have killed me, boys, but you must never give up the field!" Minutes later Bartow died, the first high-ranking casualty of the growing war.

Soon after his death, five fresh regiments of Virginians reached the field. Led by a former instructor at Virginia Military Institute, they stood their ground on top of Henry Hill against withering fire. Brigadier General Barnard Bee, awed at the way in which the Virginia leader repulsed wave after wave of attacks, cried out, "Look! There is Jackson, standing like a stone wall. Rally behind him!" Killed shortly afterward, Bee did not know that his tribute would cause Brigadier General Thomas J. Jackson to become universally known as "Stonewall" Jackson.

During two hours of constant heavy fighting after noon, confusion multiplied. Combatants on both sides wore whatever uniforms they could get. Two Federal batteries, mistakenly thinking that an advancing Confederate unit was one of their own, held their fire. When the enemies reached point blank range, they opened a withering fire that cut the regiment to pieces.

About 4:00 P.M., Confederate reinforcements arrived in time to help penetrate deep inside Federal lines. At first the defeated defenders of the Union retreated slowly and with a semblance of order. Then a Confederate gunner landed a shell on a wagon that was crossing Cub Run bridge. Destruction of the vehicle blocked the main line of retreat to Centreville. Many green recruits were thrown into panic; soon the retreat became a rout.

C.S.A. President Jefferson Davis, who had come by train from Richmond, saw the crumbling of the Federal line and the ensuing chaos. Davis noted that one of the few Federal units whose men did not panic was led by a thin, redheaded West Pointer, Colonel William T. Sherman.

Incredibly, the last shot of consequence was fired at the suspension bridge over Cub Run by none other than Edmund Ruffin, the man who gladly claimed the privilege of firing the first shot at Fort Sumter.

Casualties ran so high on both sides that the imagination of civilians was staggered. Rebels counted 387 dead and 1,588 wounded but said that only thirteen were missing or captured. On the Union side, the death toll ran to more than 450 and about 1,200 were wounded. Confusion in the rout was so great that 1,315 were reported as missing; but it was hoped many of them would turn up as prisoners.

Among the hundreds who had actually been captured was an Irish-born son of a professional soldier who had risen to the rank of full colonel. It was quite a feather in Richmond's cap to have a man of Michael Corcoran's rank and prestige safely inside a Confederate prison.

"Dragging their tailfeathers," in the language of Frederick Law Olmsted, both defeated Union fighting men and the civilians who had gone for a gay Sunday picnic straggled back into the capital.

Inevitably, so disastrous a beginning of full-scale conflict called for a scapegoat. Abraham Lincoln, who didn't go to bed at all on Sunday night, berated war correspondent Russell for writing that he had seen "beaten, foot-sore, spongy-looking soldiers, officers, and all the *debris* of the army filing back in order to form crowds before the spirit stores." That kind of publicity would delay or defeat plans to persuade Britain to give moral and perhaps financial aid to the Union cause.

McDowell was accused, probably without foundation, of having been drunk during the final hours at Bull Run. Six days later, the man who had rejoiced at the opportunity of distinguishing himself was replaced as commander by a little-known former railroad executive, Major General George B. McClellan of the Ohio Volunteers.

Though the mood of rejoicing in Richmond was quite different from the despair in Washington, everyone in both capitals viewed Bull Run as a turning point. What had seemed to be a politically generated rebellion, which those in Washington thought would be brief, had become a full-scale war. Both North and South had reached the point of no return. Soldiers and civilians alike could now dimly understand Colonel William T. Sherman's first reaction to Bull Run. "When for the first time I saw cannonballs strike men and crash through the trees and saplings above and around us, I realized the sickening confusion as one approaches a field of battle and for the first time sees a field strewn with dead men and horses."

CHAPTER

18

Rose Greenhow Was "Worth Any Six of Jeff Davis's Best Regiments"

"**I**n a day or two, twelve hundred cavalry plus four batteries of artillery will cross Bull Run and cut the rail line again. For God's sake, heed this. It is positive."

Confederate leaders to whom this message was smuggled from a Washington prison had already learned to heed everything they got from Mrs. Rose Greenhow.

Her message of December 1861 warned of a new Federal build-up in a region she had helped to make famous a few months earlier. Leaders on both sides knew by then that the debacle of First Bull Run was due partly to nonmilitary factors.

Major General George B. McClellan, upon taking over the crippled army that had been led to defeat by McDowell, told aides that "from sources unknown, the Rebels knew our entire plan of operation; they had their hands on detailed orders before some of our own commanders received them."

Rose O'Neal Greenhow, who had spent her entire life in the District of Columbia, moved in the highest social circles from early womanhood. Her intimates included top military officers, senators, and at least two U.S. presidents. John C. Calhoun of South Carolina spent a great deal of time with her after the death of her husband and became widely credited with having persuaded her to spy for the South.

"I can never, never forget that my beloved father was treacherously killed by a black body servant whom he trusted," she said many times. Known to many in Washington's inner circle as the "Wild Rose," the lovely widow had a way of making instant conquests among civil servants, most of whom believed the rumor that she could make or break the career of any man in the city.

Rose Greenhow and her daughter Rose, photographed in prison. [MATTHEW BRADY STUDIO, LIBRARY OF CONGRESS]

John F. Calhoun—no relative of the South Carolina lawmaker—probably was first to confide in Rose that something big was about to take place in late June 1861. As a clerk on the payroll of the Senate Military Committee, this man, who was much younger than the seductive widow, had access to highly classified information.

"Yes, it is true," she boasted many months later. "I knew that General McDowell was moving out, even before he got official orders." Early in July she sent a secret message to Beauregard and warned him that a force of at least 30,000 men—half again as many as he commanded—would soon take the field against him. For the moment, that was all she could tell the Rebel leader.

Before Beauregard's promised reinforcements arrived, he got a second secret message. This time, it came to him in the hollow heel of a young officer's boot. According to Mrs. Greenhow, the McDowell advance was "positive" and would involve perhaps 55,000 men.

Warnings from the Wild Rose enabled Beauregard to choose defensive posts with great care. Knowing from the start that he'd be outnumbered, the shrewd Creole decided to make the most of the terrain.

Before he had completed his defensive plans, the Confederate leader learned from Mrs. Greenhow that Federal sappers would soon cut the Manassas Gap railroad. That meant the line should not be used for movement of troops under any circumstances.

Forewarned, greatly reinforced, and prepared to spring many a trap upon greenhorn Federal troops, Beauregard made the July 21 battle of Manassas, which was never called Bull Run in the South, a victory slogan. At his behest, Rose O'Neal soon received through intermediaries a telegram that read, "Our President and our General thank you. The entire Confederacy is in your debt. We rely upon you for further vital information."

Riding the wave of victory and continuing to send daily dispatches to Richmond, Mrs. Greenhow expanded her spy network too rapidly. It sprang a leak, and in August she was clapped in Old Capitol Prison to await trial on charges of espionage and treason. It was from the prison that she sent to Beauregard information vital to his conduct in the second battle of Bull Run.

Even in prison, the Rebel spy continued to get notes about private conversations of McClellan, plus summaries of deliberations by Lincoln and members of his cabinet. Her small daughter Rose often served as a courier. So did her maidservant. At least once she used a carrier pigeon to transmit urgent information that was marked "For the eyes of President Davis, only."

It was Senator Charles Sumner of Massachusetts who emphatically said that "Mrs. Greenhow is worth any six of Jeff Davis's best regiments."

Years later, Carl Sandburg confessed to amazement after having examined the record of one woman's accomplishments. Authorities, he concluded, "had every reason and right to hang Rose Greenhow under espionage laws."

That they didn't seriously consider this alternative was due to fear of scandal. If she went to trial, high-placed male friends would be implicated. Therefore embarrassed leaders, who most of all wanted to see the last of Rose Greenhow, offered her a safe conduct to Confeder-

Old Capitol Prison, Washington. [NATIONAL ARCHIVES]

ate lines, if she would promise faithfully "to be bound by the laws of war."

She laughed at the idea.

Knowing no other way to get this thorny rose out of their hair, Federal leaders decided to send her to Baltimore under military guard. From that point, she could easily proceed to Richmond.

Legal experts weren't certain that the law permitted deportation of an unconvicted citizen, but this course of action seemed to involve the least unpleasant consequences. So authorities made no secret of the fact that they looked forward to the day in June 1862 when she would be escorted to Baltimore.

Crowds of curious onlookers gathered at Old Capitol Prison on the day designated for her deportation. Many wondered why, on so warm a day, that the prisoner wore a shawl. Just before stepping into the waiting carriage, Rose Greenhow paused. She scanned the crowd, nodded to those who cheered her, and deftly lifted her shawl just enough to reveal underneath it a Confederate flag.

No man was happier to see her leave than was Allan Pinkerton, who was largely responsible for having uncovered her spy network. He was confident that the woman—intelligent and resourceful as she was— would give Federal leaders no more trouble.

Pinkerton proved to be wrong.

Jefferson Davis soon sent Rose to Europe in the role of diplomatic courier. There she collected intelligence and regularly dispatched it to Richmond.

Some information she gathered in 1864 was so urgent that she didn't trust it to messengers; she felt she must take it to President Davis in person. So she sailed on the blockade runner *Condor* and had an uneventful voyage until the vessel reached the mouth of the Cape Fear River in North Carolina.

Spotted by a Federal gunboat and forced to make a run for it, the *Condor* ran aground on a sandbar. Rose Greenhow knew that once the vessel was captured, she would be seized and searched. Accordingly, with only two companions, she set out for shore in a lifeboat, still bearing her vital information. High waves battered the little boat and soon tipped it over.

Rose might have made it to shore with her messages had she not strapped about her waist a belt bulging with two thousand dollars in gold. Weighted down by it, she drowned, carrying with her the urgent news from Europe.

Allan Pinkerton, Abraham Lincoln, and all Washington leaders were finally freed from worrying about what the Wild Rose might do next.

CHAPTER

19

Parson Brownlow Played
Both Ends Against the Middle

A few weeks before Confederate spy Rose Greenhow was deported to the South, fire-eating newspaper editor and orator William G. Brownlow of Knoxville, Tennessee, was deported to the North.

Parson Brownlow, whose universally used title came from a brief period as a Methodist circuit rider in early manhood, should have dropped into obscurity. He did not. Instead of bringing an end to his tale, Confederate authorities, who had used extralegal means to get rid of a troublemaker, watched with astonishment as he recovered from his losses and rose to heights to which even he had not aspired.

At best a quasi-legal measure, the deportation of Greenhow, Brownlow, and later of an Ohio congressman set the stage for punitive action against ordinary folk. Most of these dramatic moves were made by Federal troops in occupied territory.

Barely one year after Brownlow was forced by Confederates to leave their section, Brigadier General Thomas Ewing of Ohio was put in command of the District of the Border in Kansas, a tract that included several Missouri counties. Ewing's notorious General Order #11 required the evacuation of four Missouri counties that were believed to harbor southern sympathizers. Residents had just fifteen days to leave, and violation of the order carried an automatic death sentence that had the approval of Abraham Lincoln.

Almost simultaneously, but without presidential knowledge or approval, Major General Ambrose E. Burnside took punitive steps deep inside Union territory. All persons in the Department of the Ohio who were considered to be southern sympathizers were ordered deported to Confederate lines.

Also without the knowledge of the president, three-star General Ulysses S. Grant deported all the Jews from Memphis. His close friend and subordinate, Brigadier General William T. Sherman, deported masses of women and children from Roswell, Georgia, and later ordered Atlanta to be evacuated. Citizens of that captured city had their choice; they could go North or South as they pleased, but they could not remain in Atlanta.

A little-known sidelight of the war, the practice of deportation by both sides gave Parson Brownlow a brief interval of quiet between a fiery beginning and a triumphant ending.

"I grew up as a penniless orphan," he told audiences at every opportunity. "If I don't know the meaning of 'root, hog, or die,' no man alive does!" Self-educated during years as a carpenter's assistant, he became a Methodist circuit rider in 1826, thereby gaining his sobriquet.

Two years of riding the circuit were enough for Parson Brownlow. He smelled bigger things in the air. Although sectional differences had not split the nation in 1828, there were enough causes and parties to provide a man with a splendid platform from which to make public his views.

In his rambling, but often persuasive, speeches and editorials, something he said was likely to appeal to nearly every listener or reader. Brownlow epitomized the art of playing both ends against the middle, not in an attempt to deceive, but as a fruit of his strongest convictions.

"Yes!" he thundered at every opportunity, "I'm a born and bred slavery man! Without slavery, the South would be flat on its back! Slavery today, slavery tomorrow, slavery forever!"

That kind of talk made many Southerners hold their heads high with pride. They tried not to listen when the parson got started on another favorite subject, which made the blood of many run faster.

"Make no mistake about it," Parson Brownlow liked to say, "our glorious federal union is the grandest government ever conceived by man, under the guidance of Almighty God! I am for our federal union,

"Parson" W. G. Brownlow. [LES-LIE'S ILLUSTRATED]

now and always!"

Upholding slavery and saying prayers of gratitude for the Union, Brownlow went into John C. Calhoun's own South Carolina district and publicly condemned the states' rights doctrine that Calhoun labelled "nullification."

Regardless of a person's views, if he listened long enough or read enough of the parson's fire-eating editorials, he could find something with which he agreed. Families, towns, counties, and states became hopelessly divided by sectional strife. Somehow, Parson Brownlow managed to maintain his reason in spite of the fact that deep inside him the brother-against-brother conflict raged before, during, and after actual war.

Forsaking the pulpit for the press, the parson edited and published three newspapers, all boldly Whig in tone. Papers published in Elizabethton and Jonesboro barely survived, but his Knoxville *Whig and Independent Journal* became by far the most influential newspaper in East Tennessee.

"Stick by the Union," Brownlow urged readers as soon as talk of possible secession became common. "Have nothing to do with separation from our great Federal establishment!"

At the outbreak of war, sentiments such as Brownlow voiced were regarded in Richmond as treason. East Tennessee was a trouble spot. Unionists, many of them perhaps converted to that cause by Brownlow's papers, showed little loyalty to the emerging C.S.A.

When Brownlow got wind of the fact that marshals were on the way to Knoxville with papers authorizing his arrest, he fled into the Smoky Mountains late in 1861. Scouts tracked him down and brought him back to Knoxville to survey the ruins of his newspaper office that had been wrecked by secessionists.

Rumor had it that a Union army was about to march into the region through Cumberland Gap. It was an unfounded tale, but ardent backers of the Union didn't wait to verify reports. They formed armed bands designed to assist the invading forces, then burned bridges to prevent ready movement by Confederates.

Jefferson Davis, sensing a crisis in the making, dispatched troops from both Memphis and Pensacola and simultaneously suspended the right of *habeas corpus*. Numerous Unionists, known or suspected, were captured and imprisoned, among them, of course, Brownlow.

Acting on orders from Richmond, the Confederate commander in Knoxville told insurrectionists not actually known to have participated in bridge burning that they would be treated as prisoners of war. Convicted bridge burners were informed that they would be "executed on the spot, by hanging, with their bodies then publicly displayed in the vicinity of burned bridges."

Five men went to the gallows. Thrown into a moist, narrow little dungeon in company with twenty-four other men suspected of bridge burning but not yet convicted, Parson Brownlow didn't retreat an inch. Instead, he informed captors that he'd "continue to fight secession on the ice in hell."

So well known a prisoner posed a dilemma for captors. They pondered alternatives and decided to get rid of the fellow by sending him to Federal lines under military escort. In later autobiographical writing, Parson Brown said that he did not leave Knoxville willingly.

"I had already written and committed to memory a splendid speech to be delivered from the gallows," he said. "When they sent me packing, I had no chance to deliver that splendid speech!"

Making his way to Washington, Brownlow was briefly a celebrity. He went several times to the White House and claimed to have given Abraham Lincoln much advice that the president followed. Soon he issued a booklet entitled *Sketches of the Rise, Progress and Decline of Secession*. Naturally, it was widely hailed in the northern press.

The successful conclusion of the Knoxville campaign by Federal forces in late 1863 put Major General Ambrose E. Burnside in command of the occupied city. That's when Parson Brownlow returned in triumph to launch a campaign for elections in which only "loyal citizens" could vote.

Blacks were excluded from his proposal; he didn't think they should vote under any circumstances. Those who remained loyal to their former masters should be permitted to stay in the region, he said, but "those unruly ones who defied the prevailing order should be instantly removed to some other section—perhaps the unpopulated West."

Talk like that grated on the ears of some Federal authorities, but it enabled Parson Brownlow to gain a wide popular following. As a member of the Union Central Committee of the government of occupation, he became one of the most influential civilians in East Tennessee.

Critics called him a carpetbagger, a label that he rejected with contempt. In spite of that rejection, he aided Northerners-come-South in their bids for places of power. Then he gained their backing and was elected governor of Tennessee.

After two terms in the executive mansion, the man who had earlier challenged Andrew Johnson in a contest for a seat in the U.S. House of Representatives was triumphantly elected to the U.S. Senate. Still playing both ends against the middle by espousing causes that every sensible man knew to be contradictory, Parson Brownlow spent six years in the nation's most prestigious lawmaking body before being forced into retirement, not because of his mixed bag of views, but by ill health.

20

"The Lot Fell upon Colonel Corcoran"

War Dept., Richmond, Nov. 9, 1861
SIR:
*   You are hereby instructed to choose by lot from among the prisoners of war, of highest rank, one who is to be confined to a cell appropriated to convicted felons, and who is to be treated in all·respects as if such convict, and to be held for execution in the same manner as may be adopted by the enemy for the execution of the prisoner of war Smith, recently condemned to death in Philadelphia.*
*   You will also select thirteen other prisoners of war, the highest in rank of those captured by our forces, to be confined in the cells reserved for prisoners accused of infamous crimes, and will treat them as such so long as the enemy shall continue so to treat the like number of prisoners of war captured by them at sea, and now held for trial in New York as pirates.*
*   As these measures are intended to repress the infamous attempt now made by the enemy to commit judicial murder on prisoners of war, you will execute them strictly, as the mode best calculated to prevent the commission of so heinous a crime.*
*   Your obedient servant,*
*   JUDAH P. BENJAMIN*
*   Acting Secretary of War*
To: Brig.-Gen. John H. Winder

That long dispatch from the Confederate secretary of war to his provost marshal in charge of prisoners does not employ the word "hostage." Neither do other official documents, some of which were issued by Federal officers and some of which bore the signatures of

Confederates. But Benjamin's dispatch meant that, if obeyed, Rebels would soon be holding a Union officer as hostage.

Abraham Lincoln had signed a bold proclamation on April 19, 1861. Under its terms, all ports in South Carolina, Georgia, Alabama, Florida, Mississippi, Louisiana, and Texas were declared to be under a naval blockade.

Laughter echoed from Savannah to Galveston, then rippled across the Atlantic. British authorities went on record as considering the president's directive to be ludicrous. "With three ships in port, how can Washington hope to bar passage along 3,500 miles of coast?" a London editorial demanded.

Ludicrous or not, the order was equipped with teeth. Any person who ignored the blockade would be treated as a pirate, not as a prisoner of war, said Abraham Lincoln.

His mettle was soon tested. July 6 saw the privateer *Jefferson Davis*, licensed by the head of state whose name it bore, overtake and capture the merchant schooner *Enchantress* off the coast of Delaware. Headed by Walter W. Smith of Savannah, raiders made prisoners of the crew of the *Enchantress* and seized cargo worth $13,000.

Sixteen days later, however, the U.S.S. *Albatross*, a vessel of the Atlantic Blockading Squadron, caught up with the privateer off Hatteras Inlet, North Carolina. Walter W. Smith surrendered without a fight, and he and his men were shipped to Philadelphia for trial.

Acting swiftly in accordance with the presidential directive, the courts took just three days to find Smith guilty of piracy. Members of his crew later received the same verdict; all were remanded to Moyamensing Prison to await execution, for the conviction of piracy carried an automatic death sentence.

The noted attorney Nathaniel Harrison, who had been retained to defend the accused men, had cited numerous precedents under which international maritime law treated privateering as legal during time of war. When justices failed to heed his arguments, Harrison appealed directly to C.S.A. President Jefferson Davis.

"It is a matter of utmost urgency," he wrote. "My clients will die unless you enter into some arrangement or negotiation with the Government, leading to an exchange of prisoners of war." Harrison's appeal reached Richmond too late. A few days before it arrived, Davis had instructed his secretary of war to take steps that led to his dispatch to Winder.

On November 10 newspapers of Charleston solemnly announced that "the lot fell upon Colonel Corcoran." Readers needed no explanation. They knew that under Winder's orders, a lottery had been held at the port city's Castle Pinckney, where numerous Federal prisoners were being detained.

Colonel Michael Corcoran. [U. S. MILITARY INSTITUTE]

Most citizens of Charleston knew a bit about Corcoran, for his capture at Bull Run had generated great excitement throughout the South. Generally known to be of Irish birth, Corcoran was regarded as a "professional soldier, totally unlike Abe Lincoln's raw recruits."

As colonel of the Sixty-ninth New York Militia, he had been the subject of national publicity in 1860. Told to parade his regiment before the Prince of Wales, who was en route to Washington for a White House visit, the Irishman had bluntly refused. He would have been court martialed had not New York authorities regarded him as invaluable in raising Irish recruits.

Once more propelled into the national spotlight under terms of Benjamin's order, Corcoran was now due to receive from Confederates whatever punishment was meted out to Walter W. Smith in Philadelphia.

There were enough additional men in prison at Charleston to implement Benjamin's second order. Under its terms, thirteen more prisoners of war "of highest rank" were selected as hostages for the crew members of the Confederate ship *Savannah*. Captured and imprisoned in New York, these seamen were also charged with piracy and were awaiting trial.

One by one, the lot fell upon ten Federal field officers plus three captains. Along with Colonel Corcoran, they were put in close confinement. Winder then notified Washington of what he had done.

Friends and relatives of the men held in Charleston bombarded the U.S. war department with letters and telegrams. British diplomats let it be known that they seriously doubted the legality of Federal action that had precipitated the selection of hostages.

Judge Grier of Philadelphia, a member of the tribunal that had tried Walter Smith, acted to get Federal authorities out of the dilemma. He could not understand, he informed Washington, why men taken on the sea should be hanged, while those taken on land were to be held as prisoners or routinely exchanged.

Grier's analysis was received with gratitude by the U.S. attorney general. Soon the death sentence that had been given to Smith was countermanded.

Confederates responded by promising not to execute Colonel Corcoran.

Eventually, all men involved were exchanged. Two of those freed from Castle Pinckney and possible execution were G. W. Neff and Israel Vogdes. These brigadier generals were the war's highest-ranking Federal hostages, but were not the last to be held.

Political and military events during the summer and fall of 1861 were almost as scrambled as were legal issues surrounding "pirates" and hostages.

Not until May did the Confederate Congress get around to making a formal declaration of war upon the United States of America. Days later, Great Britain recognized not one side or the other, but both, as belligerents. Concurrently, delegates to the Virginia convention split down the middle. Many from the western part of the state announced plans to organize a separate government aimed at the creation of West Virginia as a state.

North Carolina seceded, and New Mexico came under Confederate control when Federal troops gave up Fort Fillmore. Abraham Lincoln signed a patently unenforceable measure under whose terms those slaves used by Confederates either in labor or under arms were required to be given their freedom. Four New York newspapers, labeled seditious, were banned from the U.S. mails. At Augusta, Georgia, Presbyterians of the South solemnly voted to sever ties with their brethren in the North. Secessionist governments in Missouri and in Kentucky were given official status by Richmond, a move hotly contested by Unionists in both states.

On July 2, two days before Congress was to convene in the special session called by Lincoln, he suspended *habeas corpus* in "exceptional cases." He then submitted a lengthy war message to lawmakers in which he deplored that he had been forced to employ military measures "in defense of government." Congress received the message and prepared to declare a state of war; meanwhile, the president was busy viewing the James rifled cannon.

At year's end, belligerents on both sides were greatly relieved that no one involved in the *Jefferson Davis* and the *Savannah* affairs had been executed as the presidential order required.

However, other incidents followed. Near Fredericksburg, Virginia, Confederates waved a white flag, and Union soldiers who came to them across the river at Edwards Ferry were seized by the men they had thought to be refugees. Union General Christopher C. Augur then took prompt steps in reprisal. He arrested John L. Rinker and George C. Ryan, alleged to be relatives of the bushwhackers, and promised to

Men of the Sixty-ninth New York Militia, imprisoned at Castle Pinckney. [NA-
TIONAL ARCHIVES]

treat his civilian hostages exactly as Confederates treated soldiers they
had captured by a ruse.

Again, there was a trade.

In the spring of 1863, Federal warships under Rear Admiral Samuel
F. DuPont bombarded Charleston. Knowing themselves to be outgunned, defenders sent to DuPont a warning that they intended to
take fifty Union prisoners from their cells and expose them to the fire
of their own big guns.

DuPont did not wait for the Confederates to act upon their threat.
At his request, Brigadier General John G. Foster selected fifty Confederate prisoners from a stockade on Johnson's Island and sent them to
be placed on gunboats where they would be the first to be hit by a
well-aimed shell from a shore battery. The hostages selected by Foster
included five generals, fifteen colonels, fifteen lieutenant colonels, and
fifteen majors.

Though the list of Confederates used as hostages was widely published in northern newspapers, nothing came of this show of defiance.
By arrangement between opposing commanders, two boatloads of
prisoners met in Charleston harbor to be exchanged simultaneously.

An estimated sixty bedraggled Federals straggled into Fredericksburg on May 8, 1864, and surrendered to civilian authorities.
Thereupon U.S. Secretary of War Edwin M. Stanton had sixty-four
Virginia civilians arrested and held as hostages, using them as levers
with which to secure the release of his soldiers who had voluntarily
surrendered.

After an alleged massacre at Fort Pillow, Tennessee, Lincoln
drafted, but never signed, an order to seize hostages in a bid to force
Confederates to admit having committed war crimes.

That was the last recorded attempt to resort to use of hostages during the bloody years in which leaders on both sides tacitly agreed that
punishment would often be "an eye for an eye."

21

U. S. Grant Ripped a Hole
in the Belly of the C.S.A.

Hd Qrs Army in the Field
Camp Near Donelson, Feby 16th

Gen. S. B. Buckner,
  Confed. Army,
Sir:
  Yours of this date proposing Armistice and appointment of Commissioners, to settle terms of Capitulation, is just received. No terms except an unconditional surrender can be accepted.
  I propose to move immediately upon your works.
  I am sir, very respectfully,
    Your obt. sevt.
      U. S. GRANT, Brig. Gen.

Brigadier General Simon Bolivar Buckner, who had graduated from West Point in the class of 1844, was astonished and visibly shaken when he received this message. In an earlier note, he had taken care to remind Brigadier General Ulysses S. Grant that at Fort Sumter, Beauregard had leaned over backward in giving generous terms of surrender to Major Anderson.

Though he was too much of a southern gentleman to bring the matter up, Buckner vividly remembered a personal act of kindness to the man now demanding unconditional surrender. When Grant, a graduate of the Point (class of 1843), was turning in his resignation and desperately seeking money to get back to Missouri, it was Buckner who had lent him enough to get home.

Buckner fumed to his aides, but knew what his answer must be. Superiors had pulled out of Fort Donelson, on the Cumberland River, and had taken many of their men with them. Faced by overwhelming Federal forces on an icy morning in early 1862, the Confederate leader could foresee his men being cut to pieces, or he could accept the uncompromising and humiliating terms offered by Grant.

In his reply, the Kentucky native put a formal protest into the record. Then he underscored what his opponent already knew, that thousands of Donelson's defenders had been withdrawn, and he grudgingly conceded that "the overwhelming forces under your command compel me, notwithstanding the brilliant success of the Confederate arms yesterday, to accept the ungenerous and unchivalrous terms which you propose."

Numerous journalists and artists were on hand from the New York *Times*, Washington's newspapers, and even the *Illustrated London News*. They had a field day with their reports that informed the jubilant North of "UNCONDITIONAL SURRENDER!" However, the Richmond *Dispatch* published a different version of the dramatic moment when a Confederate commander had, for the first time, been forced to ask for terms of surrender.

Harper's Weekly printed a portrait of the "Hero of Donelson" on page one of its next issue. Abolitionists danced in the street in many cities. On the night the news reached Washington, lamps burned long into the night as celebrants repeatedly toasted "Unconditional Surrender" Grant.

Fort Donelson erased, for the moment, the shame of First Bull Run. Not only military experts, but also ordinary citizens, realized that Grant had ripped a hole in the belly of the Confederate States of America, because the fall of the fort meant that it would be easy to move on to Nashville, a key rail center. From there much of Kentucky and Tennessee could be cut off from the rest of the Confederacy.

An unknown artist portrayed victorious Grant puffing on a big black cigar. An habitual pipe smoker for many years, the Federal leader had swapped his pipe for a cigar just before the informal surrender was consummated. In consequence, throughout the North jubilant patriots showered him with fine Havanas—an estimated 20,000 of them. Grant became a heavy cigar smoker, not realizing that his new addiction would eventually lead to his death from cancer of the mouth and throat.

Not all in the North were wholly delighted at what had happened on a remote Tennessee river. Major General Henry Halleck, whose subordinates derided him as "Spit and Polish Henry," immediately began

"The Storming of Fort Donelson." [1862 LITHOGRAPH]

circulating rumors that Grant had resumed the heavy drinking that earlier had led to his resignation from the army. Halleck's superior, General McClellan, took the gossip seriously enough to dispatch to the commander of the Department of the Missouri a telegram: "Do not hesitate to arrest Grant if the good of the service requires it."

Grant's rise had been altogether too meteoric to suit Halleck, or McClellan. Along with many colleagues and hundreds who were under the command of the man who swore he had given up the bottle, their knowledge of his past colored their view of his victory.

Henry Dwight of the Twentieth Ohio Volunteers, age eighteen, kept a detailed personal diary of his experiences in the thrust to open the Mississippi River to Federal vessels. Early in the campaign that culminated at Fort Donelson, he noted that he carried on his person "50½ pounds—including knapsack, haversack with rations, canteen, rifled musket, 40 rounds of cartridges, sergeant's sword."

If he correctly read his own inmost feelings, Henry Dwight was ready and willing to die for the Union and for President Abraham Lincoln. But he wasn't eager to go in a hurry, and he didn't like the stories that were told around campfires.

General Grant's disdain for clean uniforms, the stiff West Point posture, and careful adherence to regulations, had triggered some of the animosity shown by Halleck and others. Hence he was regarded by men in his command as "a great big question mark."

Many had learned that in early married life their general and his bride were slaveholders. Some fighting men did not care, but many were angry at the idea of being led against the Rebels by a man who had owned slaves.

Though Grant had resigned from the army under pressure, it was widely rumored that he'd been cashiered. "When the man got back to Missouri from a post in the West, where he took off his uniform, he failed at everything he tried," a campfire story began.

"He became a farmer and found that nothing would grow for him. Somebody got sorry for him and gave him a job in a little store, but he just couldn't hold it long. They say that he wound up trying to sell firewood on the streets of St. Louis before his folks took pity on him and began feeding him."

Though frequently embellished, that basic story was true. When made second in command to Grant for the planned operation against Atlanta in 1864, Sherman couldn't forget that he himself had seen Grant trying, with little success, to peddle wood on the streets of the big river city.

Raucous laughter erupted any time a storyteller turned to the personal foibles of their commander. "Anybody ever seen the hair on that man's chest?" became a standard query. It was posed frequently because in the weeks before the attack upon Donelson, it became general knowledge that Grant had a horror of being seen in the nude. What's more, he dreaded the sight of blood so much that he refused to eat meat unless it was cooked well done.

Instructors at West Point had noted that the cadet who ranked twenty-first in a class of thirty-nine was far more at ease with horses than with humans. Though they let him graduate and become a lieutenant in the Fourth U.S. Infantry, officials of the U.S. Military Academy didn't expect to hear much about the man whose ways of doing things seemed as scrambled as his name.

Born Hiram Ulysses, upon arrival at West Point he found that his congressional appointment identified him as Ulysses Simpson. It seemed easier to retreat behind initials than to attempt to have the error corrected. Yet it was these initials that later provided a hook upon which to hang a new and admiring title: "Unconditional Surrender" Grant.

Initially rebuffed when war clouds led him to offer his service to the Illinois militia, the man who had failed at everything he tried won the backing of Congressman Elihu B. Washburn. That was enough to enable him to put on a uniform and become colonel of the Twenty-first Illinois Infantry in June 1861. Sixty days later, 'Lys Grant was a brigadier general of volunteers.

In the chaotic days of 1861, anything could happen, and practically everything did, sooner or later.

Washington reeled when news came that London was in an uproar over the actions of Captain Charles Wilkes. Master of the Federal vessel *San Jacinto,* Wilkes had stopped and searched the British mail packet *Trent.* When Confederate commissioners James M. Mason and James Slidell were found aboard as passengers, Wilkes hauled them off the British vessel and took them to Fort Warren, at Boston, for imprisonment.

Five weeks after the international incident, Lord Lyons, the British minister to the United States, demanded the immediate release of "civilians seized from His Majesty's ship *Trent.*" It took only a week for Lincoln and members of his cabinet to conclude that the seizure of Mason and Slidell actually violated international law. Regardless of Federal anger at the audacity of the Confederates in sending official emissaries abroad, Washington dared not risk alienating Britain.

It was in this climate of defeat and near despair that Abraham Lincoln again took the initiative. General War Order No. 1, issued on January 27, 1862, established February 22 as the day for concerted advances against the enemy by the entire Union army and navy. Those who knew the president well needed few specific directives; for weeks he had been fretting over the lack of an offensive in the West.

Along with gunboat-builder James B. Eads and scores of top military experts, Lincoln was convinced that the war would have to the won in the West, the vulnerable back side of the Confederacy bordered by the Mississippi River.

It was in obedience to the presidential directive that Halleck ordered U. S. Grant and his command, augmented by the Eads-built gunboat *Carondelet* and other vessels, against forts Henry and Donelson.

Gunboats found Fort Henry on the Tennessee River to be an easy target; it fell after only a few hours of fighting. Donelson on the Cumberland was known to be much more heavily fortified, as well as packed with Confederate veterans of earlier engagements. On a strategic site atop a bluff about 100 feet high, the fortress had a rifled 128-pounder plus ten 32-pound carronades and a 10-inch columbiad, all of which were protected by earthworks and sandbags.

Brigadier General John B. Floyd, who was in command, had remained confident until he caught his first glimpse of the Federal flotilla led by the *Carondelet.* "I fear we cannot hold out twenty minutes against so many gunboats," he told aides.

Surprisingly, the big guns of the Federal vessels sat too low in the water to be effective against the fortress perched high above. But scouts brought ominous news. Union infantry units were arriving as reinforcements in droves, and by nightfall on February 15, the defenders would be outnumbered by a ratio of at least three to two.

Floyd, formerly U.S. secretary of war in the Buchanan cabinet, was terrified. He'd earlier been indicted for malfeasance in office, charged with having diverted arms and munitions to the South on the eve of secession. If forced to surrender, he'd be subject to trial on old charges. His immediate subordinate, Major General Gideon J. Pillow, was equally troubled at the thought of being bested. Everyone knew he had taken a solemn oath never to surrender and had led his men into battle crying, "Liberty, or death!" As a southern gentleman, he couldn't face the humiliation of going back on his oath.

For those reasons both Floyd and Pillow escaped from the tightening Federal noose. Reducing the strength of Donelson by the 2,500 men they took with them, they fled by boat in the night.

U. S. Grant, whose intelligence was accurate, knew that his one-time friend Buckner, left behind as commander, did not have the supplies with which to withstand a siege or the manpower with which to repel an all-out assault. Thus, fondling the locket in which he carried a strand of his wife's hair, he dictated the message demanding nothing less than unconditional surrender.

Buckner's capitulation in spite of his protest at the terms meant that Grant had given the North its first big victory: 15,000 prisoners, a strategic fort, and—most important of all—a gaping hole in the Confederacy's line of defense in the West. Despite the uncompromising terms of Grant's demand, surrender ceremonies were so informal that they were almost casual. Within an hour after Donelson was safely in Federal hands, men of opposing armies were fraternizing.

No one in Washington or in Richmond adjusted so quickly to the new situation. In the Federal capital the victory of "Unconditional Surrender" Grant signaled a call for redoubled efforts and new strikes against regions now made vulnerable. In Richmond the loss of Donelson meant that the anticipated quick and easy total victory over Northerners who didn't know how to fight was replaced by realization that the struggle would be far longer and much bloodier than any ardent secessionist had imagined.

CHAPTER
22

Marching Off to Die, Strong Men Sang a Gentlewoman's Song

"My pulse beat much faster when men of the Twelfth Massachusetts marched through the streets of Boston, on their way to our nation's capital," the wife of an ardent abolitionist recalled many years later.

"My husband, Dr. Samuel Gridley Howe, was director of Perkins Institute for the Blind. A few days after Rebels fired upon Fort Sumter in South Carolina, I was leaving the Institute when I heard singing, 'John Brown's body lies a-mouldering in the grave; His soul is marching on!'"

Heir to a New York banking fortune and a trained musician, Julia Ward Howe was "almost mesmerized" by the lively tune and its words, sung by men responding to Lincoln's call for a military build-up. Almost unconsciously, the red-haired mezzo-soprano found herself humming the melody and sometimes singing the words aloud.

In the nation's capital a few months later, she went with friends on a picnic outing across the Potomac. They failed to reach their goal when Confederate skirmishers striking at the city forced their coachman to turn and flee.

By then, Washington had become the scene of almost daily alarms. Though some claimed that it was the most heavily fortified city in the world, few who viewed it for the first time felt safe.

Awed, Julia Ward Howe noted that troops occupied the building of the Patent Office and that tent cities had sprung up everywhere there was space for them. Big field guns loomed from hallways of the Capitol and the Treasury building. Around the Capitol, there were formidable breastworks made of the iron plates that had been cast for the unfinished dome. Soldiers scurried to and from the army kitchen that had been set up in the basement of the building.

Humming "John Brown's Body" as her carriage approached the Willard Hotel, the gentlewoman from Boston whose outing had been interrupted gave a signal to her driver. Suddenly aware of a billboard not previously noticed, she wished to stop to be sure she read it correctly. Twice she read the message before its full import sank in; a charitable organization really was trying to inform the public that bodies of dead soldiers would be embalmed and shipped home without charge, as a patriotic service.

That night, Julia Ward Howe's fitful sleep was interrupted by sounds of distant cannon fire. Tossing sleeplessly, she had an experience unlike anything she had ever encountered. "While waiting for the dawn," she said, "long lines of a poem began twining themselves inside me. I did not write them; they wrote themselves."

Legend says that she scribbled many of the words upon backs of playing cards, fearful that they would escape her fully conscious mind. Five stanzas, each made up of three lines plus a refrain, formed a finished poem that began, "Mine eyes have seen the glory of the coming of the Lord."

Massachusetts Governor John A. Andrew, with whom she had earlier toured some of the army camps in and around the capital, encouraged her to publish the song. She found editorial interest only at *Atlantic Monthly* magazine, where she received a check for four dollars and a promise to publish as soon as feasible.

Her poem, superbly adapted to the melody of the already familiar song memorializing the martyr of Harpers Ferry, appeared in print during the weeks when Lincoln's plan for a Western offensive had

Julia Ward Howe.

U. S. Grant and his men preparing to strike at forts Henry and Donelson.

A few early readers of the magazine expressed a wish that the author had found a more appropriate melody. Like most persons trained in music, some of them knew that "John Brown's Body" had been set to an old camp meeting tune, a southern one, at that. William Steffe was sometimes credited with having written "Say Brothers, Will We Meet You Over on the Other Shore," a popular favorite in Charleston, South Carolina, during the 1850s.

Federal troops, possibly members of the Second U.S. Infantry, heard Steffe's hymn and memorized it without half trying. Some of them may have sung it on the day John Brown was hanged as a traitor after having been captured by troops led by Robert E. Lee.

Within weeks after "The Battle Hymn of the Republic" had appeared in a magazine, it was available as sheet music. It soared to popularity and then to lasting fame. In company after company, first of volunteers and then of draftees, men who were certain that they were marching to their death sang as they marched.

Prisoners with barely enough breath to fill their lungs sang Julia Ward Howe's song in Andersonville prison. Chaplain Charles McCabe of the Ohio Volunteer Infantry led fellow inmates of another Confederate prison in singing the "Battle Hymn" on the night they heard of the Union victory at Gettysburg. Later McCabe led a Washington crowd that included President Abraham Lincoln.

For the most part, Confederate fighting men cheered "Dixie," but booed the "Battle Hymn." Though belligerents on both sides knew it to be the most popular marching hymn of the war, with a tune of southern origin, it was widely derided in the C.S.A. because of its "northern words."

Julia Ward Howe never lifted a musket or followed the lead of Clara Barton by going to battlefields to aid the wounded; yet she put more steel into the spines of men who sang her song than did many a drill master who taught the use of gun and bayonet.

Other civilians put their influence into quite different channels. Two innovative ideas, one that would eventually affect every American citizen, and another that would cut casualties in all future conflicts, were initiated during the Civil War.

In July 1861 U.S. Secretary of the Treasury Salmon P. Chase made a special report to Congress. For the coming fiscal year, he said, the federal government would require at least $320 million for military purposes alone.

No one had ever before dared to talk in such mammoth fiscal terms in Washington. Every lawmaker knew that it was difficult to meet the peacetime budget. Where would such a sum be found?

Chase suggested that they approve a plan to borrow two-thirds of the money needed for the army and navy. He then offered a package that included the sale of public lands, plus excise taxes on everything from bank notes to liquor. Still he was nearly twenty million dollars short of his projected goal.

Nearly six months of debate produced legislation that aimed at making up the projected shortfall by a new and ingenious method. Salaries of working men, plus profits of merchants and investors, would be taxed. Anyone with a yearly income of $600 to $10,000 would pay a 3 percent tax; persons with higher incomes would pay 5 percent. During 1863, the first year in which the income tax was collected, the return fell woefully short of Chase's estimate. The new source of revenue yielded only $2,741,857 toward a now runaway federal budget.

Few things done in Washington during war years made ordinary folk more furious than the collection of the income tax. Responding to public pressure in 1871, Congress repealed the laws providing for its collection—but a fateful precedent had been set.

Also making a lasting impact was Dr. William A. Hammond. Elected to head the civilian-led Sanitary Commission, Hammond quickly found himself hampered by military red tape. More than anything else, he wanted an official ambulance service. However, most top generals scoffed at such a notion as "unmilitary." Ambulances had always been handled by the quartermaster corps and always should be, they argued.

Hammond's idea did not catch on until after the second battle of Bull Run in August 1862. Reports concerning heavy casualties led to a general call for volunteer vehicles plus experienced male nurses.

With the take-off point designated as the Treasury building, volunteers responded in great numbers. A few brought vehicles that could be used as field ambulances; most had light gigs or heavy wagons that could not be used. While waiting for orders, members of the swelling crowd began to drink. By the time they left for the battlefield, many would-be helpers were so drunk that out of one contingent of nearly one thousand men, only seventy-five reached their destination. Secretary of War Edwin M. Stanton was enraged. Although knowing that generals and admirals would protest, he set in motion a train of events designed to produce the ambulance corps suggested earlier by William A. Hammond.

"Hammond's corps," as it was called at first, proved to be one of the lasting innovations of the war. It became the prototype for all modern military medical services.

23

James J. Andrews Lost a Race but Became a Folk Hero in Both North and South

"**M**y business is railroads—Rebel roads. Tell General Mitchel that the matter is urgent. Yes, I'm prepared to wait—all night, if necessary."

James J. Andrews, author of the note, was already known to some members of the headquarters staff of the Army of the Ohio, having brought in bits and pieces of intelligence about enemy movements. Most of his information had been accurate. Usually posing as a smuggler, he had proved that he could penetrate Confederate lines and return with little or no problem.

Brigadier General Ormsby M. Mitchel, an 1829 graduate of West Point, had been chief engineer of the Ohio and Mississippi Railroad at two separate periods. Widely acclaimed as a charismatic speaker on astronomy, he was said to consult the stars before making any major decision.

Mitchel was known to chafe at the lax discipline among the troops commanded by his superior, Major General Don Carlos Buell. But the Kentucky native took every opportunity to laud Buell for the large and growing spy network that he had developed and personally controlled.

When Mitchel learned that one of Buell's best spies planned to wait all night, if necessary, in order to see him, he was sure that something big was in the offing. Scuttlebutt among members of Buell's command post had it that plans were afoot to send a raiding party into Alabama to cut a rail line. Perhaps that might be the business about which the fellow Andrews had come.

When he was ready to see the thirty-two-year-old spy, Mitchel dismissed subordinates.

"No," Andrews responded in reply to the general's initial question,

"I have not come about the Memphis and Charleston Railroad. Those plans are not yet mature, as you undoubtedly know."

Mitchel nodded as though he had been sitting with the group planning to strike at the rail line somewhere near Huntsville, Alabama, although he hadn't been included in preliminary discussions.

"You remember that we tried to blow up some of the bridges in north Georgia a few months ago," Andrews said. "My job was to set the explosives. Those bridges would have gone up, too, if our party had reached the targets.

"We failed because most of the fellows in the outfit were scared of their shadows," the spy/saboteur continued. "Now I want you to detail some of your best men—or work out a plan to get volunteers on the quiet—and assign them to me. With the proper backing, I can wreck the Western & Atlantic line."

Mitchel was visibly interested. Like every other top Federal commander in the region, he knew that the one-track railroad between Atlanta and Chattanooga was properly called "the lifeline of the Confederacy." On it supplies from the deep South rolled northward toward Confederate armies, day and night.

"Just what do you propose?" he demanded. "And why come to me instead of to General Buell?"

"General Buell has his hands full with other operations, so has given me a two-week leave," Andrews explained. "Otherwise, I wouldn't have the time to come to your tent. But I have the name of a railroad engineer in Atlanta who's a solid Union man standing ready to help us any time we can strike."

"Your idea has possibilities," Mitchel admitted. "How would you implement it?"

"Let me sound out men in your units, one at a time," Andrews urged. "This time, I want only the best. When I have enough volunteers, I'll put 'em in civilian clothes. We'll travel singly, or maybe in pairs, to avoid attracting attention. We'll take over a train, head north, and burn every bridge and trestle we cross. We can make the Army of Northern Virginia hungry, I tell you!"

Andrews's bold proposal intrigued the Kentucky-born general. Within hours, he relayed the proposal to General Don Carlos Buell, who gave full approval. "Andrews is one of my best," he said. "I would direct his enterprise myself, were it not for other urgent matters. I'm glad he came to you."

April 7, 1862, saw Andrews lead his followers out of Shelbyville, Tennessee. Their clothing and conversation labeled them as border-country farmers who wanted nothing to do with armed forces, North or South.

At Chattanooga they boarded a southbound train and got off at Marietta, Georgia, a station close to the Chattahoochee River. April 12 found the Marietta ticket agent of the Western & Atlantic Railroad unusually busy. He had many more passengers than usual, and the strangers had selected half a dozen destinations.

Big Shanty (later Kennesaw) was the breakfast stop for the Chattanooga-bound train. While fellow passengers ate and drank, Andrews and his men slipped aboard the waiting locomotive *General*. A veteran trainman in the band uncoupled the train. Then, with an experienced engineer at the throttle, the locomotive plus its tender and three cars lit out with twenty-one hijackers as crew and passengers.

William Fuller, conductor of the stolen train, had no notion of what had happened, but he did not stand around wringing his hands as his train disappeared around a curve.

Fuller let out a yell that brought two of his aides to his side. Then he led them lickety-split along the railroad track—on foot. Some of the Confederate soldiers and civilians at Big Shanty nearly split their sides with laughter.

Along with master mechanic Anthony Murphy and engineer Jeff Cain, Fuller hoofed it as fast as his lungs and legs would permit. By the time they had run about a mile, Fuller began to understand. A band of drunks or pranksters had not stolen his train; they were Yankees, clearly bent upon some diabolic end!

Puffing to the spot where a section crew was working, Fuller requisitioned their small work car. He and his comrades then propelled the car by pushing it with long poles.

At Etowah station, the Confederate railroaders found the rickety old locomotive *Yonah*. They took it over and began puffing after the hijacked locomotive under the power of steam. Up ahead, Andrews and his raiders stopped at intervals to cut telegraph lines and to try to set fire to wooden bridges and trestles.

Soon Conductor Fuller flagged a southbound freight pulled by a Danforth & Cook locomotive called the *Texas*. Veteran engineer Peter Brachen was at the throttle. At Fuller's demand, he uncoupled his load, and the pursuers of the stolen train jumped aboard. Fuller took up a position on the back end of the tender, then signaled for Brachen to give the *Texas* steam for full speed ahead—running backward.

Perched on the tender in order to see ahead and signal to Brachen, Fuller was swung from side to side as they rounded curves. Meanwhile, the raiders periodically dropped some of their wooden fuel on the track, hoping to wreck the pursuing locomotive. When the *Texas* hit a large piece of wood, Fuller sometimes bounced as much as two feet into the air. Yet the backward-racing *Texas* covered the ten miles from Adairsville to Calhoun in just under twelve minutes. With his four comrades, Fuller chased the train thieves about fifty-five miles.

Twice, the Federal force dropped a box car. Twice, pursuers picked it up in motion without major damage. Both cars were left on a sidetrack at Resaca. Soon the Rebel trainmen caught sight of the raiders and began pouring on more steam.

With her valve wide open, the *Texas* was running under 165 pounds of steam. At the all-important tunnel, seven miles north of Dalton and

Captain W. A. Fuller, who led the chase for the stolen locomotive. [ATLANTA HISTORICAL SOCIETY]

Before seven raiders were hung simultaneously, one was permitted to speak to Confederate onlookers. [ATLANTA HISTORICAL SOCIETY]

within striking distance of Chattanooga, Fuller signaled to his engineer to slow down. Smoke in the tunnel made it impossible to see whether they were in danger of ramming their quarry from behind.

Emerging from Tunnel Hill about one-fourth mile behind the *General*, the *Texas* again picked up speed. Still running backward, the huge iron horse slowly gained on the forward-running locomotive that now pulled only one car.

Just north of Ringgold, the Confederates saw the hijackers begin jumping from their locomotive and dashing into thick underbrush. They had burned their last piece of wood; only wisps of smoke, nearly white, came from the stack. Search parties found and captured all of the raiders, plus two who had inadvertently been left behind at Marietta. They were thrown into tiny Swims jail in Chattanooga.

Eight days after he was captured, James J. Andrews got a swift trial and a sentence of death. Late in May 1862, twelve of his followers were shipped to Knoxville for court martial; seven were selected to be tried, not as prisoners of war but as spies who had penetrated enemy lines disguised as civilians.

The condemned men were brought to the Fulton County, Georgia, jail on June 7. That afternoon, Andrews was hanged before a cheering crowd. Ten days later the seven who were condemned in Knoxville were also executed in Atlanta.

Eight raiders of the group left in Swims jail pulled a break on October 16. After wandering through the Cumberlands for days, six were recaptured and sent to Castle Thunder in Richmond, where one week later they were exchanged. These six reached Washington on March 24, 1863, not quite a year after having taken part in one of the most dramatic raids in the annals of America.

With John A. Wilson of the Twenty-first Ohio Volunteers as their spokesman, survivors of the raid contacted the White House. Abraham Lincoln had Wilson and his comrades brought to the executive mansion. There, Secretary of War Edwin M. Stanton had an inspiration. Weeks earlier, lawmakers had authorized a new medal that was to be bestowed for conspicuous heroism. Why not present it to each of the men who had tried to cut one of the most important supply lines in Rebel territory?

That's how the hijacking of a Georgia train led to the first ceremony in which soldiers were presented with the Congressional Medal of Honor. In time, most members of Andrews's band, plus survivors of those hanged in Atlanta, received the coveted medal.

In the interval between the initial planning of Andrews's raids and the escape of some of the raiders from a Chattanooga jail, many other things took place.

Late in January 1862, Federal officials launched the ironclad warship *Monitor*, designed by John Ericsson to meet the threats posed by the Confederate *Virginia*, which had been converted from the captured U.S.S. *Merrimack*.

In February, U. S. Grant captured Fort Donelson, making Nashville an easy target. It was occupied by Federal forces without bloodshed, becoming the first Confederate state capital to fall.

March saw a five-hour battle between the *Monitor* and the *Virginia* end in a draw, no ordinary draw but one which made wooden warships obsolete and changed naval warfare forever. At the April battle of Shiloh, also a draw in terms of military results, commanders on both sides realized that tens of thousands could die with nothing accomplished.

Also in April, about the time of the Andrews raid, Captain David Farragut's fleet of seventeen Federal vessels captured New Orleans, thereby closing the Mississippi River to Confederate traffic. But Confederate forces under Stonewall Jackson seized most of the Shenandoah Valley and remained poised only fifty miles from Washington.

Three months after Andrews's raid ended in capture and death, Lincoln read to his cabinet the first draft of a document aimed at the emancipation of slaves in Rebel territory. Soon afterwards, blacks from New Orleans formed the "Chasseurs d'Afrique," the first regiment of free blacks offered to the Union, but they found that their services were not wanted for the present.

In August, Federal forces were defeated at the second battle of Bull Run in north-central Virginia. Though the presentation of medals to the hijackers of a Rebel railroad would gain the interested attention of the entire North, it was quite clear that it would take much more than a few daring raids to bring the bloody war to an end.

CHAPTER

24

Carl Schurz Spoke for 200,000 Germans in Blue

"It was nothing; Frau Kinkel was the person really responsible," Carl Schurz modestly replied in answer to a question. Speaking in German to a packed audience at a New York Republican rally, the bespectacled thirty-year-old acted as though he really didn't want to tell the story of the best-known rescue during the recent German revolution.

However, responding to pleas from his listeners, he gave a capsule account.

"Frau Kinkel came to me by night. 'My Gottfried will die unless you go to his aid,' she said to me."

Schurz, then only twenty-one years old, held the professor at the University of Bonn in high esteem. He knew that Kinkel was imprisoned at Spandau, near Berlin. But until his teacher's wife made an impassioned appeal, he had not thought of mounting a rescue attempt.

From his refuge in Switzerland, where he had gone after the failure of the revolutionary movement for which he had fought, Schurz entered Germany twice under false passports. He spent months planning to get Kinkel from a prison considered to be escape proof.

"In the end, it was easy," he assured his New York audience. "With the help of friends, a turnkey was bribed. Then we managed to lower Kinkel to the street from an attic window in November 1850.

"The attic window had no bars," he explained with diffidence.

Waving aside renewed calls for a detailed account of the flight to Mecklenburg and Rostock by carriage and then by schooner to England, the man who had settled in Wisconsin turned to his main theme. He called the new Republican party "the party of liberty and freedom." Castigating the staid old Democratic party as "content to lie in bed with slavery," he called for listeners to go to the polls and help send Abraham Lincoln to the White House.

Memories of the 1860 campaign flooded the mind of Carl Schurz on June 10, 1862. That is the day on which Major General John Charles Frémont, the man for whom he had worked ardently in the election campaign of 1856, sent word for Schurz to drop whatever he was doing and hurry to the command tent.

Face to face with the commander of the Western Department, the civilian who had resigned as U.S. minister to Spain to offer his services to the Union army expected to receive an order. Instead, Frémont handed him a parchment. "Congratulations!" exclaimed the man who'd been the first Republican nominee for the presidency. "The man you helped send to the White House has not forgotten you; Lincoln has made you a brigadier general!"

Taking command of units that included veterans of nearly a year of fighting, Schurz led the corps that took the brunt of Stonewall Jackson's attack at Chancellorsville. At Gettysburg, battlefield deaths of superiors put him at the head of the famous Twenty-first Corps. Soon afterward, the man who had come from Germany as a political refugee became a major general.

By then, he had been in correspondence with Abraham Lincoln for many months. As head of the Wisconsin delegation to the Republican convention of 1860, he had been a staunch supporter of front-runner William H. Seward. But when a sudden surge made Lincoln the nominee, Schurz managed to win a place among the committee named to convey to him the official news that he had been chosen.

Lincoln was barely in the White House before Schurz tactfully suggested that "it would be well to remember your foreign-born supporters." Both men knew that Lincoln's successful bid for the backing of this important segment of the electorate had been vital to his victory.

Schurz himself had hit the campaign trail for the man whom he had not backed at the convention. He spoke at rallies in Indiana, Illinois, Ohio, Pennsylvania, Wisconsin, and New York. Attracted to the nation's largest city because of its big and influential German community, he began to enlist volunteers for the First New York Cavalry, the "Lincoln Riders," immediately after the fall of Fort Sumter.

Instead of putting on a uniform as colonel of the unit he'd organized, Schurz went to Spain at the request of Lincoln. However, unable to stay out of the growing struggle in his adopted country, he kept his ministerial post for less than a year. To the end of his life, he insisted that he was "overcome by surprise" when informed that he had become a brigadier general by presidential appointment.

"Schurz looks superb in uniform," Lincoln reputedly told aides after the unit commanded by his friend passed in review as part of the Army of the Potomac, "but his real value lies in his ability to motivate our German-speaking citizens."

Many of these citizens did not speak or read English. But when urged to fight for the Union and for freedom by speakers who used their own language, these new citizens responded in droves.

Early organizers of a body of German volunteers in St. Louis got such response that they had to establish two units instead of one. Some of them were drilling when a soldier/civilian clash, much like that in Baltimore, broke out. As in the seaboard city, southern civilians goaded and perhaps attacked men in uniform. Again, a person unknown fired the first shot.

A band of Confederate sympathizers then gathered in the engine house of Fire Company No. 5. Squads of soldiers surrounded the building and poured volley after volley into it. When more than twenty-four hours of street fighting ended in May 1860, at least twenty-eight were dead. As yet not one man in blue or in gray had been killed in conventional battle. English-language reports filled newspapers, but it was German-language accounts of the St. Louis fighting that brought recruits trooping to enlistment centers.

Before the war was over, Carl Schurz and a host of German-speaking aides and colleagues persuaded at least 200,000 of their countrymen to fight for the Union they understood only dimly. Along with Italians, Scandinavians, Irish, and French soldiers, they were mocked by many as "cannon fodder for the Confederates."

But it was the foreign-born soldiers, with Germans in the lead, who tipped the scales in terms of manpower for the struggle. At the height of its military strength on January 1, 1864, the C.S.A. had only about 427,000 men in active service, just over twice as many as Germans who fought for the Union for a few months or for the duration.

Carl Schurz was too busy with nonmilitary matters, with White House contacts at the top of his priority list, to be concerned about military advancement. Yet in the aftermath of Gettysburg he was promoted to the rank of major general.

Three of his countrymen also became major generals: Samuel P. Heintzelman, Franz Sigel, and Peter J. Osterhaus. Along with subordinates, they had helped to recruit many of the men they led into battle. Brigadier General Alexander Schimmelfenning had brought thousands into the Pennsylvania Volunteers. Brigadier General Ludwig Blenker, a folk hero during the war that had made Carl Schurz a refugee, encouraged at least 31,000 Germans of Missouri to don blue uniforms.

At that, Missouri provided only six German regiments. Ten were formed in New York, six in Ohio, five in Pennsylvania, four in Wisconsin, and three in Illinois. Heintzelman and his Pennsylvanians were selected for the all-important task of defending Washington when it appeared that the Confederates were about to strike at the capital during the summer of 1862. Blenker's chief of staff, who spoke only German, was a monocle-wearing member of Prussia's minor nobility, Prince Felix Salm-Salm.

Germans and other Europeans brought to the Union army experience and talents sorely needed. Their discipline and bearing set them apart from raw American recruits. Only one high ranking officer was charged with having brought disgrace to both his native and his adopted country. Widespread tales, never supported by hard evidence, alleged that Brigadier General Schimmelfenning found refuge in a pig pen at Gettysburg, hiding there for three days.

That tale, if based in fact, was in sharp contrast with hundreds of stories about bravery and gallantry on the part of foreign-born men in the armies of the North. To a degree not fully realized then, and usually overlooked now, immigrants made the vital difference between the manpower of the Union and of the Confederacy.

Because the C.S.A. had no big industrial cities to attract immigrants by the boatload, no more than about 150 companies of foreign-born soldiers fought in gray. At most, these units numbered perhaps 10,000 to 12,000 men, compared with the 500,000 foreign-born soldiers who fought in blue. Heros von Borcke of Prussia became chief of staff to C.S.A. Major General J. E. B. Stuart. Camille Armand Jules Marie of France and Patrick R. Cleburne of Ireland became Confederate major generals. But the overall impact of Carl Schurz plus other foreign-born soldiers was heavily weighted in favor of the North.

At war's end, the one-time refugee who spoke no English when he entered the United States at age twenty-three was asked to perform a special service for his adopted nation. President Andrew Johnson badly needed an impartial firsthand report of conditions in the South. Reluctant to take on the task because he personally believed that the franchise should be extended to ex-slaves before one-time Confederate states were readmitted to the Union, Carl Schurz traveled for months in order to prepare a detailed summary. Johnson angrily suppressed the German's report, but Congress demanded that it be made public. As a result, it was the body of findings by the man who earlier had spoken for 200,000 Germans in armies of the North that helped to shape the course of Reconstruction in the defeated South.

CHAPTER

25

"The Sharpshooter" Brought Men to Recruitment Offices in Droves

"**N**othing since the receipt of news that Rebels had fired upon our Fort Sumter has done so much to bring men to the colors," a veteran recruitment officer told a reporter for the New York *Illustrated News* in June 1862.

His glowing response to a canvas, painted not on a battlefield but in a Manhattan studio, was all the more remarkable because it paid tribute to an artist on the staff of a rival paper.

Boston native Winslow Homer, age twenty-six, took this and all tributes in stride. He was the best of the wartime artists, and he knew it. *Harper's Weekly* had consistently paid him sixty dollars for two-page spreads of drawings and sketches. No competitor was paid anywhere near that rate.

After an apprenticeship to a lithographer in his native city, Homer audaciously opened his own studio. It was so successful that in 1859 he moved to New York City. While studying at the National Academy of Design, he earned his keep by contributing drawings to *Harper's Weekly*.

"Most good artists depict what they see," a member of the newspaper's editorial staff once said. "Winslow is different; he puts on paper and on canvas the things that he feels."

Because *Harper's* wished to convey to the nation the feelings that swept over Washington in the aftermath of secession, Homer was sent to the capital to sketch the inauguration of Abraham Lincoln. Before the year ended, he had filled thick sketchbooks with drawings made while Major General George B. McClellan's army was camped near the capital.

About the time that his canvas, produced in a studio from drawings made in the field, created a sensation in the North, some fighting men in blue were expressing their disgust for the artist and other camp followers.

"General McClellan is said to have at least 75,000 men near here," an unidentified officer wrote to his wife from Williamsburg some time in May. "At that, we are outnumbered badly. Not by the Rebels; we can take care of them. We are outnumbered by the Bohemian Brigade."

Artists and newspaper reporters ranked at the top or near the top of most lists of those making up this motley company of camp followers. "Ladies of the evening," seldom ladylike by any standard, went everywhere with the armies. So did horse thieves, peddlers of herb medicines, small-time clothiers, liniment and salve salesmen, and anyone else hopeful of making a few dollars, along with many wives of officers.

Artists and reporters were especially scorned because many fighting men thought they should be in uniform. Others resented what they called "helter-skelter sketching." Sometimes agonizingly accurate, many pieces of art actually were badly incorrect in details and in overall emphasis.

It was the North that benefited, not only from a canvas that brought joy to recruitment officers, but also from distribution in newspapers that tried to give readers sketches of notable leaders plus both stirring and everyday events far from home. There were no illustrated newspapers in the South.

New York was the center toward which battlefield art flowed and from which it was distributed in the form of woodcuts and engravings.

Every good stream invited grimy fighting men to "Wash Day." [LESLIE'S ILLUS-TRATED]

A coward is drummed from the corps. [HARPER'S WEEKLY]

Harper's Weekly vied with *Frank Leslie's Illustrated Newspaper* for reader loyalty, but the *Illustrated News* had its own coterie of faithful readers. In London, the *Illustrated London News* relied largely but not exclusively upon the pen of Frank Vizetelly. Because London's sympathies were tipped toward the South, citizens of the metropolis saw many more visual interpretations of the war than did persons living in the C.S.A.

Winslow Homer's battle scenes were vivid and memorable, but it was his capacity to sketch life in army camps and among civilians that most endeared him to the masses.

English-born Alfred R. Waud, also a staffer at *Harper's* after having served an apprenticeship at the *Illustrated News*, was the first to get sketches of Bull Run to editors. He was in the thick of the fight at Antietam and produced scores of drawings at both Chancellorsville and Gettysburg. At the siege of Petersburg, Waud nearly fell victim to a sniper's bullet because he insisted on standing, sketch pad in hand, at elevated sites that put him in full view of Confederate marksmen.

Theodore Davis, like Homer and Waud of *Harper's*, was eager to give readers an accurate view of a typical uniform worn by an officer in gray. Unable to get his hands on such clothing any other way, he went to the battlefield and stripped the corpse of a dead captain.

Arthur Lumley of the *Illustrated News* took a different kind of risk. Eager to get a bird's eye view of action, he climbed into a gas-filled balloon and soared to a height of 1,100 feet. Swinging in the cage of one of Dr. Lowe's brand-new contraptions, Lumley sketched furiously in an attempt to depict the surging panorama beneath him.

At least once, Alfred Waud went too far, in the opinion of his editors. He sent them a graphic portrayal of a man being carried from a field hospital on a stretcher. A mass of bandages covered the stump left behind when surgeons had sawed off a shattered leg. Grim-faced edi-

Ladies sewing for soldiers; havelock is worn by lady at left. [WILSLOW HOMER, *HARPER'S WEEKLY*]

tors ordered engravers to reverse the position of the wounded man, so that in the printed version there was no sign of his having undergone an amputation.

Though none of them achieved the wartime fame of several *Harper's* artists, *Leslie's* employed at least two dozen men to depict glorious Union victories, ignominious Northern defeats, and everyday life among soldiers and camp followers.

Many sketches were made in haste and in partial ignorance, and the best of them were subject to transformation at the hands of artisans who prepared plates for use by publishers. Even the great Winslow Homer was not always a stickler for accuracy. His sketch of northern ladies making havelocks (special kepi covers adapted from the British military who fought in India) shows a fashionable lady wearing one of the odd headpieces. Though specialists consider such headgear to have been reserved exclusively for masculine use, Homer's painting that includes a woman wearing a havelock today hangs in the Metropolitan Museum of Art.

Thomas Nast, who perfected his own special style as a battlefield artist, later gained lasting fame as creator of both the Republican elephant and the Democratic donkey. Homer's postwar paintings made him rich and famous. Waud was commissioned by the son of Georgia's wartime governor to come to the state to illustrate *Mountain Campaigns in Georgia*, a volume designed to lure tourists to Georgia's battlefields.

The impact of Winslow Homer's "The Sharpshooter" established his reputation. Nostalgic pieces, landscapes, and Civil War art produced from memory many years after the conflict made him one of the most sought-after artists of his era. But it was the poorly paid and little-known staffers for illustrated weeklies whose work provided, and continues to provide, a means for genuine viewing of the war, even though at a distance and through a glass darkly.

CHAPTER

26

Lincoln's Master Spy Brought Joy to the Hearts of Rebels

"**W**e're trapped. Outnumbered and outgunned," mused Joseph E. Johnston. Aides gathered at his Richmond headquarters for their usual early-morning conference nodded agreement.

Drumming with his fingers on the table before him, the West Pointer of the class of 1829 who was fourth in seniority among C.S.A. full generals demanded: "Why in the name of God does the man not attack?"

He received no reply and expected none. Major General George B. McClellan of the West Point class of 1846 was notoriously cautious. His years as a railroad executive had taught him not to make hasty decisions or rush into action less than fully informed. But poised to strike at the Confederate capital in May 1862, "Little Mac" had no need for caution.

Many of the big guns that ringed Richmond were dummies, made of wood. Johnston was positive that the enemy was aware of the ruse and would not be deceived. He was equally sure that McClellan's overwhelming superiority in manpower meant that a quick and bold thrust would force Confederates to evacuate their capital.

Yet the Federal force of 105,000 men made no move. Day after rainy day dragged by with no sign of action. As May drew to a close, weather came to Johnston's aid. Flood water washed away bridges over the Chickahominy River, leaving at least four divisions of men in blue stranded near the Virginia villages of Seven Pines and Fair Oaks.

Still puzzled that McClellan had failed to make the most of his advantage, Johnston took the initiative. With C.S.A. President Jefferson Davis planning to tour the battle area, Confederates struck at Federal units cut off from the main body of their troops by the swollen river.

Brigadier General Edwin V. Sumner, age sixty-five, heard firing at

Major Allan Pinkerton. [LIBRARY OF CONGRESS]

his headquarters tent north of the river. Without waiting for orders, he marched the men of his command through swamps to the scene of battle. His quick action prevented a Union debacle. During indecisive fighting, Johnston took two bullets and, though not critically wounded, was forced to ask for leave to recuperate.

By June 1, Johnston had been succeeded by Robert E. Lee, for the first time in command of a major army that soon would become known as the Army of Northern Virginia. Lee pulled back into Richmond and waited. Like Johnston, he was puzzled that McClellan did not mount an all-out assault. Such a move would have meant heavy casualties on both sides, of course; but it also could have meant the fall of the Confederate capital and an early end to the war.

McClellan was far more active than his foes realized. Every day he spent hours reading and digesting intelligence reports about enemy positions and strength, then discussing these reports at length with his intelligence chief.

Major Allan Pinkerton, who had received his commission from McClellan soon after First Bull Run, had long and close ties with the Federal commander. For that reason McClellan unhesitatingly accepted Pinkerton's verdict that "We're facing perhaps as many as 200,000 rebels, certainly no less than 180,000."

It was the vastly inflated estimate of enemy strength that accounted for McClellan's failure to mount an attack. Incorrectly believing himself to be greatly outmanned, he waited for reinforcements or a shift of Confederate troops, then waited, and waited some more.

For the first time, colorful Allan Pinkerton, whose career had begun as a maker of barrels in his native Scotland, was badly misinformed by his own intelligence gathering.

Pinkerton came to the United States in 1842 at age twenty-three and set up his own cooper's shop in northern Illinois. While cutting hoop poles on a deserted island, he stumbled across a hideout used by counterfeiters. Leading a posse he had assembled, the barrel maker captured the counterfeiters and became a local celebrity. He was rewarded with the post of deputy sheriff of Kane County.

Soon afterward he was given the same office in Cook County. By 1850 Pinkerton was attached to the Chicago police force as its first detective, but after a few months he resigned to launch a private detective agency, one of the nation's earliest.

Pinkerton and his operatives cracked a number of cases involving robberies of the Adams Express. With widespread newspaper publicity, suddenly he was a national celebrity. When his agency won a contract to provide protection for the Illinois Central Railroad, Pinkerton became a friend of the line's vice president, George B. McClellan.

It was McClellan who urged the detective to take his information "to the very highest levels" when Pinkerton learned that southern sympathizers in Baltimore might make an attempt upon the life of president-elect Abraham Lincoln, an attorney whose clients included the Illinois Central. In obedience to Pinkerton's instructions, Lincoln made part of his journey to Washington in partial disguise. Regardless of how he was dressed, the tall man from Illinois did go through Baltimore in the dead of night and did know that Pinkerton's had 200 men guarding railroad bridges and trestles to foil any attempt at sabotage.

Within weeks after taking the oath of office, Lincoln conferred at length with Pinkerton about the possibility of establishing within the federal government a new secret service department. Though nothing came of it at the moment, it was Pinkerton who, by a mandate from Abraham Lincoln, later launched the Secret Service as a special agency of the Army of the Potomac.

McClellan's sudden elevation to top command in the wake of the Federal debacle at First Bull Run led to an urgent call for the services of his old friend Pinkerton. Himself wearing a disguise and using an alias, the detective traveled through much of the South gathering intelligence for McClellan. Then he established a headquarters tent near the general's to provide for him full and accurate information about enemy military strength and movements.

So long as he functioned as a detective or head of a large and growing spy network, Pinkerton was superb. He had discovered what Rose Greenhow was doing for the Confederacy and had seen to it that she was deported. Then he had sent his own spies into Richmond to keep him informed about activity in the Confederate capital.

But Lincoln's master spy had no military background or training. Having spent his life among civilians, he now relied upon civilians for information. Day after day he interrogated camp followers of the Union army, stragglers brought in from Confederate villages, and ex-slaves who were fleeing from their masters. Many or most of these persons probably gave him the best information they had, but all of it was secondhand or thirdhand.

Repeatedly, he warned McClellan that "Richmond is an armed camp; rebels have flocked there in such numbers that the city is defended by at least 200,000 men."

Actually, Lee had only 68,000 men when he took command in early June. The arrival of Stonewall Jackson with another 18,000 men still left Confederates outnumbered nearly three to one. McClellan's own command included more than 100,000 men, and other Federal forces poised to strike at Richmond numbered another 100,000.

Backed by McClellan, Allan Pinkerton managed to get an audience with U.S. Secretary of War Stanton. "Sir," the great detective urged firmly, "you must move heaven and earth to bring the Army of the Potomac up to at least 300,000 men. Failure to do so will invite disaster at the hands of rebels who have 150,000 well drilled and well equipped troops between Washington and the Potomac, alone."

While McClellan hesitated to take the offensive, C.S.A. Major General J. E. B. Stuart led cavalry units in a daring ride completely around the Federal force. When Stuart reported to Lee that the enemy's right flank was unprotected, the Confederate commander pulled 47,000 troops out of Richmond. Leaving the capital protected by only 25,000 men, he struck hard at the exposed right of the Union army on June 26.

On the following day, Confederates managed a break-through at Gaines Mill. That erased any doubts harbored by McClellan. Convinced that he was surrounded and outnumbered, he ordered a hasty withdrawal to the James River in a move designed to "save this army."

McClellan refused to recognize that he had acted on false information and in a telegram to Lincoln complained, "I have lost this battle because my force was too small." Pursuing Confederates took heavy losses at Malvern Hill, but in spite of this rebuff the Federal threat to Richmond was, for now, eliminated.

Only a few weeks passed before Washington discovered how woefully inaccurate Pinkerton's intelligence reports had been. But he

Allan Pinkerton (left) *in conference with McClellan.* [LESLIE'S ILLUSTRATED]

remained a favorite of McClellan and stayed close to his side until the fearful battle of Antietam caused McClellan to be removed from command.

Pinkerton gave up his military rank and privileges and returned to his Chicago detective agency. As for McClellan, who still refused to believe that the great detective had overestimated enemy strength by 300 percent, a brief return to command was followed by being placed on inactive duty for an indefinite period.

McClellan, who was probably correct in believing Abraham Lincoln to be personally responsible for his humiliation, retaliated by consenting to become an 1864 candidate for the presidency on a peace platform, which practically guaranteed him the support of immense numbers of Northerners who were by then sick and tired of the killing.

27

Near-dictatorship Evoked the Wrath of "Blackjack" Logan

Aug 30, In the Field

Hon. Abraham Lincoln
Executive Mansion

Sir: Through pages of the Tribune, I have just received astonishing news. Dr. Israel Blanchard of Murphysboro in Illinois has been placed under arrest by Marshal David L. Phillips.

Dr. Blanchard is said to be en route to Old Capitol Prison charged with the crime of having attending on August 10 a meeting of subversive nature. Herewith, I append evidence proving that he could not have been there. Please act promptly in accordance with this information.

JOHN A. LOGAN, Brigadier General
of Volunteers

In the nation's capital, the president needed no words of introduction or explanation. Logan, whose nickname stemmed from the blackjack oak widely used by railsplitters, was famous for his fiery temper. His terse and unceremonious letter was proof positive that he was fighting mad.

Like the chief executive, Logan had risen to prominence from a background as an Illinois attorney. Four terms in the Illinois legislature, followed by four years as district attorney, had given him a springboard from which to win election to Congress.

Abraham Lincoln well remembered that Logan was the congressman, unidentified in most news dispatches, who had snatched up

John A. ("Blackjack") Logan,
brigadier general of volunteers.
[NATIONAL ARCHIVES]

a uniform and donned it to join in the fighting at First Bull Run. Like Lincoln, Logan's military experience was limited to a few weeks during the Black Hawk War many years earlier. But it was his long-time colleague, the president himself, who had named Blackjack a brigadier general in March 1862.

Ostensibly a reward for heroic service at forts Henry and Donelson, the promotion from the rank of colonel was a typical White House gesture. Lincoln went out of his way to select prominent Democrats, such as Logan, for recognition.

On October 9, 1862, barely one month after receipt of Logan's letter and the detailed evidence sent with it, the president sent a terse message to Secretary of War Edwin M. Stanton: "I strongly incline to discharge Dr. Blanchard."

Released from prison, the physician returned to southern Illinois and won a seat in the state senate. He was one of the fortunate few who, charged with subversive or questionable activities or sentiments, had a powerful friend whose influence brought him quick release.

Blanchard's brief imprisonment came as part of a series of sweeping changes in civilian life. In the aftermath of the Baltimore riot that led to the first bloodshed of the growing conflict, a grim Lincoln leaned upon his legal experience and took drastic action. In the interest of national security, on April 27, 1861, he suspended the right of *habeas corpus* along the line of communication that linked Philadelphia with New York.

Attorney Lincoln considered it unwise, and probably illegal, to implement his order through normal channels. Hence he sent it to U.S. Secretary of State William H. Seward and to General Winfield Scott, as a military measure. Scott soon established at Annapolis a new military department under Brigadier General Benjamin F. Butler. Butler, in turn, sent two regiments to Relay House, just eight miles from Baltimore, to cut the route used by Confederates to send men and supplies to and from Harpers Ferry.

Lincoln's mandate gave military authorities a free hand to act swiftly and decisively "in order to suppress an insurrection against the laws of the United States." As put into practice by Butler, that directive meant that anyone believed to harbor seditious thoughts was subject to arrest without warrant and to being jailed without recourse to a writ of *habeas corpus* allowing release while awaiting trial.

Dozens of citizens caught in Butler's net were obscure people; a few were prominent. One of them, Ross Winans, was a member of the Maryland legislature who at age sixty-five was reputed to be worth fifteen million dollars, earned from machine shops and locomotive building.

Winans employed Baltimore's most distinguished attorney, a long-time acquaintance of Lincoln's, to present to the president himself a request for release. Reverdy Johnson, who had resigned from the U.S. Senate to become Tyler's attorney general, persuaded the president to release his wealthy client. During their conversations and exchanges of notes, Lincoln made a promise that he soon had cause to regret. "I have no purpose to invade Virginia," he told Johnson.

Few political prisoners in a nation moving dangerously close to a military dictatorship had powerful brothers-in-law or top-level attorneys with unlimited expense accounts. During a period of about eighteen months, civilians were hauled off to military prisons at the rate of at least 1,000 per month, often on secondhand or thirdhand evidence that wouldn't have been admitted in any court.

William H. Seward, who had every reason to be confident that he would become the Republican nominee at the Chicago convention of 1860, became U.S. secretary of state one day after Lincoln's inauguration. Furious at Washington's *National Intelligencer* and *Evening Post* newspapers for criticizing wholesale arrests without warrants, Seward confided in W. H. Russell. Editors could grumble all they pleased, he said. "Whenever I wish to have a suspect apprehended, I have only to touch this little bell on my desk."

Horace Greeley, a long-time ardent abolitionist, laid before the secretary his personal protests. Congressman Lyman Trumbull, early in the December 1861 session of Congress, introduced a resolution that would have required Seward to tell how many persons were under detention and to cite the laws they were accused of having broken. Henry W. Halleck, briefly general-in-chief of the U.S. Army, wrote that he believed "Treasonable acts, in the Loyal States, should be left

U.S. Secretary of State William H.
Seward. [U.S. SIGNAL CORPS]

Lieutenant General Winfield Scott.
[*HARPER'S WEEKLY*]

for trial by the courts, as provided by Congress."

These and other protests against the continuing and spreading ero-
sion of civil liberties had no effect. Even the chief justice of the U.S.
Supreme Court found himself impotent. Roger B. Taney, the key figure in the Dred Scott decision, consented to hear the case of John
Merryman. Arrested for having preached Rebel doctrines at
Cokeysville, Maryland, he was imprisoned by one of Butler's subordinates, General George Cadwalader. Taney issued a writ requiring Cadwalader to bring Merryman into court for a hearing. Cadwalader
ignored the order; so Taney sent a marshal to serve him with a citation
for contempt of court. Armed soldiers barred the marshal from Fort
McHenry, where Cadwalader had his headquarters and Merryman
was imprisoned.

Then Taney sent a lengthy statement to Lincoln, reminding him of
the historic importance of *habeas corpus* and calling upon him to en-
force the laws of the land. Lincoln responded by turning to his attorney general. Edward Bates, who had assumed the office left vacant
when Stanton became secretary of war, dutifully issued an opinion
stating that the suspension of *habeas corpus* was both legal and correct.

Internal troubles of the C.S.A. led Jefferson Davis to attempt to
follow the route being followed by Lincoln. But the Confederate chief
executive was hampered by states' rights advocates in the Confederate
Congress. However, they approved revocation of the right of *habeas
corpus* in invaded territory as a means of quelling civil disorder and
later authorized military officers to arrest civilians during a period of

thirty days. In Atlanta, Knoxville, and other cities most judges refused to obey the order from Richmond. Repeated attempts by Davis to suspend civil liberties within the Confederacy won only limited and brief support.

Back in Washington, lawmakers took belated action in March 1863. In spite of widespread indignation, they passed an act that legalized proclamations by the president and by Secretary of War Edwin M. Stanton, and authorized suspension of *habeas corpus* in the future.

Arbitrary arrests continued in the North throughout the conflict, though their number dropped sharply after mid-1863. No citizen who was jailed in this fashion ever had a civil trial. Attorney General Bates repeatedly instructed subordinates to make certain that no case should go to trial unless conviction was certain. Apparently not a single case ever met that standard.

But failure to take a case to court did not mean that accused persons were set free. Many of them spent long months behind bars. Overcrowding of jails and prisons produced flagrant abuses so widespread that Henry W. Bellows of the Sanitary Commission yielded to pressure and investigated some of them. In New York he found twenty-three men, two-thirds of them in irons, massed in a tiny cell without beds, bedding, "or the commonest necessaries."

Prisoners at another institution managed to smuggle to friends a remonstrance that friends sent to Washington. Addressed to President Lincoln, their pleas described their condition as "like that of slaves on the middle passage." Like most other protests against wartime abuse of civil liberties, this was never answered.

"You have reason to be thankful that I picked the right brother-in-law," Dr. Israel Blanchard often told patients in the aftermath of his experience. "General Logan would have staged a one-man assault upon the Executive Mansion, had he not secured my release."

In spite of close ties with a powerful Federal officer, Blanchard may actually have been guilty under the order originally issued by Lincoln, which was greatly stiffened by an August 8, 1862, directive of Secretary of War Stanton. Under Stanton's order, "all U.S. marshals, superintendents and chiefs of police of any town, city, or district" were told to arrest and imprison any person suspected of giving aid or comfort to the enemy. If Blanchard didn't actually enroll in a Confederate military unit—as charged—he clearly was in sympathy with the enemy.

But his fiery brother-in-law who came to his rescue was never reprimanded. Instead he was elevated to the rank of major general a few months later. In postwar years Blackjack Logan commanded Union veterans who formed the Grand Army of the Republic, 500,000 registered voters who made up one of the nation's most powerful political organizations ever.

Part Four

Order of the Day: Survival

Bridge over Antietam Creek, later derisively called "Burnside's Bridge." [HARPER'S WEEKLY]

CHAPTER

28

Rebel Error and Federal Fear
Blended to Yield
the Deadliest Day Ever

"Whoopee! Lord Almighty! Wh-o-o-pe-e-e-e!" Barton W.
Mitchell of the Twenty-seventh Indiana was acting as
though the war was over. Uncertain records make it impossible to be
sure he was still a buck private or had become a corporal in Colonel
Silas Cosgrove's unit.

"Three of 'em!" shouted Mitchell, waving a fist that held objects he
had picked up on the ground. "The secesh boys done left us three
cigars—*whole* cigars!"

By September 13, 1862, tobacco had become increasingly scarce
among northern fighting units. There were rumors that at many
points of contact between opposing forces, men in gray were swapping
tobacco for morphine, quinine, and other essentials no longer easily
obtained in the South.

Many prisoners whiled away time by producing elaborately carved
pipes, whether or not they had tobacco with which to use them. Before Grant and Lee had put their signatures to the surrender documents at Appomatox, men of their armies were busy exchanging food
for tobacco.

Three whole cigars found on ground vacated only hours earlier by
Confederates under Major General Daniel H. Hill meant hours of
fondling, smelling, and tasting before the sheer ecstasy of lighting up.

"What's that piece of paper, Bart?" demanded Sergeant John M.
Bloss.

Earlier too busy chortling over his discovery to notice anything else,
Mitchell examined for the first time the paper in which his cigars had
been wrapped. One glance revealed that it looked official.

"Who's Chilton?" Mitchell responded.

133

Bloss shook his head. "Colonel Cosgrove ought to know," he suggested.

Together the soldiers took the cigars plus the paper to their leader. He couldn't identify Chilton either, but he was positive that the paper ought to be bucked right up the line, all the way to General McClellan himself.

At a crossroad where he was being lauded by a group of civilians living close to Frederick City, Maryland, Major General George B. McClellan was interrupted by an aide. A whisper in his ear led the commander to take a careful look at the paper handed him.

No doubt about it, the document had been signed by Colonel Robert H. Chilton. Every top officer in the Army of the Potomac was familiar with that name. Chilton was adjutant general of Robert E. Lee's Army of Northern Virginia.

"Here is a paper with which if I cannot whip Bobbie Lee I will be willing to go home!" an ecstatic McClellan told an aide shortly afterward.

For the paper in which Bart Mitchell's cigars had been wrapped was one of seven copies of Special Order No. 191, issued by Lee on September 9. From that paper, pronounced genuine by Allan Pinkerton, McClellan learned Lee's plan of action.

Lee had sent three of his four main bodies of troops southward from Frederick to surprise and overcome the Federal garrison at Harpers Ferry. That meant the remaining Rebels in the vicinity would be relatively easy targets, difficult only because there were so many of them left.

C.S.A. General Robert E. Lee.

With scouts reporting Lee's remaining troops to be moving toward Sharpsburg, McClellan decided to meet him there, only a few miles from Harpers Ferry. However, he cautiously waited until Sunday, the fourteenth, to get under way.

The Confederates spent Monday and Tuesday choosing positions and digging in for the decisive battle they expected. Hoping to surprise them, McClellan struck at dawn on Wednesday. Veterans of Major General Joseph ("Fighting Joe") Hooker's First Corps raced along a turnpike and across a forty-acre cornfield. In spite of heavy fire from men under Stonewall Jackson, the Federals managed to seize control of the field.

Troops surged back and forth across that field twice more during the morning. C.S.A. Major General John B. Hood directed a charge that momentarily gave the spot to the Rebels. Then Union Major General Joseph Mansfield sent men of his Twelfth Corps to recapture the field and move into the woods that bordered it. Next, two fresh Confederate divisions arrived in time to rake the enemy from three sides. In twenty minutes of carnage, 2,200 Federals fell, dead or wounded.

As the battle shifted toward the south, Lee's center split open, offering foes a chance to divide his forces and conquer them. Union Major General Ambrose E. Burnside could have been decisive to the conflict, but he was not. At nearby Antietam he hesitated to send his men across the creek that named the village.

Small and shallow, Antietam Creek could be easily waded at many points. Burnside preferred to send his men across a stone bridge, sturdy and elegant but so narrow that Confederates easily thwarted attempts to take it. Delayed at the bridge for more than three hours, Burnside's force was hit by Rebels under Major General Ambrose P. Hill not long after the creek was crossed. Official reports blamed "confusion in command" for the indecisive Federal action but said nothing about dawdling on the part of Burnside.

General Robert E. Lee had exhausted his reserve; his grand plan to move toward Washington and take the Federal capital was gone. The Army of Northern Virginia was on the brink of collapse.

But at Harpers Ferry, where Hill had made short work of the Federal garrison, orders came soon after dawn. Hill and his Light Division should be on the double to Sharpsburg at once. Wearing his red battle shirt, their commander pushed his men hard. But the day was hot and seventeen miles in the dust seemed to be fifty. Man after man fell from his unit, exhausted, and lay there watching as the army moved on toward Sharpsburg.

Barely 2,500 tired Confederates reached the scene of battle late in the day. Many of them proudly wore blue uniforms taken from the armory at Harpers Ferry. With shots raining from an apparently fresh

Alexander Gardner photographed the dead at Antietam. [NATIONAL ARCHIVES]

unit that numbered hundreds of men who seemed to be Federals, Mc-Clellan's forces wavered and then fell back abruptly.

When the battle ended with no clear-cut victory, opposing commanders counted their losses. More than 26,000 men were dead, wounded, or missing as a result of the bloodiest single day of the war. Because a staff officer, never identified, had lost a copy of his battle plans, Lee's hope of striking at Washington was gone.

McClellan briefly congratulated himself that he'd managed to fight to a draw, while holding an entire army in reserve. He'd done so because Pinkerton's intelligence convinced him that the 25,000 reserves might be essential in some nearby sector, at a moment's notice.

But in Washington, strategists who studied McClellan's reports plus news of the battle became furious. Had the overcautious Federal commander thrown his entire force into the fray, there was little doubt that Antietam would have been a triumphant victory instead of an indecisive day of butchery. General-in-chief Henry W. Halleck demanded and got action. By presidential order, McClellan was again relieved from active duty, this time permanently.

C.S.A. Colonel Robert H. Chilton, whose signature was appended to the lost order that helped to determine the shape of the war's bloodiest day, never quite got over what had taken place. Pondering that three cigars were so precious that they were wrapped in the only available paper and then lost where a tobacco-hungry Hoosier could find them, he observed, "The god of battles alone knows what would have occurred; but certainly, the loss of this battle order constitutes one of the pivots on which the war turned."

29

Elias Boudinot Led Tribesmen into the Promised Land of the C.S.A.

"**U**ncle, I believe the time has come for me to take off my uniform and find a place to live in Richmond."

C.S.A. Colonel Stand Watie nodded in understanding and agreement. "You have done all that you could here," he said. "Richmond offers the only hope for our people and those of the other tribes."

Elias Boudinot was universally known among American Indians and had already made something of a name for himself among whites. As lieutenant colonel of the Cherokee regiment raised for the Confederacy by his uncle, he had spent little time with the unit. Instead, he ranged far and wide recruiting other native Americans for military service.

The outbreak of war between the North and the South had been seen as a godsend by many tribesmen. For the first time in decades they were in a bargaining position. Both Federal and Confederate units were eager to get their help, particularly in the West.

Long-time Cherokee leader Cooweescoowe, known to whites as John Ross, made repeated trips to Washington. There he sought and got frequent interviews, but few promises, from Abraham Lincoln. As late as September 1862, barely thirty days before Elias Boudinot resigned from military service, Ross was again in the Federal capital, again presenting Indian claims at the White House—with no result.

Elias Boudinot, whom Ross had known since childhood, was the third man of distinction to bear that name. Revolutionary War leader and Continental Congress President Elias Boudinot had signed the treaty of peace that ended the war between Britain and her colonies. A man of wide interests who was the first president of the American Bible Society, Boudinot had become keenly interested in a bright young Cherokee from distant Georgia.

Attending a missionary school in the North, Buck Watie found a patron in Boudinot and a sweetheart at the school he was attending in Connecticut. Watie took Harriet Gold as his bride and, with the blessing of his patron, also became known as Elias Boudinot.

It was the younger Boudinot who returned to his tribesmen and became editor of the famous Cherokee *Phoenix* newspaper. Both Boudinot and Stand Watie signed the treaty under whose terms Cherokees were removed to the West. When angry tribesmen murdered Boudinot, his children were sent to relatives in Connecticut.

The third Elias Boudinot landed in Manchester, Vermont, with an aunt. Reaching maturity and becoming a member of the Arkansas bar, he followed his father's footsteps by working part-time for the *Arkansian* newspaper.

Boudinot was named chairman of the Arkansas Democratic state central committee just as simmering sectional strife erupted into violence. When a secession convention was called, he became its secretary.

The outbreak of war persuaded the bright young attorney, who was striking in appearance and a dynamic public speaker, that Cherokees and members of other tribes now had a chance to win concessions. However, when Federal leaders offered nothing but a series of rebuffs, Boudinot helped Stand Watie recruit men for the Confederacy.

October 1861 saw John Ross reach long-term agreements with C.S.A. Brigadier General Albert Pike. A Massachusetts native, Pike had gone into Indian country with plans to raise 5,000 warriors to serve as a buffer against Federal forces. Jefferson Davis, earlier U.S. secretary of war and personally familiar with much of the West, had given the enterprise his blessing.

Terms given by Confederates to the Five Civilized Tribes were extremely generous. They gained rights denied them for years in Washington and were on the verge of being recognized as citizens of the C.S.A. Jubilant tribesmen, vociferous in expressing their gratitude to Boudinot, Watie, Ross, and Pike, enlisted in droves. Nearly all asked and got permission to join cavalry units. Cherokees, Creeks, Chickasaws, Seminoles, and Choctaws rode off to battle sometimes wearing some small symbol of the C.S.A. but often without identifying gear.

At Pea Ridge, Arkansas, early in 1862, native Americans in Confederate service did what some experts had said was impossible: They stood up to the withering artillery fire of Federal units and actually charged cannoneers under Colonel Peter Osterhaus, breaking the Union line.

Most engagements in which tribesmen took part were small, however. They were far more valuable as scouts than as soldiers. But

Elias Boudinot the Younger. [LI-
BRARY OF CONGRESS]

whether on scouting expeditions or in combat, they frequently re-
verted to tribal ways and mutilated the bodies of dead enemies. Some
who rode in Confederate units dangled Federal scalps from their belts.

Northern newspapers gave much attention to "atrocities committed
by Indians in the service of the Rebels." As fear and anger mounted in
the North, it was increasingly clear that there could be reprisals in the
future. Hence Elias Boudinot decided he'd be worth more as a political leader than as a soldier. He campaigned for election to the Confederate Congress, won without opposition, and set out for Richmond.

A few Confederate leaders opposed seating him, but terms worked
out by John Ross persuaded the Congress to accept his credentials. He
was seated in October 1862 and told he'd be permitted to vote on all
issues except those involving Indians. The one-fourth Cherokee,
twenty-six-year-old congressman, won such respect that he was named
a member of the Indian Affairs Committee.

Meanwhile, a small band of his own people was gaining renown in
battle. This band was made up of the Cherokees who had eluded deportation to the West and remained in the Smoky Mountains. Called
to the Confederate colors by frontier entrepreneur William H.
Thomas of North Carolina, it formed the nucleus of what its leader
expected to become the Thomas Legion.

However, the grandiose plans for a legion having infantry, cavalry, and artillery units operating under a single commander never quite materialized. Most of Thomas's men were armed with squirrel rifles, some of which had been bored in order to admit larger bullets, but all having percussion locks and using loose powder.

With William W. Stringfield, also a white man, as his first captain, Thomas managed to recruit an estimated 500 Cherokees, plus a sprinkling of Anglo-Saxon mountain men. Small as it was, this unit was formidable. Unlike most in the West, it was continually in the field.

The Thomas Legion fought throughout North Carolina and eastern Tennessee, then went north to join the forces of C.S.A. Major General Jubal Early. The mostly barefoot Cherokees were conspicuous among raiders who plundered the Shenandoah Valley and briefly considered trying to free 15,000 Confederate prisoners at Point Lookout, Maryland.

A far more tempting prize than the prison camp loomed in sight, however. Early's raiders, Cherokees included, moved toward Washington. Since Major General David Hunter's forces had withdrawn behind the Alleghenies, the capital was protected only by forces quartered there. The raiders reached the outskirts of Washington but fought only minor skirmishes; arrival of reinforcements made an all-out attack impossible.

Back in the familiar Smokies a few months later, a veteran of the long campaign told vivid stories of his adventures. Typically he ended his account by admitting that "we took a whipping before it was over, but it was worth it; we scared hell out of Abe Lincoln!"

Meanwhile, in Richmond Elias Boudinot failed in his chief objective. He did manage to get fresh concessions and new promises, but the Confederate government was unwilling or unable to deliver results envisioned by lawmakers. Along with everyone else in the C.S.A., native Americans experienced shortages, inflation, and loss of loved ones in battle. Instead of improving, the lot of the Indian grew worse. Tribal lands were devastated, Federal raiders confiscated livestock and burned crops and homes. Captured Indians were refused exchange as punishment for their battlefield atrocities.

Peace brought the price of the strange alliance so strongly favored by Elias Boudinot higher than he had ever imagined it could be. Because members of the Five Civilized Tribes had taken up arms against a benevolent government, said U.S. lawmakers, Congress had no choice. In a series of sweeping new enactments, it wiped out all existing treaties with native Americans. With hearts burning with anger at military defeat and tribal lands laid waste by raiders, those who followed Elias Boudinot into the C.S.A. were left with virtually no rights during the time masked by the seemingly positive title of Reconstruction.

CHAPTER

30

An Ex-congressman from Ohio Got a Special Sentence— Banishment

"I have a proposition for you," Clement L. Vallandigham said to Brigadier General William S. Rosecrans on an evening late in May 1863. "Draw up your soldiers in a hollow square tomorrow morning. Then announce to them that Vallandigham desires to vindicate himself.

"I will guarantee that when they have heard me through, they will be more willing to tear Lincoln and yourself to pieces than to escort Vallandigham out of the nation he loves."

Barely able to restrain a smile, Rosecrans politely refused the offer. Not long afterward, he did remark to an aide that his prisoner didn't look a bit like a traitor in spite of what everyone was saying.

Guarded by a military party that displayed a huge flag of truce, Vallandigham was hustled to Murfreesboro, Tennessee, at that time the advance post of the Union army in the West. May 25 saw him ceremoniously escorted into Confederate territory and released. Banishment to Confederate territory was the punishment decreed by President Lincoln, who was forced to enter the case because prominent Democrats supported the man convicted of treason.

Elected to Congress from Ohio in 1858, Vallandigham quickly became a thorn in the flesh of the administration. With war clouds growing darker by the month, he clamored for peace. Appealing especially to unskilled and semiskilled immigrants of the sort who had helped to elect Lincoln, the orator from Ohio would be termed a populist today. Since that term hadn't yet come into vogue, people with his outlook were known as the Peace Democrats. Because they often wore copper pennies as identifying symbols, members of this dissident group became known as Copperheads.

An ardent and articulate champion of states' rights, Vallandigham staked his political future upon a peace platform. "I had rather my right arm were plucked from its socket and cast into eternal burnings, than aid or sanction anything leading to war," he told fellow congressmen late in 1860.

When war erupted, he became a tireless and eloquent critic of nearly everything done or proposed by the Federal administration. He attacked military leaders and their actions, proposals for finding funds with which to expand the military budget, abolitionists in general, and Horace Greeley in particular. Above all, he hammered away at presidential decisions that he dubbed "clearly and unequivocally false to the letter and spirit of the United States Constitution."

Neither attempts at conciliation nor unveiled threats stopped the man's tongue. Hence Ohio officials loyal to the administration drew up a new set of lines for congressional districts of the state. Somehow (they never could explain quite how it occurred) they managed to place a strongly Unionist county into Vallandigham's old district.

While that move cost him his seat in Congress, it by no means silenced him. Instead, he reached new peaks of eloquence in denouncing the recently arrived Union commander of the Department of the Ohio. Brigadier General Ambrose Burnside, whose conspicuous failures at Antietam and at Fredericksburg made him constantly angry, had been told to bring the work of Ohio Copperheads to an end.

Early 1863 saw a stream of directives from Burnside. One of them, General Order No. 9, prohibited citizens from criticizing policies of the administration. That, of course, simply prodded Vallandigham to new heights of eloquence.

By the time General Order No. 38 went out, Burnside had decided to prohibit "all declarations of sympathy for the enemy." In practice, that meant he intended to press charges of treason against any man who voiced opposition to anything the government did in pursuing the war.

Ohio Congressman Clement L. Vallandingham. [MATTHEW BRADY STUDIO, NATIONAL ARCHIVES]

Vallandigham, now a candidate for the governorship of Ohio, was in his element at Mount Vernon on May 4. Nearly 20,000 persons pushed and jostled for a chance to hear him speak. Though a man of official bearing was next to the speaker's platform in order to take down in shorthand everything that was said, Vallandigham raged that he not only despised General Order No. 38, but he "spit upon it and trampled it under his feet." Shortly after midnight, wearing the garments in which he slept, the former congressman was placed under arrest.

Instead of putting an end to Copperhead activity in Ohio as he had planned, Burnside soon found that he had created a new symbol. Though less potent than Dred Scott, John Brown, or Uncle Tom, it still was one to reckon with. As a result, Dayton, Ohio, exploded into a full-scale riot in which a mob destroyed the offices of the pro-Union Dayton *Journal* before slashing hoses at fire houses and putting businesses to the torch.

Brought before a tribunal of eight military officers, Vallandigham challenged their right to try him. Quickly convicted, he appealed without success to the federal district court and then to the U.S. Supreme Court.

New York Governor Horatio Seymour exploded when he learned that Vallandigham was to be placed in close confinement for the duration of the war. Backed by other men with powerful political connections, Seymour demanded that the president intervene in the case. Lincoln's handling of that case, said the New York official, "will determine in the minds of more than one half of the people of the Loyal States, whether the war is being waged to put down rebellion at the South, or to destroy free institutions at the North."

Pondering his options, the president decided that he would neither free the accused man nor affirm the verdict of the military commission that convicted him. Banishment from Union soil, he felt, would be a middle course that would be the least offensive course of action.

Vallandigham remained on Confederate soil for less than one month. Then, by a circuitous route that included Bermuda and Nova Scotia as stopping points, he reached Windsor, Canada, and resumed his campaign for the governorship of Ohio. Soundly defeated, he refused to cease his fight for peace.

Still forbidden to enter the United States, he put on a disguise and took to the campaign trail in the presidential election of 1864. Authorities could not have failed to know the identity of the bearded man who flailed at "King Lincoln" in major cities of Ohio, Pennsylvania, and New York. By now, however, he was too notorious to be rearrested.

At the Democratic national convention in Chicago, the man subject to arrest on sight managed to frame and then to win passage of a

Ambrose E. Burnside at his head-quarters tent near Bull Run Creek. [NATIONAL ARCHIVES]

"peace plank" that called for an immediate end to the war and a systematic plan under which to heal wounds of "the Federal Union of the States."

It was under Vallandigham's peace plank that George B. McClellan accepted the nomination for the presidency. On the hot August day that saw McClellan win by acclamation on the first ballot, delegates to the Chicago convention and citizens throughout the North were sick and tired of war. To many, including Abraham Lincoln and members of his cabinet, McClellan's election seemed all but assured without a series of battlefield victories.

It was a time of pride and disappointment. Lincoln's Emancipation Proclamation, issued on January 1, 1863, applied only to areas in rebellion, and although it had tremendous psychological effect, it freed few, if any, slaves.

The bad news for Lincoln was that the Conscription Act of March 3, a Federal draft applying to all males between ages twenty and forty-six, had triggered violent protests. Nevertheless, the Union defeat at Charleston, South Carolina, had been followed by glorious victory at Vicksburg, Mississippi. Washington had been threatened when Confederate troops crossed the Potomac, and near-panic had broken out in the capital, but Gettysburg had been counted as a great victory in spite of the fact that Meade suffered 23,049 casualties against Lee's 20,451. Chattanooga and Knoxville had been taken by Federal forces, but in sum "the year of the great battles" had produced a North far from triumphant, reeling from almost daily reports listing the dead and wounded.

By taking what seemed to be a prudent middle course with respect to Vallandigham while battles raged, the president appeared to have dug his own political grave. Lincoln and his advisors feared that with McClellan riding upon Vallandigham's peace plank, Lincoln's administration—and the war—would come to an inglorious end.

31

From Start to Finish, Abraham Lincoln Really Was Commander-in-Chief

"The lawyer from Springfield spent half the afternoon at the New York Avenue shop," a clerk in the telegraph office of the U.S. War Department confided.

"That means our fingers will be marching in double time tomorrow," a colleague responded. "Wonder who the lucky ones will be, this time?"

Major General John Adams Dix, commander of the Department of Virginia and the top-ranking Union volunteer officer, proved to be one of "the lucky ones." War Department clerks sent him, not one, but two urgent telegrams from the president on June 8, 1863.

"We have dispatches from Vicksburg of the third siege progressing. No general fighting recently. All well," the first dispatch informed Dix.

A few hours later, Abraham Lincoln gave Dix another of his innumerable personal reports to commanders in the field: "Have had here for three or four days the substance of news of fight at Port Hudson. We know that Gen. Sherman was wounded. We still have nothing of that Richmond newspaper story of Gen. Kirby Smith crossing and of Banks losing an arm."

No armchair commander, Lincoln was deeply and intimately involved in the conflict from start to finish. He planned strategy, examined and approved or disapproved new weapons, frequently paid visits to fighting men in the field, personally selected officers for promotion, accepted or rejected major policy decisions of his commanders, and almost daily fired off telegrams with information, questions, or detailed instructions to military leaders.

When it had become obvious that the Fort Sumter situation re-

Over and over, the commander-in-chief reviewed troops from the steps of the Executive Mansion. [HARPER'S WEEKLY]

quired a clear-cut decision to yield the installation or fight for it, U.S. Secretary of State William H. Seward spoke bluntly. As the man whom Republicans initially favored in the 1860 election, he had been hesitant to join the cabinet of "a prairie lawyer." Once in it, he intended to shape major policy decisions.

"Sumter is not worth a fight," he said repeatedly. "Give it up; do not launch this administration with blood on its hands."

Backing up words with action, Seward entered into communication with South Carolina officials. A go-between went so far as to promise South Carolina Governor Pickens that Sumter would be evacuated without a struggle.

Eleven days after his inauguration, Lincoln polled his cabinet for views about Fort Sumter. It was clear that Seward's views were regarded as definitive. Only the postmaster general voted with Lincoln; all the others voted to yield the installation without a struggle.

On April 7, the day after Lincoln signed an order for the military relief of Fort Sumter, Seward still insisted that he would prevail. "Faith as to Sumter fully kept," he wrote to John A. Campbell of Alabama, who had conveyed messages between the capital and Columbia, South Carolina. "Wait and see," he promised.

In direct opposition to the known views of his secretary of state, the president sent an April 8 dispatch. It notified the governor of South Carolina that Fort Sumter would be supplied with provisions. Once that message was in their hands, Confederate authorities had two alternatives: They could swallow their pride and retract their ultimatum, or they could use military force and become branded as aggressors who fired the first shot.

C.S.A. President Jefferson Davis and his advisors did precisely as Lincoln had expected. Therefore, since the South had "fired upon the

North," Lincoln moved swiftly. Congress was not in session and was not scheduled to convene until July 4. Instead of calling lawmakers into a special session, the president delivered a series of hammering blows at the enemy.

On Monday after the news of Sumter's fall reached Washington on Sunday, Lincoln called for 75,000 soldiers "to repossess the forts, places, and property which have been seized from the Union." It was a staggering demand. On January 1, 1861, the armed forces of the United States included less than 20,000 men.

Governor Claiborne F. Jackson of Missouri labeled the president's call for troops as "illegal, unconstitutional and revolutionary—inhuman and diabolical." Congressman Clement L. Vallandigham issued an urgent appeal for a special session of Congress, insisting that "Congress and only Congress is empowered to lead our great nation into war."

Few persons in leadership roles paid any attention to carping critics. The president had spoken, and his wishes must be obeyed. Nearly 100,000 men, whose enlistments were for only ninety days, were provided by loyal governors.

Two weeks after the first call for soldiers, Lincoln requested 42,034 more volunteers, this time for three years of service in the regular infantry and cavalry plus the tiny navy. Simultaneously, he used unappropriated funds of the U.S. treasury for military purposes.

Still without congressional authorization and knowing that the Union had just twenty-nine steam-powered naval vessels, plus sixty-one old-time sailing ships, Abraham Lincoln proclaimed a blockade of nearly 2,000 miles of southern coastline. Long before that mandate could be even fumblingly implemented, ninety-day enlistments of the first 75,000 volunteers were about to expire.

The Confederates, who already had scores of West Point graduates in places of command and whose rank-and-file citizens were far more familiar with guns and the outdoors than were typical city dwellers of the North, had assembled a sizable army. As the clock began to run out on Lincoln's volunteer force, another clear-cut choice presented itself: Fight at once, or perhaps not at all.

General Winfield Scott, a long-time veteran of both combat and command, wanted nothing to do with the foolhardy attempt to launch an attack. However, his commander-in-chief overrode "Old Fuss and Feathers" and sent Federal soldiers marching to the debacle of First Bull Run. Once Horace Greeley and other fire-eating northern editors learned that the glorious Union fighting force had suffered 2,896 casualties, there was no stopping the war fever. Congress or no Congress, it would now be a fight to the finish!

America has never seen anything quite like the first four months of the Lincoln administration. By the time Congress convened on July 4, actions of the president had made a formal declaration of war perfunctory. Old-timers in the nation's capital wagged their heads knowingly. "He learned well from old Stuntz," they said.

Seeking a gift for his beloved son Tad, the newly installed president had wandered to the toy shop of Joseph Stuntz, a crippled veteran of the Napoleonic wars. Miniature soldiers and toy weapons fascinated the chief executive; he spent hours playing with them on Stuntz's counter and discussing with the veteran the great battles in which he had fought.

No one knows exactly how much the immigrant influenced Abraham Lincoln, but personal direction of top-level strategy was only one of his many interests as commander-in-chief. Fascinated with mechanical devices in general and weapons in particular, the man from Springfield seldom refused to give time to a person who wished to present the claims of a new or an improved weapon. After watching tests of Sherwin's rifled cannon, he ordered immediate construction of a trial six-pounder. With Postmaster General Blair in tow, he watched experiments with Maynard's rifle and Alexander's cartridge.

In October 1861, he notified General McClellan, "A battery of repeating guns, on wheels, can be seen at the arsenal any hour. Could you, without inconvenience, see them at 3. or 4. o'clock—please answer."

Lincoln inspected and tested new kinds of gunpowder, the "Rafael" repeater cannon, the Spencer rifle, the Ferris gun, an electric detonator, rockets, signals, fuses, and even Greek Fire. When wealthy Baltimore secessionist Ross Winans won release after arbitrary arrest, rumor had it that he'd bribed the president, not with a bundle of cash, but with the promise to deliver to him the steam gun Winans had built for Confederate use.

It was the commander-in-chief who picked "born loser" U. S. Grant for command. Lincoln personally handed him his commission as major general in the U.S. Army.

During periods when he was sending orders and policy decisions to commanders in the field, the commander-in-chief found time to see Peter Peckham, inventor of Peckham rifles and cartridges. In a weed-covered lot between the Executive Mansion and the unfinished Washington Monument, Lincoln personally tried out the Marsh breechloading rifle and recommended that it be thoroughly tested at West Point. When the army's chief of ordnance decided not to use the weapon, the president overruled him and ordered the purchase of 25,000 Marsh rifles.

At Lincoln's directive, barrels of incendiary fluid for use in hollow shells that produced Greek Fire were shipped to McClellan. Samuel

Winans' steam cannon. [*LOSSING'S PICTORIAL HISTORY OF THE CIVIL WAR*]

Gardiner's hollow bullet that could burst inside the body of a person whom it hit intrigued Lincoln. Short-tempered Brigadier General James W. Ripley, head of ordnance, snorted with disgust when asked to take a look at the brutal new weapon. Despite Ripley's feelings, the War Department soon placed an initial order for 100,000 of "the Gardiner bullets."

Hardly anything was too small or too large for the attention of the commander-in-chief. December 1861 saw Lincoln demanding of McClellan: "Is it true that Gen. John M. Schofield is to be ordered East? My expectation & wish was for him to remain in Mo. Please answer." Writing to Halleck in September 1863, he pointed out that he believed George G. Meade, a major general of volunteers, should in his opinion "move upon Lee at once in manner of general attack. I think this would develop Lee's real condition and purposes better than the cavalry alone can do. Of course my opinion is not to control you and Gen. Meade."

No one was deceived by the commander-in-chief's frequent disclaimers. Though he tried to couch his "little suggestions" as softly as possible, both the sender and the recipient knew that they constituted inflexible orders.

Lincoln's steel came through when he was forced to countermand actions of a commander with whom he disagreed.

John Charles Frémont, the first Republican nominee for the presidency, was one of four men hand picked by Lincoln to become major

An angry commander-in-chief went to Antietam to demand explanations from McClellan (facing him from the left). [NATIONAL ARCHIVES]

generals at the outbreak of war. Placed in command of the Western Department, Frémont, on August 30, 1861, issued a proclamation declaring the slaves of Missouri to be "forever free." Lincoln promptly and firmly countermanded this emancipation declaration. He did the same thing the following May when Major General David Hunter abolished slavery in the Department of the South. As a tool of war, a declaration of emancipation was of potential significance, but it would only come at the time and in the form stipulated by the commander-in-chief.

Just as Abraham Lincoln had almost single handedly moved the nation from exchange of insults and threats to all-out war, so he was adamant when the peace movement gained momentum in both North and South. Confederate commissioners came to Hampton Roads, Virginia, late in January 1865 to discuss possible terms of peace. Their arrival inside Union lines coincided with a spurt of support for the Copperhead movement in the North, led by Vallandigham.

C.S.A. President Davis had ordered his representatives to negotiate terms of peace between the belligerent parties, but Lincoln was adamant. Reunion, and only reunion, would be discussed. There would be no talk of an armistice of any sort, said the Union commander-in-chief, until Confederates surrendered their weapons, agreed to reunion, and accepted emancipation.

Under these inflexible terms, the war ground to its bitter end, with the finish as well as the beginning guided by the man for whom the presidency often seemed secondary to his role as commander-in-chief of the armed forces of the United States.

CHAPTER

32

Grant of Maine Built State-of-the-Art Fortifications for Atlanta

Richmond Va 11 July 1863

Col. L. P. Grant,
Department of Georgia
Loss of Vicksburg to the Federals has made railroad centers even more important than before. It is imperative that steps be taken at once to defend Atlanta in the unlikely event that the enemy will send raiders there in order to destroy railroads. Please acknowledge.
Jeremy F. Gilmer, Bureau of Engineers

Before July 1863 ended, Grant had made plans that were approved by Colonel M. H. Wright, commander of the Confederate garrison in Atlanta. Surveys were already under way, in preparation for mapping much of the region between the city and the Chattahoochee River. Captain Arnold, at the large arsenal in Augusta, had complied with a request for 100 picks and 100 shovels.

Writing at length to Gilmer in the War Department, Grant reported that it was already clear that "fortification of this city presents problems second only to the defense of Richmond." It would take a line of more than ten miles, plus special fortifications at the river, to defend the rail center.

Hardly more than a growing town at the beginning of the conflict,

151

Atlanta had become the center from which munitions and supplies were shipped to the Army of Northern Virginia. Miles of the single-track Western & Atlantic Railroad had already proved too tempting for Andrews's raiders to resist. Sooner or later, Federal forces were sure to strike at the spot where the W&A was linked with three other lines.

Governor Joseph E. Brown forbade the shipment of cotton over the state-owned W&A. His ostensible purpose was to prevent speculators from taking it into Tennessee for possible sale to the enemy. Actually, Brown by now realized that military matters must have first priority.

Residents of Atlanta were ordered to replace wooden shingles of their houses with tin. This costly transformation was made to reduce the likelihood of a fast-spreading fire. Such a conflagration could spread to arsenals and government warehouses, crippling the war effort.

By the time raider James J. Andrews and his men were hanged, government agents were combing the city and surrounding countryside for lead, which was desperately needed for manufacture of bullets. All over Atlanta pipes, window and door hinges, and some roofing sheets were seized.

Sheet copper, earlier imported from Mexico, became critically short in supply. Mines at Ducktown, Tennessee, shipped their entire production south on the W&A, but there never was enough to meet demands of the young but fast-growing Confederate arsenal.

Lemuel P. Grant, a native of Maine who had come to Georgia as an engineer for fast-expanding railroads, had no military experience. Yet his commission from the engineering bureau in Richmond was given with the expectation that he would be put in charge of fortifying Atlanta, with little or no help from the central government. While waiting for specific orders, which did not come until after the July 4 fall of Vicksburg, Grant personally surveyed the fast-growing hospital center he was expected to defend.

Earlier, Georgia's legislature had ordered the W&A Railroad "to provide all the passenger cars need for transportation of sick and wounded soldiers." When that proved to be impossible, all railroad superintendents were asked to "attach to each passenger train one or more ambulance cars, equipped with bunks and containing sacks of straw or cotton or hay."

Checking off an informal list, Grant discovered that nearly all of the city's public buildings had been converted into hospitals. Before peace eventually came, more than 80,000 Rebels and at least 2,500 Union soldiers were treated in Atlanta.

Thousands of civilians who had fled to Atlanta as refugees had erected flimsy shacks in vacant areas. Some who could not afford

"Rebel works in front of Atlanta, No. 1." [GEORGE BARNARD PHOTO, NATIONAL ARCHIVES]

building material had taken up residence in abandoned boxcars. No keeper of a hotel or boardinghouse was permitted to receive any traveler who failed to produce a permit, which had to be inspected and approved by the provost marshal.

Stripped of his official power by military authorities, Mayor James M. Calhoun had been named "civil governor." That action, taken on August 16, 1862, had the practical effect of turning the rail center into a military post.

Lemuel P. Grant, age forty-six in 1863, had been a railroad builder in Alabama, Louisiana, Mississippi, and Texas before coming to Georgia. Confederate authorities acknowledged quite early that Atlanta needed a system of fortifications. So did Vicksburg, Richmond, and Petersburg; no experienced military engineer was available for the small center remote from battle lines.

Having initially rejected a commission sent him from Richmond, Grant had no choice in July 1863. He must take charge of building Atlanta's defense or risk punitive action. There would be little or no help from elsewhere; he would have to use men and material at hand to the best of his ability.

Two major resources were available to the man from Maine. Many owners of slaves were glad to hire them out at token rates of twenty-five dollars a month or less; anything was better than permitting them to remain idle on plantations that couldn't be worked for lack of seeds and tools.

In addition to manpower, Grant had trees. Most of the hills and ravines around Atlanta were heavily wooded. Besides oak, poplar, walnut, and hickory trees, there were slash pines by the hundreds of thousands.

Somewhere, Lemuel Grant had come across an old European military manual, which he studied carefully to develop a master plan of defense. He designed a system of twenty strong redoubts, each to be built on a prominent hilltop. Rifle pits were to be attached to these installations, with breastworks and sometimes trenches linking the entire system.

While hundreds of slaves were building the defenses proper, thousands more worked in the forests. They chopped down trees, then cut off limbs in such fashion that they formed networks of outward-pointing spears.

From the battered old European manual, Grant had learned that Napoleon's engineers placed great reliance upon the deceptively simple *chevaux de frise*. For this protective device, big trees were not needed. Saplings were cut down and their tops were sharpened. Then these palings were fastened together to form a crisscross pattern of pointed trees.

In addition, Lemuel Grant put gangs of slaves to work erecting twelve-foot palisades before points he considered especially important. Made of trees no less than one foot in diameter, the palisades were arranged so that defenders could fire between tree trunks, but no attacker could squeeze through.

To complete his readiness for attack, the railroader had all trees and shrubs cleared away from defensive positions for a distance of about one thousand yards. Attackers would have to charge across open ground while being fired upon by the five big guns that each redoubt was designed to hold.

When completed, the system of fortifications virtually ringed Atlanta at a distance of about one and one-half miles from the center.

With slave labor, slash pines, and red mud, a railroad builder from Maine created in just over a year a ring of defensive works that he considered adequate. No civilian had ever done anything comparable. When the crucial test came, Grant's work proved its worth. Though the rail center fell when Confederate defenders pulled out after the Union army cut all rail lines to prevent resupply, not one soldier in blue penetrated Atlanta's defenses by force of arms.

Most key coastal cities of the South were defended by conventional forts. In addition to Atlanta, numerous inland sites prepared for the worst. Shallow trenches that originally served to defend Vicksburg, Mississippi, were extended to miles of elaborate works designed to withstand a siege. Richmond was ringed by earthworks that sheltered big guns. Petersburg, Virginia, had so many forts, redans, trenches, and abatis hardly distinguishable from Atlanta's *chevaux-de-frise* that the Confederate center withstood a ten-month siege.

In the North, the nation's capital became by far the most conspicuously fortified city. Separated from the Confederate capital by only a three days' hard march, it was a tempting target. Major John G. Barnard of the engineer's corps, U.S. Army, was assigned to erect defensive works.

By the time Lemuel Grant had the defensive protection of Atlanta well under way, at the end of 1863, Washington was surrounded by thirty-seven miles of unbroken fortifications. Eventually the system was expanded to include twenty miles of rifle pits that intersected with sixty enclosed forts, plus ninety-three batteries housing seventy-four mortars and at least 760 heavy guns.

Yet no system of fortifications—North or South—was fully secure. Vicksburg, Atlanta, Petersburg, and Richmond fell as a result of overpowering military might, siege, or encirclement. Washington experienced few months in which citizens felt entirely safe. Rumors abounded, and it was known very early that though Robert E. Lee was recuperating from severe injuries to his wrists, he had high hopes of leading men in gray along Pennsylvania Avenue in triumph.

Washington's biggest scare came after many Confederate armies had been battered to pieces. Twelve months after Lemuel Grant began to plan for the fortification of Atlanta, men under C.S.A. Major General Jubal Early actually probed Washington's Fort Stevens on the Seventh Street Pike running toward Silver Spring, Maryland. As the conflict raged the firing of big guns could be clearly heard by the president and his family in the White House and by lawmakers in the U.S. Capitol.

33

Armies Were Expanded— at the Cost of Riots and Escalating Abuses

S aturday, July 11, 1863, saw an order penned for the fortification of Atlanta. In most respects, it was a routine day in Rebel territory. Not so in the North. For the first time in the history of the federal government, there was a drawing that determined what males would be required to don blue uniforms.

Even top-ranking military officials generally opposed opening their ranks to men who didn't want to fight. It was believed they would make poor soldiers.

Yet all other expedients had failed. Under a 1795 statute, it was illegal to require militia companies to serve more than three months during any year. Even patriotic paintings and songs, plus the oratory of fiery abolitionists, were not enough to produce the hordes of volunteers needed to whip highly motivated Confederates.

So March 3, 1863, saw enactment of a Federal conscription law. All males ages twenty to forty-five were required to register, but there were numerous exemptions and loopholes. Only the urban poor were expected to feel the full force of the new statute.

For the first drawing of names, New York City leaders picked what they considered to be a docile district: part of Manhattan above Fortieth Street. They paid little attention to a note sent to his police precinct headquarters by Detective Dusenberry:

A man named John Andrews is stirring up the people to action against the draft and against the colored. He is making treasonable speeches about the 10th Ward and especially along Allen Street. I am sticking with him. Dusenberry.

Several men chosen on Sunday for immediate military duty were members of the Black Joke Engine Company No. 33, a hard-fighting, hard-drinking band of volunteer firemen. Insulted at the very notion of being drafted, they launched a movement designed to burn the draft office and the papers it contained.

Promptly at 10:00 A.M. on Monday, a hose cart loaded with cobblestones stopped at 677 Third Avenue, location of the draft office. Rocks were thrown through the windows, and angry Black Jokers broke down a door, chased officials out of the building, and set fire to it.

Once begun, physical resistance to the military draft snowballed beyond the wildest fears of authorities. John Andrews and other known Copperheads had already created a climate of hostility; once volunteer firemen defied the law by acts of mob violence, latent hostility provided plenty of fuel for the growing flames. Hundreds, then thousands, then tens of thousands joined in the rioting.

Rail lines were torn up. Jewelry stores were battered open and stripped bare. Saloons were looted. A Second Avenue rifle factory was invaded, providing splendid weapons for new waves of assault.

By noon on Monday, many rioters were beginning to focus upon black targets, whom they dubbed "the cause of the war." Fifth Avenue's Colored Orphan Asylum, haven for about 229 children, was wrecked and then set ablaze.

Harper's Weekly had a reporter on the spot who recorded one of the first killings:

> A mob of men and boys seized an unfortunate Negro cartman of Carmine Street on Monday evening. Having beaten him until he was in a state of insensibility, they dragged him to Clarkston Street and there hung him from a branch of one of the trees that shade the sidewalk by St. John's Cemetery.
>
> The fiends did not stop here, however. Procuring long sticks, they tied rags and straws to the end of them, and with these torches they danced round their victim, setting fire to his clothes and burning him almost to a cinder.

Too late, Mayor George Opdyke wired Washington asking for troops. Secretary of War Stanton calmly replied, "The government will be able to stand the test," then dispatched orders requiring military forces to converge upon the stricken and reeling city.

Soldiers poured into New York from forts in the harbor. A full company rushed to the scene from West Point, and New York militia regiments in the Army of the Potomac were detailed to join in preventing anger at the draft from getting out of hand.

Even the Tribune *office, one of the city's strongest buildings, was a target for the mob.* [NEW YORK PUBLIC LIBRARY]

During the three days it took to quell the disturbance, mobs controlled many streets. Much as revolutionists had done in European cities, rioters dug up cobblestones and formed barricades that were gunproof. In spite of such protection, a few were killed and many were wounded by musket and rifle fire. Blacks, the chief targets of the erupting wrath, fared badly.

No one knows precisely how many persons would have been included had a casualty list been drawn up when order was restored. Contemporary newspaper accounts say that the dead numbered 300 to 1,000. Many later analysts concluded that the numbers were greatly inflated. Perhaps no more than about 100 citizens died in one of America's worst riots.

New York Governor Horatio Seymour grimly reminded Lincoln that he had warned of serious consequences if the draft orders were implemented. Governors of Kentucky and of New Hampshire resorted to the old southern argument—states' rights—in pleading that they be permitted to suspend or modify the draft. Disturbances broke out in stalwart Unionist places such as Bucks County, Pennsylvania, and Albany, New York. In Milwaukee, a mob made up mostly of immigrants who spoke no English attacked the draft headquarters with stones and clubs.

Nevertheless, Abraham Lincoln did not swerve in his purpose. To Seymour's plea that the draft be suspended, at least for the time being, the president responded:

Time is too important for the nation to take such a course. We are contending with an enemy who, as I understand, drives every able-bodied man he can into his ranks, very much as a butcher drives bullocks into a slaughter pen. This produces an army with a rapidity not to be matched on our side if we first waste time to re-experiment with the volunteer system.

With fires of rebellion that had flared throughout the North quenched before overpowering military force, the draft was formally resumed as earlier scheduled, on August 19. Seymour of New York railed angrily that "the long arm of the president now reaches into the shops and homes of every hamlet, town, and city in the nation!"

In New York, military authorities arrested 443 persons, but less than half of them were indicted on any charge. Eventually, 67 persons were convicted of having taken a leading part in America's worst civil disturbance. Some who were convicted of killing a black received sentences lighter than those usually handed out for stealing a side of bacon.

When conscription had been initiated nearly a year earlier in the Confederacy, Georgia's Governor Joseph E. Brown sent a long and angry letter to Jefferson Davis. Many in the South managed by legal maneuver or by subterfuge to evade the draft, but there was no outbreak of mob violence. No matter how much they disliked it, most southern whites agreed that conscription was necessary to resist tyranny in Washington. Slaves, who were not affected, kept their mouths shut and tried to stay out of trouble.

Resumption of the draft did bring some badly needed men into Federal military forces. It did not, however, correct flagrant abuses already linked with the insatiable demand for manpower to defeat the South.

Almost on the heels of Lincoln's first call for 75,000 ninety-day militia, local, state, and federal agencies began offering men cash incentives to go to war. Bounty for enlistment, initially pegged at three hundred dollars, produced the derisive song, "We Are Coming, Father Abraham, Three Hundred Dollars More."

As the conflict widened and the need for men became more imperative, bounties were doubled and then doubled again. To a man needed to fight at a wage of about thirteen dollars a month, some sparsely settled western counties offered a bounty of fifteen hundred dollars upon enlistment for a three-year hitch.

Such a system inevitably produced a network of commercial brokers who helped to provide men for a fee over and above the bounty. A group of "runners," flourishing especially in seaboard cities with large immigrant populations, specialized in supplying recruits who collected their bounties before being found disabled when given a perfunctory physical examination.

An aged New Yorker was attacked for no reason except his color. [HARPER'S WEEKLY]

Even worse than abuses spawned by the bounty system were the evils that grew out of the system of substitutes. Under Federal provisions, any male called for service could avoid it by providing an able-bodied substitute. For reasons no biographer has ever managed to plumb, Abraham Lincoln, who was not subject to conscription, hired a substitute for himself.

"Immigration societies" sprang up in many cities. Sending agents to Europe, they recruited men who would come to a Federal center and sell their services as substitutes. Since the supply of manpower secured in this fashion was sometimes inadequate, substitute brokers began relying upon the tactics of the press gangs of old. They kidnapped runaway boys and newly arrived foreigners by plying them with drinks before knocking them in the head. The poor fellows woke up wearing blue uniforms. Before the fighting stopped, bounties paid by federal, state, and local governments amounted to several times the military budget for the first year of fighting.

Though enforced by bayonets, the draft actually called only about 168,000 men into service. Of these, at least 117,000 were hired substitutes, frequently but not always sent straight to a German-speaking unit that looked to Carl Schurz for leadership. At least 86,000 men, one of them being a Buffalo, New York, law enforcement officer named Grover Cleveland, hired substitutes without resorting to a broker as an intermediary. No stigma was attached to what Cleveland and tens of thousands of other relatively affluent males did.

Tolerated briefly in the C.S.A., the practice of allowing substitutes drew even more fire than the original conscription act. As a result, an 1863 act made the practice illegal throughout the South. Yet in the North as in the South, the war-shaped society came to regard it as normal and right to do anything and everything possible to evade the dictates of the central government. Regardless of whatever else it did, the prolonged North/South conflict helped to produce a lasting climate of suspicion and hostility directed toward Washington, the center of the nation eventually reunited by force of arms.

CHAPTER

34

Mary Walker Got Her Medal— And Kept It

"**Y**ou were right. I did need more training. So I left the hospital and spent a year at the Hygeio-Therapeutic Center in New York."

Wearing modified bloomers, his diminutive visitor smiled at Major General George H. Thomas sprawled at the foot of a tree in McLemore's Cover near Chattanooga, Tennessee.

Suddenly very serious, she drew herself erect and gave a smart salute. "Mary Walker, M.D., reporting for duty, sir," she said.

Thomas laughed. "A woman in the army? You're mad. Rosecrans would cry 'harlot' and Washington would explode."

"Would that be so bad, general?"

Mary Walker, who had known Thomas casually when both were in the nation's capital, had picked her target carefully. She knew that he had balked when asked to serve under Major General William S. Rosecrans at the time the Army of the Cumberland was created in October 1862, for earlier Rosecrans had been his subordinate. However, after protesting, Thomas accepted command of the Fourteenth Corps as subordinate to Rosecrans.

One reason he yielded, as nearly everyone acquainted with Thomas realized, was the cloud that still hung over him in Washington. He had demonstrated his loyalty at Shiloh, Perryville, and Stone's River; yet many in the Lincoln administration were unable to forget his strong Confederate ties.

Given a commission in the artillery after his 1840 graduation from West Point, he very early made it clear that he expected to be a career officer. By 1860 he was a major in the Second Cavalry.

Stationed in Texas, his unit was surrendered by General David E. Twiggs, and many officers took off their U.S. Army uniforms to accept Confederate commissions, including Albert S. Johnston, William H. Hardee, Robert E. Lee, and John B. Hood.

Torn between loyalties, Thomas took a leave of absence. Against strong family pressure, the Virginia-born officer finally made up his mind to stay with the Union. Friends and relatives cut him off, and many men in high places were suspicious of his motives. A refusal to serve under Rosecrans would have revived the old questions, and Thomas knew it. Therefore he swallowed his pride and spent the early months of 1863 in east Tennessee and Alabama.

"Something big is in the works," Mary Walker said, interrupting his reverie. "Everybody in Murfreesboro knows it. There will be lots and lots of casualties. I'm not here to fight; I came to tend the wounded."

"You can't do that in your ridiculous costume," responded Thomas. "Get into a proper uniform, and go to work!"

Without consulting superiors, Thomas gave Mary Walker a commission as assistant surgeon, the only woman to serve the Union in such capacity. Wearing a uniform but keeping her curls "so I can be known for what I am," she was assigned to a field hospital.

Days later, on September 19, furious fighting erupted at Chickamauga. Rosecrans's divisions, previously scattered, had been concentrated to drive C.S.A. General Braxton Bragg and his gray-clad troops from Chattanooga. Moving to block Rosecrans's return to the city and himself to re-occupy it, Bragg met the Federals head-on at Chickamauga Creek.

Halfway through the second day of continuous battle, bad judgment by Rosecrans left a hole in his line. Confederates poured through and were on the verge of sudden victory when Thomas deployed his men on Snodgrass Hill, where they stood firm against wave after wave of attackers. It was this exploit that made the man with strong Confederate ties a national hero, acclaimed as the "Rock of Chickamauga."

Mary Walker got all she was seeking, and perhaps more. With just under 10,000 Federals wounded, she and her colleagues worked without a break for more than thirty-six hours. Tossing her curls when a superior asked her what on earth she was doing with a Rebel, the assistant surgeon tended a wounded man in gray as carefully as one in blue.

Neither reprimand nor danger stopped the New Yorker who had graduated from Syracuse Medical College and had tried to set up a practice before deciding that she was needed by the U.S. Army. Rebuffed in early attempts to enlist, she worked for a time as a volunteer nurse at the Patent Office hospital in Washington. There she met George H. Thomas, who tried to get rid of her by suggesting that she needed more training before entering battlefield service.

Herself a minor celebrity in the aftermath of Chickamauga and the subsequent siege of Chattanooga, Dr. Walker became a prisoner as a result of insisting upon aiding a wounded Rebel. Confederate forces captured her and sent the strange-looking Union medical officer to Richmond's Libby Prison.

At the war's end, the only woman who had managed to serve the Union as an assistant surgeon received a Congressional Medal of Honor for gallantry in battle. Years later, in 1919, Congress decided that too many Medals of Honor had been awarded, and a Board of Medals review led to the revocation of Dr. Walker's award.

Notified of the official action and still wearing male attire complete with top hat, bow tie, and wing collar, Mary Walker shook her stubborn head and responded, "I'll never give it up!" She died clutching her precious medal. In 1977 the only Medal of Honor awarded to a woman during the Civil War was reinstated, and the recipient became the subject of a commemorative U.S. postage stamp.

Neither woman knew it at the time, but the ranks of the C.S.A. included a close counterpart to Mary Walker.

Though trained only as a nurse, not as a physician, Sally Louisa Tompkins opened a hospital in Richmond and used her own money to operate it for months. Many such enterprises in the Rebel capital had

Medal of Honor winner Dr. Mary Walker. [U.S. POSTAL SERVICE]

Major General George H. Thomas. [*LESLIE'S ILLUSTRATED*]

tremendously high casualty rates; Tompkins's did not. Her work was repeatedly praised by Jefferson Davis, who said that even the official army hospitals didn't return so large a percentage of patients to active duty as did Tompkins's.

Almost a year before Mary Walker bulldozed her way into service as an assistant surgeon, Sally Tompkins received an unequalled honor. Abuses in privately operated Confederate hospitals led to an order that only military personnel could operate them. To circumvent that regulation, Jefferson Davis gave Sally Tompkins a commission as a captain of cavalry, making her the only woman to hold a Confederate commission. During the forty-five months in which Tompkins's hospital treated more than 1,300 wounded men, only 73 died.

Part Five

The Devil Take the Hindermost

Brigadier General James A. Garfield. [LIBRARY OF CONGRESS]

CHAPTER

35

James A Garfield Harvested Political Hay in the Aftermath of Chickamauga

July 27, 1863
Army of the Cumberland

Hon. Salmon P. Chase
Sec. of the Treasury
For a long time, I have been wanting to write to you confidentially. I have refrained hitherto, lest I do injustice to a good man, and say to you things that were better left unsaid.

I cannot conceal from you the fact that I have been greatly tried and dissatisfied. For many weeks I could not but feel that there was not that live and earnest determination to fling the weight of this great army into the scale and make its power felt in crushing the shell of this rebellion. I feel that the time has now come when no plea should keep this army back from the most vigorous activity.

James A. Garfield
Brigadier General

Excerpts from Garfield's long letter to a nonmilitary leader who was one of Lincoln's most trusted advisors reveal that Rosecrans's subordinate desperately wanted Washington to know that his commander was dragging his heels.

A member of the Ohio senate at the outbreak of hostilities, Garfield won no battlefield honors. His powerful political connections, however, led to rapid advancement in rank, as well as election to Congress late in 1862.

Fitz-John Porter, major general of volunteers, may have made serious blunders at Second Bull Run. When formal charges were brought again him, Brigadier General James A. Garfield was a member of the court-martial that heard evidence. Porter was cashiered out of the army in January 1863 and "forever disqualified from holding any office of trust or profit under the government of the United States."

Though he lacked combat experience, thirty-two-year-old Garfield now had firsthand understanding of how rapidly a commander could fall, and how far. Assigned to the Army of the Cumberland, he was angry that a congressman-elect did not pull more weight. That anger was fed by his growing fury that his commander—a Democrat— seemed to be dragging his feet. It was a situation that practically invited political meddling.

With Lincoln openly pressing for Rosecrans to take the initiative, the commander polled his staff in early June 1863. All seventeen commanders of troops thought an immediate advance would be unwise. Garfield—not included in the poll because he didn't command troops—took up his pen and dashed off a long memorandum. Addressed this time to Rosecrans, it enumerated nine distinct reasons for an immediate all-out advance.

It was insubordination of this sort that had led Garfield and colleagues to cashier Fitz-John Porter. This time, however, the situation appeared different to the ambitious civilian-general from Ohio.

When action did come a few weeks later, it was a debacle for Federal forces. Rosecrans was described by Garfield as riding along silently, "abstracted, as if he neither saw nor heard" the carnage at Chickamauga. Some firing was still being heard, however, so the congressman-elect volunteered to ride off for a quick look at the battle lines. It was Garfield, therefore, who boosted Thomas to national fame as the "Rock of Chickamauga."

Retreating into Chattanooga and immediately besieged by Rebel forces, Rosecrans was relieved of command just thirty days after Garfield's epoch-making ride that brought disgrace to his commander and fame to Thomas. Ulysses S. Grant took command of the re-organized Western armies, brought William T. Sherman to Nashville, and formulated plans for the Atlanta campaign. With Thomas as his second in command, Sherman began his methodical move southward, while Grant went north to face the Army of Northern Virginia.

Meanwhile, Garfield wore his uniform to the December 1863 sessions of Congress and was soon rewarded by promotion to rank of major general. Intimate ties with such key Republican leaders as Salmon P. Chase paved the way for his eventual successful bid for the White House, for which Chickamauga was the springboard.

The Battle of Chickamauga. [*LESLIE'S ILLUSTRATED*]

Some generals in gray, notably C.S.A. Major General John B. Hood, criticized their commanders in much the same way that Garfield sniped at Rosecrans. Hood's letters to Jefferson Davis probably led to the downfall of C.S.A. General Joseph E. Johnston. But instead of going to Congress and then to the White House, Johnston's critic was given command of the Army of Tennessee, destined to be crushed by Sherman.

Garfield harvested political hay in the aftermath of Chickamauga, but he was not alone in following that path to glory. The North/South conflict sent more men to the White House than did all other wars of the United States, combined.

Ulysses S. Grant, who was regarded as a failure prior to 1861, gained early glory at Fort Donelson. Abraham Lincoln was unwilling to give him a free hand, however. It took Vicksburg, Lookout Mountain, and Missionary Ridge to convince the president that in Grant he had—at last—just the man he had been seeking.

March 1863, saw the president personally elevate Grant to general-in-chief at the revived three-star rank, which previously had been permanently held only by George Washington. It was as the triumphant conqueror of the Army of Northern Virginia that Grant was swept into the White House.

Another chief executive, a civilian-soldier like Garfield, enlisted in the Seventieth Indiana Infantry as a second lieutenant. After being made a colonel, Benjamin Harrison admitted that he had "no more relish for a fight than for a good breakfast, and hardly so much." But he fought through the entire Atlanta campaign and was rewarded by promotion to brigadier general, a title that helped him to win the Republican nomination and the presidency.

Private William McKinley enlisted in the Twenty-third Ohio Volunteer Infantry soon after the fall of Fort Sumter. At war's end, he was only a brevet major, but he had seen enough battlefield action to be lauded as a veteran and a hero when Republican party boss Mark Hanna picked him as a likely candidate for the presidency. Perhaps least known today of the six Civil War generals who won the White House, Chester A. Arthur entered the New York militia before the outbreak of hostilities. During the years of conflict, he became quartermaster general of state forces, with the rank of brigadier general.

McKinley's commander, Rutherford B. Hayes, served with the Twenty-third Ohio Volunteer Infantry from start to finish. He began as a major and ended as a major general. Campaign strategists for the 1876 Republican nominee for the presidency listed fifty engagements in which he fought and rejoiced that somehow he had managed to survive having four horses shot out from under him. While still a lieutenant colonel, he was badly wounded at South Mountain. His real military glory stemmed, though, from his having fought with Morgan's Raiders during the summer of 1863 and in the Shenandoah Valley campaign of Major General Philip H. Sheridan the following year.

Ohio Republicans saw him as a sure winner in the congressional race of 1864 and nominated him in spite of what he had said earlier: "An officer fit for duty who at this crisis would abandon his post to electioneer for a seat in Congress ought to be scalped." Hayes did not have to eat his words. He won easily without campaigning and was on his way to the White House as the fifth Civil War veteran to win the nation's highest office.

Major General William. S. Rosecrans.
[KEAN ARCHIVES]

36

The Youngest General Captured the Most Wanted Fugitive

At the Lanier Hotel in Macon, Georgia, on May 6, 1865, Brevet Major General James H. Wilson scrawled a hasty signature. An aide hurried to a portable printing shop and barked orders. Before night, dozens of villages and towns were plastered with bold-print posters:

ONE HUNDRED THOUSAND DOLLARS REWARD IN GOLD will be paid to any person or persons who will apprehend and deliver JEFFERSON DAVIS to any of the military authorities of the United States. Several millions of specie reported to be with him will become the property of the captors.

For Wilson, born and reared in the region of southern Illinois where Abraham Lincoln spent many of his early years, capture of the most wanted fugitive of the war would come as the capstone of a colorful career.

After one year at McKendree College, eighteen-year-old Wilson entered the U.S. Military Academy in 1855. Graduating sixth in the class of 1860, he had worn his second lieutenant's uniform only a few months before he took part in the Federal expedition against Port Royal, South Carolina, and Fort Pulaski, Georgia.

Wilson was at the telegraph key when orders came from Washington for Rosecrans to relinquish command of the Army of the Cumberland. A few days later Wilson received the telegram that ordered Grant to proceed to Chattanooga and take command.

Not yet having led a substantial body of troops into battle, the man who was close to the men who shaped the plans of the U.S. Army in the West was named brigadier general of volunteers on October 31, 1863. That gave him two separate distinctions. He was the only officer ever promoted from Grant's headquarters' staff to command troops in the field. And, at age twenty-six, he was the youngest general officer in the history of the U.S. Army, the youngest man ever to command an army in the field except Alexander the Great and Napoleon.

Half the age of many officers in his command, Wilson fought with Grant at Chattanooga before being sent to the Army of the Potomac as head of the Third Cavalry Division. He was at Richmond and in the Shenandoah Valley with Major General Philip H. Sheridan before being transferred to Sherman's cavalry as a brevet major general at age twenty-seven.

Young as he was, the Federal officer moved into Alabama and out-witted C.S.A. Lieutenant General Nathan B. Forrest, the only man in blue who could make such a claim. For the first and only time during the North/South conflict, Forrest was both outmarched and out-maneuvered.

In a lightning raid originally aimed at Selma, Alabama, Wilson and his men moved across the state line into Georgia in April 1865. It was there that he got news that Jefferson Davis and his cabinet had fled from Richmond and were believed to be *en route* to Mexico by way of Georgia.

Four days after Wilson plastered middle Georgia with reward posters, the fleeing former head of state was seized near Irwinville, Georgia. Captain James H. Parker and private Andrew Bee of the Fourth Michigan Cavalry contested for the glory of having captured Davis. Escorted under heavy guard to a room in the hotel where Wilson made his headquarters, the ex-president of the C.S.A. spent the evening in conversation with his captor. They talked about West Point and mutual friends, the assassination of Lincoln, and President Johnson's charge that Davis had masterminded the murder plot.

May 12 saw two formal dispatches from Wilson go to U.S. Secretary of War Stanton. They underscored that Davis had, indeed, been cap-tured and reported that at Davis's own request, he would be shipped to the capital by water.

On the following day, Wilson sent a much longer message to the War Department. In it, he reported that the fugitive, surprised by Federal soldiers at dawn, "hastily put on one of Mrs. Davis's dresses and started for the woods, closely pursued by our men, who at first thought him to be a woman, but seeing his boots while running sus-pected his sex at once."

Throughout the northern press, the story of Jeff Davis's capture in one of his wife's dresses provoked hilarity, applause, and cartoons. A few editors noted, very early, that the account given by Wilson was "strikingly like that retailed about President Abraham Lincoln, on his

Brigadier General James H. Wilson (seated) *with Brigadier General Alfred Torbert.*
[MATTHEW BRADY STUDIO, LIBRARY OF CONGRESS]

way to his first inauguration in a Scotch-plaid garment borrowed from his wife."

Only a few months passed before the colorful tale of Davis's capture was hotly disputed. James H. Parker told editors of the Portland *Argus*, "I am no admirer of Jefferson Davis. I am a Yankee, full of Yankee prejudices, but I think it wicked to lie about him. I saw the whole transaction from the beginning; he did not have on any garments such as are worn by women."

Private Andrew Bee penned his own description of the man he claimed to have captured with his Colt: "He had on a military suit, cavalry boots and all, and a gray flannel blouse."

Did Wilson manufacture the story of Davis in women's clothing as a counterpart to the tale of Lincoln's going to his inauguration in disguise? Or did he accept without question embroidered versions retailed by his men?

No one knows for certain. But once circulated, the fabricated account of Davis's capture gained a life of its own and was told and retold for decades. Regardless of why Wilson circulated that story, his capture of the fugitive ex-president was momentous in its own right. Six weeks after the youngest of all brigadier generals made Davis his prisoner, James H. Wilson was advanced to the permanent rank of major general. Again, he was the youngest man of that rank on record.

37

"Rightly Used, a Few Hand Guns Could End This Bloody Business!"

Loungers within earshot in the bar of Willard's Hotel, Washington, put their drinks aside and turned to listen. Someone had asked, "How many men will you have with you, colonel?"

Slim, soft-spoken Colonel Ulric Dahlgren, looking even younger than his twenty-two years, eyed the questioner up and down before responding, "Plenty to do the job."

By February 1864 Dahlgren had become the topic of daily gossip in the capital. Everyone who knew anything at all was aware that something big was in the works. Brigadier General Judson Kilpatrick was said to be behind a scheme that had all the makings of a circus.

Rumors were correct.

Kilpatrick, whose cavalrymen commonly called him "Kill Cavalry," half as a term of respect and half in recognition that he seemed to care little for his own life or those of his men, spent much of his time in battle and the rest cultivating influential persons. During the recent Gettysburg campaign he had shown poor judgment by leading a third-day charge that ended in disaster. Now it was imperative that he plan and execute an operation that would restore him to favor.

Major General Benjamin Franklin Butler, generally regarded as the most incompetent of Lincoln's many political generals, had bungled once more late in 1863. His idea was fine enough; it was its execution that had gone awry.

From his headquarters at Fort Monroe, near the spot at which the James River pours into Chesapeake Bay, Butler took a long, hard look at Richmond. News from a spy network, secondhand or thirdhand by the time it reached Butler, said the city had only a few hundred defenders. If the Army of the Potomac would show enough activity to keep Lee and the Army of Northern Virginia on the move, Butler reasoned, his own Army of the James could move swiftly up the peninsula and seize Richmond with little or no resistance.

In its early stages, the operation of the plan was all but perfect. Lee moved farther and farther away from the Confederate capital. Butler's men were within striking distance when they came to a structure much like the one that had stymied Burnside at Antietam, an ordinary bridge. However, this time the bridge, which was a few miles below Richmond, was badly damaged and about to fall into the stream it spanned.

"'Spoons' Butler sat there looking at that bridge for half a day," laughed wags at Willard's Hotel in telling and retelling the story. "Finally he gave up, turned around, and went back to Monroe. By then, of course, Lee had tumbled to what was going on. He poured men into Richmond and made it as tight as a bottle."

During the months after Butler's bungled raid, Confederate leaders nad begun to relax. No one else would dare to repeat Butler's mistake, they believed. So Richmond was once more ripe for the plucking.

At least, that's what "Kill Cavalry" told Abraham Lincoln and Secretary of War Stanton during the winter evenings he spent with them at the White House. He spouted information about distances, guns, and men so convincingly that the top Union leaders decided to give him a free hand.

Kilpatrick's own commander, Major General Alfred Pleasonton, wanted nothing to do with the business. He was boiling mad that the president had bypassed the chain of command to listen to an officer famous for rash actions. So Pleasonton sent properly diplomatic protests to the White House where he was overruled without a hearing.

Under orders from the president, a secret cavalry raid would be launched before the coming of spring. It would be led by Kilpatrick with about 4,000 men, aided by an elite smaller body headed by Ulric Dahlgren.

No one in Washington, and few in the Union military, had to be told who Ulric Dahlgren was. His father was famous everywhere as the inventor and manufacturer of the 25,000-pound smooth-bore Dahlgren cannon and as commander of the Washington Navy Yard. Lincoln had wanted him for the post at the outbreak of hostilities, but there was a catch. By law, command of the yard was limited to a man with the rank of captain or above, and Dahlgren was only a lieutenant in the U.S. Navy.

As he did in scores of other instances, the commander-in-chief got his way. Lincoln persuaded Dahlgren to take over the naval yard, law or no law. Then he twisted arms in Congress so that lawmakers passed a special act making the appointment legal. Soon also named chief of ordnance, Dahlgren was a rear admiral by the summer of 1863 and was on the water commanding the South Atlantic Blockading Squadron.

His son Ulric was the apple of the admiral's eye. Because of his close ties with the White House, he also was a man to take seriously.

As developed by Kilpatrick and Dahlgren, the raid upon Richmond would serve more than one purpose. Lincoln was eager to have hundreds of copies of his December 8, 1863, amnesty offer distributed in Confederate territory. Many who read that proclamation, said the president, would accept its terms and come over to the Union side. What better place to distribute the message than in the Confederate capital?

A second goal of the cavalry raid was release of prisoners held at Belle Isle, near Richmond. No one knew just how many were there, but an educated guess placed the number at about 15,000. Liberated, these men would join forces with Kilpatrick and Dahlgren and would return to Washington in triumph.

Top secret or not, the general plan of the operation was well known in the capital long before it was launched. That is why Ulric Dahlgren, living in his father's home and beginning to become accustomed to the use of an artifical leg fitted for him after battlefield surgery, parried questions at Willard's bar evening after evening.

At least once, says Washington lore, he let his guard down and informed listeners in a mysterious high-pitched whisper, "Rightly used, a few hand guns could end this bloody business!"

No one then knew what he meant. But the secret was out, once the raid upon Richmond proved to be a fiasco and Ulric Dahlgren had become a casualty.

Insiders knew that the raid was starting when Kilpatrick led about 4,000 men out of camp on the evening of February 28, 1864. They rode all night in the direction of Ely's Ford on the Rapidan River and made splendid time. Just as the sun was rising, Dahlgren took 500 picked men and left the main body of the Federal force. It was the mission of the smaller body to cross the James River and enter Richmond from the south at precisely the time Kilpatrick's main body hit hard from the north.

Kilpatrick's troopers were in sight of Richmond's defensive lines before evening on March 1. From a distance, wooden cannon looked deceptively real and the constantly moving Confederates seemed to number many more than the 500 actually manning genuine guns. While Kilpatrick hesitated and considered waiting until dark to launch his attack, Confederate cavalry struck his lines and persuaded him to withdraw down the peninsula.

Dahlgren fared far worse.

Rear Admiral John A. B. Dahlgren, leaning against one of his immense guns.
[LIBRARY OF CONGRESS]

Instead of the knee-deep stream that he had anticipated, the James River was swollen by late winter rains and melting snow. Since it was obviously too high to cross at most points, he searched for and found a guide, a black known only as Martin. When the spot to which Martin led Federal troops proved to be as turbulent as other points, Dahlgren had Martin hanged from a big oak. Obviously, he concluded, the fellow who had pretended to be eager for freedom was a traitor who didn't deserve so easy a death.

Foiled—or tricked—by Martin's ignorance or treachery, Dahlgren was forced to remain north of the river. That prevented him from making the planned quick strike from the south at the hour Kilpatrick was supposed to hit from the north. Turned back by Confederates as they approached Richmond from the wrong direction at the wrong time, Dahlgren's men were thrown into confusion. With less than 100 followers, he tried to swing halfway around the city, hoping to join forces with Kilpatrick. Instead, he ran into a Confederate ambush in rural King and Queen County.

When Confederates opened up on the raiders, their volley put four bullets into Dahlgren's body. Jubilant fighting men in gray surrounded the dead Federal colonel. One seized his wooden leg as a trophy; another cut off a finger for the sake of a fine ring it sported. His watch was snatched up, and even the clothing was stripped from his body. Then Ulric Dahlgren was dumped into a pine box for shipment to Richmond.

Before his body reached the capital, Confederates had found papers strangely reminiscent of the lost copy of Robert E. Lee's Special Order No. 191 used as wrapping paper for three precious cigars. Dahlgren had no cigars to carry; but when his clothing was searched, his pockets were found to be stuffed with important-looking documents.

Within days, "the Dahlgren papers" were the talk of both North and South. Bearing the signature of the son of Admiral John Dahlgren, a man who surely had access to Abraham Lincoln and his top advisors, the documents revealed that the planned Richmond raid had involved much more than release of prisoners and distribution of amnesty offers.

According to the papers, once Belle Isle prison camp and Libby Prison were in Federal hands, raiders were to put Richmond to the torch. During the confusion created by the burning of the city, picked men were to use those hand guns of which Dahlgren had spoken at least once. Their chief target was to be Jefferson Davis, with members of his cabinet as secondary targets.

Most newspapers of the North denounced the Dahlgren papers as "blatant forgeries." Even the hasty hanging of black Martin won the editorial approval of the New York *Times* as "a fate he richly deserved."

However, throughout the South and especially in Richmond, the Dahlgren papers were taken at face value and the plot to assassinate Jefferson Davis was denounced in high places and low. C.S.A. Secretary of War James A. Seddon favored executing some of the captured raiders as reprisal for the plot. His colleague who served as chief of ordnance, West Point graduate Josiah Gorgas, said Seddon's proposal was far too mild, that the C.S.A. should retaliate for "the Northern war of extermination" by adopting its own Black Flag policy, under which all men taken prisoner would be summarily executed.

Drawn into the bitter controversy against his will, General Robert E. Lee sent a formal protest to Major General George G. Meade, then commanding the Army of the Potomac. Meade made a perfunctory investigation, concluded that no one outranking Dahlgren had been informed of the plot, and persuaded Lee to persuade Confederate leaders to shelve their investigation.

Battles on land and on the sea soon caused the name of Ulric Dahlgren to drop from headlines of newspapers other than the Richmond *Examiner*. One faithful reader of the *Examiner*, who followed every bit of evidence pointing to a Federal plot to assassinate the president of the C.S.A., may have been inspired by it to formulate a counterplot of his own. If the Federal plan to put a few hand guns to good use in Richmond did not actually plant the seed in the mind of John Wilkes Booth, it clearly influenced him in formulating his own successful scheme to use a tiny derringer upon Abraham Lincoln.

38

Lauded in the South, Forrest Was Vilified in the North

T*here were also 2 negro women and 3 little children standing within 25 steps of me, when a rebel stepped up to them and said, "Yes, God damn you, you thought you were free, did you?" and shot them all.*

They all fell but 1 child, when he knocked it in the head with the breech of his gun.

Private William J. Mays had earlier testified about the conditions at Fort Pillow prior to arrival of Confederate troops. His deposition, dictated to a secretary, was one of the most detailed included in the lengthy published report of the congressional Joint Committee on the Conduct of the War, issued in Washington late in 1864.

Another Tennessee Unionist, Mack J. Leaming, added details:

The enemy carried our works at about 4 p.m., and from that time until dark, and at intervals throughout the night, our men were shot down without mercy and almost without regard to color. This horrid work of butchery did not cease even with the night of murder, but was renewed again the next morning, when numbers of our wounded were basely murdered after a long night of pain and suffering on the field where they had fought so bravely.

As forts go, Pillow wasn't much. Located sixty miles north of Memphis by river and thirty miles as the crow flies, the earthworks installation squatted on a bluff overlooking the Mississippi River. However, its strategic site was important because guns in the fort could halt river traffic with its flow of supplies to the armies. Possession of the site seesawed back and forth, and in April 1864, it was held by Union forces.

The defenders at the time it came under fresh Confederate attack consisted of the Thirteenth Tennessee Cavalry plus the Eleventh U.S. Colored Troops and a handful of men from the Fourth U.S. Colored Light Artillery.

Leading 1,500 men of Major General Nathan B. Forrest's Cavalry Corps, C.S.A. Brigadier General James R. Chalmers hit Fort Pillow at 5:30 A.M. on April 12. Almost immediately, the Federals found that artillery could not be used against the attackers, as it was impossible to train guns downward at a sufficiently acute angle.

Confederate riflemen swarmed over nearby knolls and kept the Union forces inside the crude installation pinned down. They threw so much fire against the little *New Era* gunboat, standing by to defend Fort Pillow, that Captain James Marshall was forced to keep the port- holes closed. That meant that the 282 rounds of shrapnel and canister that his men managed to fire were totally ineffective.

Major Lionel F. Booth, commanding the defenders, had earlier boasted that he could defend Pillow "against any force for at least forty-eight hours." But a Confederate sharpshooter picked him off be- fore the fight was four hours old. The command passed to Major William Bradford, who earlier had been described in dispatches as being "a very young officer, entirely inexperienced."

Forrest himself, one of the most daring cavalry leaders on record, rode up before 10:00 A.M. with his main body of cavalry and took charge of the continuing assault. During the following five hours, he had three horses shot from under him, just one less than the four-year total of Rutherford B. Hayes.

Unaware that the command had passed to Bradford, but certain that the defenders could not hold out much longer, Forrest rigged a flag of truce about 3:30 and sent a squad of men forward. A message ad- dressed to Booth demanded immediate surrender, promising that cap- tives would be treated as prisoners of war.

"Should my demand be refused," Forrest concluded, "I cannot be responsible for the fate of your command." Though far less rigid than the unconditional surrender demanded by Grant at Fort Donelson, from which Forrest had escaped with 1,500 men before the final show- down, the terms seemed to include veiled threats.

Bradford hastily composed a reply. He asked for a full hour in which to consult with officers and with Captain Marshall of the *New Era*. During that time, he proposed that neither side should "make addi- tional preparations."

When his response to the demand for surrender was finished, Brad- ford signed the name of his dead commander to conceal from the en- emy that Booth had fallen hours earlier. However, before Bradford's proposed terms could be delivered to Forrest under a flag of truce, a small flotilla of steamers moved toward the bluff. One of them was

Forrest had three horses shot from under him in five hours.

clearly crowded with Federal soldiers.

Suspecting a ruse on the part of Pillow's defenders, Forrest sent a new message forward. In it, he gave the Union force twenty minutes in which to decide to give up or to continue the fight. Before that time had elapsed, a reply came from the inexperienced commander inside: "I will not surrender."

With one eye on the steamers inching their way forward, Forrest threw everything he had against Fort Pillow. By then, the impotent *New Era* had dropped downstream and was out of the fight. A Confederate charge drove the defenders from Pillow and pushed them to the river bank into murderous fire from a line of riflemen who had been stationed there an hour earlier.

When the carnage was over, 231 of the 550 Union defenders lay dead and another 98 were wounded. Although eighty-six Confederates were wounded, Forrest counted only fourteen men dead. The South had scored an overwhelming victory in a minor engagement.

Why had so many men in blue died and why were a majority of the dead blacks? If black women and children actually were at Pillow, as charged by Mays but denied by fellow Unionist survivors, they were not listed in official records.

Forrest, already a folk hero in the South, was everywhere lauded for his gallant and brilliant victory. But in the North, charges of butchery directed against black soldiers erupted as soon as news of the battle was made public. Abraham Lincoln ordered Stanton to investigate; Stanton delegated the job to Grant, who turned it over to Sherman with telegraphed instructions: "If our men have been murdered after capture retaliation must be resorted to promptly."

Eventually, Sherman's failure to call for retaliation was taken to mean that there was no proof of murder after surrender. Lincoln, who had drafted a lengthy paper establishing a system of hostage taking in reprisal for what happened at Fort Pillow, never signed the document. But long before it was formally published, it was generally known that the report of the congressional committee would say that Fort Pillow was the site of the most barbarous atrocities of the North/South struggle.

Labeled "a onetime slave dealer from Memphis," Forrest (who actually did trade briefly in slaves during early manhood) was vilified throughout the North. Emotions were so strong that forty years later *Harper's New Monthly Magazine* published a series of sketches depicting atrocities at Fort Pillow, sketches made by an artist who was never near the site he depicted.

As in the cases of John Brown and Ulric Dahlgren, tales that circulated in the South were different from those in the North. Yet, statistically, the summary was damning for Forrest: Only 20 percent of the black members of Pillow's garrison were taken prisoner, while 60 percent of the whites who served as defenders walked away as prisoners.

Had he been questioned by a congressional committee, Nathan Bedford Forrest probably would have cited his surrender terms as generous by comparison with Grant's at Donelson. Also he would have told of the forgery of replies by an inexperienced commander. Surely he would have noted the wild confusion of battle and, perhaps with a gleam in his eye, he might have asked, "What about atrocities committed upon Confederate prisoners by Ulysses S. Grant?"

In 1864 Forrest and every other Confederate commander was keenly aware that Grant had demanded, and had gotten, a change of rules regarding prisoners of war. Almost exactly one year before Pillow, Grant had seized a new strategic advantage. With manpower growing very short in the South but still abundant in the North, he had called a halt to the exchange of prisoners.

Captured Confederates could no longer count on being returned to uniform, and the impoverished South would have to feed its prisoners instead of getting rid of this burden by exchange. Also, Federal soldiers in Confederate prisons were often close to the end of their terms of enlistment. Why make exchanges to get men who would take off their uniforms a few weeks after gaining their freedom?

In April 1864 neither Forrest, Grant, Lincoln, nor Davis fully realized the effect that ceasing to exchange prisoners would have upon already overtaxed stockades like Andersonville. But all men knew that a lot of black soldiers had died at Fort Pillow. Many southern whites rejoiced; most Northerners cried "Foul!"

39

Jubal Early Swapped a Day for a Wagon Load of Gold

Like Fort Pillow and dozens of other sites, control of the city of Frederick, Maryland, seesawed back and forth between Federals and Confederates.

Robert E. Lee did not even mention Frederick during a long conference with C.S.A. Major General Jubal ("Jubilee") Early in mid-June 1864. Conferring at Cold Harbor, the Confederate general-in-chief told his hard-drinking, hard-riding subordinate that this time there was a real chance to strike a decisive blow in the heart of the Union. Prodding his Second Corps to move at top speed, "Jubilee" could cross the Potomac somewhere in the vicinity of Harpers Ferry. Storming through western Maryland, he would be poised to hit Washington City. Ringed by unmanned fortifications, the capital seemed to be a plum ripe for the picking. With only 15,000 men, Early couldn't hope to hold and occupy it, but with skill and luck and, above all, proper timing, he could hit the Treasury Department, the War Department, the Naval Yard, and other vital targets.

June 18 saw an urgent telegram from Lee: "Strike as quickly as you can. If circumstances permit, carry out the original plan. Otherwise move upon Petersburg without delay."

One week later, long columns of gray-clad troopers solemnly filed past the grave of their revered former leader, Stonewall Jackson. Many broke into sobs; some, including Early, vented their emotion by making vows to avenge his death. Damaged and rusty cannon were shoved aside; for this lightning strike, they would only be impediments. With forty good guns and a dozen light field pieces, the Confederates prepared to move on Washington.

"The road to glory can't be followed with much baggage," their leader told his subordinates when he ordered them to include in their personal belongings whatever underwear they would need. For each 500 men, Early set aside only one skillet wagon to transport cooking

C.S.A. Major General Jubal Early. [LI-
BRARY OF CONGRESS]

utensils.

July 2, the anniversary of unforgettable Gettysburg, saw the gray
columns still in the Shenandoah at Winchester, Virginia. There, Early
sent one corps north through Martinsburg and the other east toward
Harpers Ferry, with plans to converge in forty-eight hours. Thousands
of Confederates crossed the Potomac on July 6; the invasion was under
way and precisely on schedule.

Following Robert E. Lee's detailed plan, a cavalry brigade dashed
off in the direction of Baltimore with the objective of freeing 18,000
prisoners confined at Point Lookout. Early himself crossed South
Mountain and occupied Hagerstown, Maryland. He considered burning the town, but when a delegation of citizens offered to pay him to
leave it undamaged, he settled for $20,000 and pulled out quickly.

Approaching Frederick after leaving Hagerstown, "Jubilee" sat on
his horse and surveyed the thriving city through a glass. It was easy to
see that the predominantly German citizens knew how to make money
and to keep it; undamaged despite successive waves of occupation,
Frederick was a sparkling jewel. If Hagerstown could fork over
$20,000, there was no telling what Frederick could do.

Early's half-formed plan was partly shaped by anger. It was at Frederick, so everyone said, that Stonewall Jackson had swallowed a public
insult. According to the story told in North and South alike, Jackson
was at the head of a column moving through Frederick when a woman
deliberately humiliated him. The woman, Barbara Fritchie, had stood
at her window waving a Union flag in the face of the Confederate
leader.

Amplified and embroidered, the incident was made the subject of a stirring poem that gained wide circulation. It glorified Barbara Fritchie and Frederick at the expense of Stonewall Jackson and every loyal Confederate.

Wanting to avenge the insult to Jackson and thinking of the gold extorted from Hagerstown, Jubal Early had a clear-cut proposal in mind by the time he reached Frederick. He would give officials two options: They could clear the place of people before he burned it, or they could deliver a wagon load of badly needed gold.

Aghast but also terrified, a deputation of civic leaders decided to negotiate. After a period of dickering, they agreed to pay Early $200,000 as ransom for their city, but they warned him that the city itself did not have that kind of money. It would have to be borrowed from banks, and that would take time, at least forty-eight hours.

With one eye on the promised ransom and the other on a battle strategy that required him to move without a lengthy stop, Early agreed to give them twenty-four hours in which to pay or to suffer. As they had indicated, officials had to turn to banks, which advanced $200,000 against the promise of a bond issue to repay the loan. Repayment dragged on so long that the city paid out $600,000 in interest before retiring the Civil War debt.

Satisfied with the trade, in which he had given up a single day in return for $200,000, Early again turned toward his goal, the nation's capital.

Strangely, there was no panic in the city. Word-of-mouth reports had doubled the number of Confederate raiders to 30,000, and everyone knew that Washington City was guarded only by a few units of militia and maybe 200 U.S. Marines. Settlers flocked in from the countryside, seeking refuge. Clerks scurried about searching for weapons with which to arm companies of volunteers from government departments. Prices of foodstuffs doubled and then redoubled. An exception was beef, which dropped because plentiful supplies were available from herds driven south to escape the Confederates.

Assistant Secretary of War Charles A. Dana, who didn't want to go on record as criticizing Henry W. Halleck for permitting defenses to get in such deplorable shape, sent an urgent telegram to General Grant: "Unless you direct positively and explicitly what is to be done, everything will go on in the deplorable and fatal way in which it has gone the past week."

Gleeful secessionists boasted that they could see the dust from Confederate columns as Congress hurried to adjourn at noon on July 2. In the Capitol, Abraham Lincoln sat solemnly in the president's room. Aides handed him bill after bill, which he signed after glancing at the heading. However, when he came to the Wade-Davis bill, he defiantly pushed it aside.

Occupied Frederick, Maryland, in September of 1861.[HARPER'S WEEKLY]

Secretary of the Navy Gideon Welles, with whom the chief executive conferred on many topics not related to the navy, had realized a month earlier what the bill meant. "In getting up this law," he confided to his journal, "it was the object of Mr. Henry Winter Davis and some others to pull down the Administration."

Clearly having been influenced by ardent abolitionist and South-hating Senator Charles Sumner, the congressional act spelled out the fashion in which the legislative branch of government, not the executive, would deal with the rebellious states whose ultimate defeat or capitulation was now widely taken for granted. When he heard what was in the works, Lincoln said he might neither sign the bill nor veto it. Instead, he might put it in his pocket a while and think about it.

The idea of a "pocket veto" infuriated many of the president's most loyal followers. Horace Greeley of the New York *Tribune*, who had thumped for action from the time of the Dred Scott decision, thundered that Lincoln had become timid and "almost pro-slavery." With the re-election of the president already in deep trouble, campaign strategists admitted that they saw no way out of the new difficulty.

At about the time Jubal Early was taking his first good look at Frederick, Maryland, from a distance, Lincoln put out a public statement concerning his failure to say yes or no to Congress about the Wade-Davis bill. He liked some provisions, he said, but needed time to ponder implications of others. "What an infamous proclamation!" exclaimed powerful Congressman Thaddeus Stevens of Pennsylvania.

Furor over the pocket veto was pushed aside on the afternoon of July 11, when Washingtonians heard the dull booming of cannons at a distance. This time—their third try—the Confederates would surely penetrate the defenses of the city!

But the one-day delay at Frederick, waiting for his "wagon load of gold," had cost Jubal Early and the Confederacy dearly. Grant dispatched the veteran Sixth Corps by steamer, and three brigades of veterans reached the Sixth Street wharf on Monday, July 11. Now the hospital patients, who, though barely able to walk, had been hastily armed, were suddenly in the way, instead of representing Washington's last, feeble hope.

Within hours, three more brigades arrived. With 10,000 battlefield veterans in the city and the Nineteenth Corps steaming up the Potomac, the probability that Washington would be burned by Confederates rapidly eased, but did not entirely disappear.

Few in the city failed to hear Confederate rifle fire, and Early's raiders actually penetrated the outskirts of the capital. At Fort Stevens, where Federal forces had decided to launch a counterattack, Abraham Lincoln insisted on being present for the action. When a minié ball dropped a surgeon who was standing very close to the commander-in-chief, a brash young captain—so the tale goes—yanked at the coat tails of the very tall man who made a conspicuous target. "Get down, you damned fool!" shouted Captain Oliver Wendell Holmes, son of the man who had glorified Barbara Fritchie and himself destined to be a member of the U.S. Supreme Court.

Whether or not that rebuke took place as reported, Abraham Lincoln saw that Early's raiders were too late. Had they been one day earlier, the outcome might have been different. As it was, they were forced to retire from the field after having inflicted less than 100 casualties upon Washington's defenders.

Back at the White House, the president realized that public confidence in his leadership, already waning, would drop to a new low upon word that Confederates had actually fired upon the capital. Almost daily, he received word that the man in whom he had most confidence, Ulysses S. Grant, was now being castigated as a bloody handed butcher.

Failure though it was, Early's raid had brought the Union to a new level of humiliation. That caused enlistment officers to sit idle as the once-hearty stream of volunteers dried up entirely.

Admitting to himself frequently and sometimes to others that he now had little or no chance to hold the White House for a second term, the commander-in-chief decided to take the offensive once more. In spite of overwhelming public opinion that cried for peace at any price, Abraham Lincoln solemnly issued a call for another 500,000 fighting men, with unfilled quotas of states to be met by means of the universally hated draft.

40

In the South and in the North, Stricken Atlanta Was Seen Through the Eyes of George Barnard

"**G**et your wagon ready to roll; we move into the city tomorrow."

George Barnard, photographer of the Military Division of the Mississippi, acknowledged the curt order with a nod. During the months he had traveled with Sherman's army, he had learned to spring into action as soon as he was told that troops would be on the move. With the northern press still publishing letters and editorials about Jubal Early's raid aimed at Washington City, the Connecticut native was himself eager to see what fallen Atlanta looked like.

Twenty years earlier, in 1843, he had opened a daguerreotype gallery in Oswego, New York. It was there, a decade later, that he took the nation's first news photographs, action shots of an immense industrial fire. When new processes made the daguerreotype obsolete, Barnard took to the road in a wagon and shot landscapes and villages until he became associated with Matthew Brady. For Brady, Barnard photographed much of the countryside surrounding Bull Run Creek; then he worked independently until Sherman made him his unofficial military photographer.

Barnard prepared to capture Atlanta on glass plates four inches square. They first were sensitized by being dipped into a chemical mixture, made ready on the spot and used while still wet. Hence the distinctive "watermelon wagon" of the photographer and the little tent that was his darkroom became familiar as he trailed behind Sherman's army as it moved slowly southward from Chattanooga during the early months of 1864.

Alexander Gardner is believed to have inspired Barnard to become a Civil War photographer. [LIBRARY OF CONGRESS]

During the campaign, Barnard made numerous photographs of forests and rivers and bridges. One of them, which he mistakenly labeled as "Etawah Bridge" (instead of Etowah) stretched across a 620-foot span. To the photographer who captured it on a wet plate, the most remarkable fact about the structure was that it had been built in just six days by 600 men.

Hastily evacuated by Confederate forces when the last rail line was cut, Atlanta would be entirely different from the countryside with which he had grown familiar. Elaborate fortifications and war-scarred ruins would make splendid photographs.

As always, George Barnard was methodical. His eyes were caught by a two-story house standing near a formidable line of *chevaux-de-frise*. Immediately he used one of his precious plates. Knowing that his slow emulsions made it impossible for him to capture the scene and the looming clouds above, he double-printed: exposing his plate for the foreground, and adding clouds from another negative.

When at war's end he issued a book made up of sixty-one large photographs at the incredibly high price of one hundred dollars, the reception in the North was more than he could have expected. *Harper's Weekly* lauded the photographer for his "care and judgment in selecting the point of view, for the delicacy of execution, for scope of treatment, and for fidelity of impression." Editors told northern readers that Barnard's shots "surpass any other photographic views which have been produced in this country—whether relating to the war or otherwise."

In the South, the reaction was equally high key, but entirely different in nature. Enraged ex-Confederates seized upon Barnard's photographs as indisputable evidence that Sherman had, indeed, turned his wrath upon Atlanta as had no other military leader in any other

Photographer's darkroom tent plus wagon on the Atlanta battlefield. [NATIONAL ARCHIVES]

city.

One shot depicted railroad iron piled on crossties, soon to be set afire so that rails could be bent into "Sherman's neckties" when red hot. Another showed the ruined roundhouse of the Atlantic & Western Railroad, while a companion shot portrayed a bank building gutted beyond recognition.

To southern eyes, far the most compelling of Barnard's photographs showed iron wheels and axles of railroad cars against the background of a burned-out factory. As far as one could see, the desolate wreckage stretched along the track. Clearly, concluded the first to see this wartime photograph, "the beast, Sherman," wantonly destroyed anything and everything he couldn't carry off with him.

No doubt about it, Barnard had captured the soul of the Atlanta campaign as no other photographer captured any other campaign. His caption for photograph no. 44 was meticulously accurate, too: "Destruction of Hood's Ordnance Train."

But what Barnard did not say, because he assumed that everyone knew it, was that C.S.A. General John B. Hood—not Sherman—was responsible for the scene of desolation Barnard had captured. On the evening before pulling out of Atlanta, Hood ordered his sappers to burn or to blow up everything the enemy might be able to use. When his men fired his own eighty-one-car ammunition train, explosions set the nearby Atlanta Gas Works on fire, a graphic scene of wanton destruction later made vivid in the movie *Gone With the Wind*.

Had Barnard not been along to document desolation and had he not failed to label it as the work of Confederates, Sherman would still be hated in the South, but perhaps not quite so violently.

Matthew Brady, who was briefly Barnard's employer, achieved far more fame than did any of his subordinates. Specializing in portraits of presidents, generals, and celebrities, Brady put his name upon anything and everything in his studio. Many of his images were purchased or secured by barter; that made no difference—all were "Brady photographs" when offered for sale.

Brady's close ties with Abraham Lincoln gave him access to the most powerful Federal leaders. Many of them remembered that it was Brady who had produced for Lincoln a campaign portrait that was credited with having helped him win the White House.

Reckless as he was about claiming credit for the work of subordinates, nevertheless Matthew Brady did more than any other man to preserve for the future a set of visual images of the North/South conflict. One reason is that all of the really great photographers of the conflict—Brady himself, George Barnard, Alexander Gardner, and Andrew J. Russell—were at one time or another associated with the Brady Studio. Timothy O'Sullivan, Guy Fox, T. C. Roche, James Gibson, William Pynell, and a score of other military photographers worked for Brady or for Gardner or for both. It is through their cameras that persons and events of the tumultuous war years can be seen. Thousands of engravings and woodcuts published in the illustrated weekly newspapers were based upon photographs, most of which were destroyed.

Hampered by scarcity of essential supplies and a shortage of experienced men, the South produced only a few good wartime photos. Julian Vannerman of Richmond did the best he could. So did George F. Cook of Charleston and A. D. Lytle of Baton Rouge. Most of the photographs they made perished, but those that survive lack the compelling qualities of the best Union-produced prints.

Like vivid tales about Uncle Tom, Dred Scott, and Rose Greenhow, photographs were subject to interpretation from the standpoint of the pro-Union or staunchly Confederate viewer or listener. But even though the story of a photograph such as Hood's Ordnance Train continues to be twisted to fit neatly into strongly held beliefs, our American heritage would be vastly poorer without the work of George Barnard and his fellow war photographers.

41

Northern Medics Produced America's First Big Wave of Drug Addicts

*S*urgeons *tried to have their operating tables placed in the open where the light was best. Some of them were partially protected against the rain by tarpaulins or blankets stretched across poles.*

There stood the surgeons, their sleeves rolled up to their elbows, their bare arms as well as their linen aprons smeared with blood, their knives not seldom held between their teeth, while they were helping a patient on or off the table.

A man already under the influence of opium was given ether, if it was available. The surgeon snatched his knife from between his teeth, wiped it once or twice across his apron, and the cutting began. When the amputation was concluded, the surgeon would look around with a sigh and cry, "Next!"

As a postwar speaker, Carl Schurz gave that description of a Union field hospital to many audiences. Nearly always, at least one listener hobbled up to him to say, "I wish I'd been like Johnny Reb—made to bite the bullet, because the medics were out of painkillers."

U.S. Surgeon General Joseph K. Barnes, who gained that title and the rank of brigadier general in August 1864, was dismayed when he made the first official survey of long-term effects of battlefield surgery. *Addiction* had not yet entered the vocabulary of physicians, much less of ordinary citizens. So Barnes simply estimated that a minimum of

Ambulance office of the Federal Ninth Corps, near Petersburg, Virginia (1864).
[NATIONAL ARCHIVES]

many thousands of Union veterans "required regular doses of morphine, with dosage increasing sharply as time passes." No one knows how many veterans who had worn gray were dependent upon the needle until death.

Pioneer reformer Dorothea Dix, who toured America's insane asylums, said that especially in the North, but also in the South, she found "legions of heroes whose minds were sound, but who had been committed because of effects produced by morphine and opium."

In the aftermath of First Bull Run, the mortality rate among seriously wounded men was astronomical. Optimistic generals, prodded by their commander-in-chief who was eager for action before ninety-day enlistments ran out, had given little advance attention to medical needs. Soon, though, the capital was dotted with hospitals whose number continued to increase until their beds held the largest number of wounded men of any city in the world.

By Second Bull Run in August 1862, Federal forces had adopted an innovation called the "ambulance." Earlier, wounded men had been carried from the field on stretchers or on the backs of comrades. A one-horse ambulance was little more than a square box mounted on the axle of a single pair of wheels. Yet it was so handy that many general officers requisitioned ambulances to carry their papers and personal belongings.

In an early demonstration of his strategic skill that made him famous, Robert E. Lee split his army of 48,000 in order to strike the 75,000 men of Major General John Pope from two sides simultaneously. When three days of carnage near Bull Run Creek ended with a brilliant Confederate victory, Pope's units counted at least 5,900 wounded men. Rifle bullets had done about 95 percent of the damage, with artillery fire accounting for most of the rest and bayonet and saber wounds amounting to less than ½ percent of the total.

Standard ambulances, supplemented by a few of the new four-wheel variety that were slow and clumsy, but much more comfortable, swung into action. They could not begin to handle the most serious cases, so troopers of every unit were detailed as stretcher bearers.

By the time the immense wave of wounded reached Washington and its hospitals, men who were unable to get battlefield amputations were usually gangrenous. They reached the capital begging to have an arm or a leg cut off, but it was too late.

Federal officials soon realized that the conflict would be much longer than anyone had expected. Standard-issue medical panniers were prepared for use in tents that served as field hospitals. These all-purpose kits held fifty-two bottles and vials, of which seven were pure opium, pure morphine, or other medications heavily laced with the addictive substances.

Sixty days before Second Bull Run, at Pittsburg Landing in Tennessee, the Federal armies of the West counted 8,408 wounded men when Confederates left Shiloh battlefield. Sherman chalked up a record, of sorts: Four horses were shot from under him in a single day. A reporter for the Cincinnati *Times* described "men with their entrails protruding, others with bullets in their breast or shoulders still lying where they fell, and one poor wretch whose eyes had been shot away entirely."

Those who were seriously wounded and who were lucky enough to survive were sent to Washington by river steamers whose stench often identified them as hospital ships.

Two years later, in May 1864, Abraham Lincoln's armies were still ill prepared to deal with wounded men. In a three-day strike directed against Robert E. Lee's Army of Northern Virginia by Grant (actually commanded in the field by Meade) more than 12,000 men in blue were wounded.

Medics had long ago learned how to turn a school, a church, or even a farmhouse into an impromptu field hospital; this time, the vast marshland of the wilderness that had been the field of battle had few buildings. An awestruck observer, violently ill from what he saw, described the seemingly endless stream of vehicles that converged upon Fredericksburg, Virginia.

Sufferers looked ragged as well as bloody, for most pockets had been ripped off or slit, for the sake of watches and cash. Surgeons, he noted, had done the best they could to sort out the wounded. Those too far gone to be moved were often shoved aside; those who had to be carried were stuffed into every available ambulance and wagon. Amputees were often grouped by category. By putting into a wagon only men who had lost their right leg, and who could therefore lie on their left side, it was possible to pack more cargo into a given amount of space.

Every public building in Fredericksburg became a hospital. So did mills, warehouses, and churches. Straw spread on the floor for bedding ran out before the first 4,000 men were placed. Those who reached the city later lay on the bare floor, hoping desperately that one of the thirty surgeons on hand would soon get to them.

With no break except an occasional short nap, one surgeon spent four days amputating arms and legs. By the time limbs were piled head-high around him, with more wounded arriving every hour, he called it "a scene of horror that beggared description; God forbid that I should ever see such again."

Working against time, surgeons in field hospitals of the North were helpless without alcohol, morphine, and opium. They used narcotics

Bringing the wounded to Culpeper Court House after the Battle of Cedar Mountain, Virginia (1864). [EDWIN FORBES IN *HARPER'S WEEKLY*]

not only for the relief of pain, but also in treatment of dysentery, camp fever, and other common maladies.

Dr. S. Weir Mitchell of Philadelphia had put his national reputation behind use of opium. "This mighty painkiller is among the best weapons in the doctor's arsenal," he wrote. "Especially if administered by use of the hypodermic needle, it is without equal."

Throughout the land, it came to be expected that as an amputee began to regain consciousness, he would respond to mounting pain by shouting, "More opium! More opium!"

All opium and most other major drugs came from overseas, hence the ever-tightening Federal blockade made them increasingly scarce behind Confederate lines. Some Confederate surgeons secured morphine and opium from runners who regularly traded in the North. Many could only tell a man about to undergo surgery to fill his stomach with brandy and—literally, not figuratively—bite a soft lead bullet to avoid cutting his tongue off with his own teeth.

A few Confederates tried to use medications prepared from common red poppies of the garden variety. Sufferers sometimes found this better than nothing, but most reported that it did little to dull the pain felt when knife and saw were used.

Because of the drastic shortages faced in the Confederacy as the war dragged on, comparatively few men in gray became morphine or opium addicts. In contrast, their opponents in blue, who often seemed to fare better at the time of battlefield surgery, were far more likely to become dependent upon a painkiller.

Once hostilities ceased, men on both sides who had become drug dependent while in uniform eked out their remaining years as "opium eaters," always able to get it, because no laws governed the importation or use of the drug.

At the University of Illinois, historian Dee Brown conducted an exhaustive survey that led him to conclude that an immense but uncounted number of Americans were addicted to opium during the decade of the 1870s. Men who contracted the habit while under treatment by members of Dr. Joseph K. Barnes's U.S. Medical Corps, said Brown, were to be found "throughout the whole country—in towns and villages and rural districts as well as in all of the great cities."

Part Six

Every Fire Eventually Burns Itself Out

Political powerhouse Major General William T. Sherman. [NATIONAL ARCHIVES]

42

Sherman Tipped the Scales in Favor of Lincoln's Re-election

Grim-faced cabinet members converged upon the White House on August 23, 1864, in response to an urgent summons from the president. Having called the meeting to order, the chief executive handed each man a piece of paper that had been folded and sealed so that the message it conveyed could not be read.

Promising that in due time he would reveal the contents of the paper, the president solemnly ordered each man to sign the copy he held. Usher of Indiana, a particularly critical state because of the Copperhead-dominated legislature, hesitated.

"Sign!" the president sternly ordered with a gesture that clearly implied that he meant, "Sign at once, or resign!"

When that fateful memorandum was opened nearly three months later, startled readers saw what the beleaguered president had written:

> *Executive Mansion*
> *Washington, Aug. 23, 1864*
> *This morning, as for some days past, it seems exceedingly probable that this Administration will not be re-elected. Then it will be my duty to so co-operate with the President elect, as to save the Union between the election and the inauguration; as he will have secured his election on such grounds that he can not possibly save it afterwards.*
>
> *A. Lincoln*

Having secured what amounted to a written pledge to support his successor, Lincoln calmly dismissed the cabinet and turned to routine business that included signing an order for sale of land in the Winnebago Indian reservation.

In the aftermath of the nearly successful attempt by Confederates under Jubal Early to penetrate Washington City and destroy many of its facilities, Lincoln's political power had reached a new low.

Most of the war news had been bad for months. A long-planned Union attack upon Richmond stalled in May. Against terrific odds, Robert E. Lee held out against a three-day frontal assault at Cold Harbor, near Richmond, in June. Grant found himself bogged down, with 100,000 men rendered ineffective, by the siege of Petersburg.

There had been a few bright spots, to be sure. June 19 saw the U.S.S. *Kearsarge* overcome the most famous and most feared of Confederate vessels, the C.S.S. *Alabama*. At Mobile Bay, Rear Admiral David G. Farragut had scored an impressive win on August 5. Signs pointed to the probability of a Sherman victory in the drive for the vital rail center of Atlanta.

All in all, however, the future looked bleak indeed when Lincoln commanded his cabinet members to help preserve the Union in spite of his expected defeat at the polls. Everywhere, folk were weary of war. So vital was the issue of preserving the Union seen to be that the Republican party made a one-time change of name in order to make Lincoln the June nominee of the National Union Party.

There was much talk of Salmon P. Chase for president—so much so that he resigned from the cabinet in July and was replaced by little-known William Fessenden of Maine.

In the entire North, only the Radical Republicans still wanted to press the war. At their national convention in Cleveland, they adopted a platform that called for "suppression of the rebellion by force of arms, without compromise." Then they nominated for the presidency John C. Frémont, who had made an unsuccessful try as the first Republican nominee in 1856 and who had seen his emancipation proclamation for Missouri countermanded by the commander-in-chief. Though not numerous enough to be decisive, the Radical Republicans were loud and bothersome. They could not be ignored.

According to a story that gained wide circulation in early October when first told by Michigan Senator Zachariah Chandler, "Abe Lincoln may look like a farmer, but he's smart as a fox. Knowing he had to get Frémont out of the way, he looked for bait with which to tempt him.

"He couldn't offer Frémont a cabinet post; that would never do. So he poked around until he found that Frémont hated Montgomery Blair—[Blair had represented Dred Scott before the Supreme Court] Then smart old Abe got Frémont to drop out of the race in exchange for making Blair resign as postmaster general."

Exactly what trade was struck has never been revealed. But Frémont did withdraw on September 17, three weeks after the fateful cabinet meeting, and Blair did resign September 23.

With Frémont out of the way, the man who had never wavered in his insistence that the Union must be put first, last, and always ahead of every other consideration, turned his guns upon his one-time favorite general whom Democrats had nominated on a peace platform.

George B. McClellan, who had been shelved by Lincoln after Robert E. Lee's 1862 invasion of Maryland, was affectionately known by soldiers as "Little Mac." But in the upcoming presidential election, he had to be reckoned as a giant.

Powerful Horace Greeley of the New York *Tribune* expressed what he sensed to be a national yearning for peace: "Nine-tenths of the whole American people, North and South, are anxious for peace on almost any terms and are utterly sick of human slaughter and devastation. If the Rebellion can be crushed before November, it will do to go on; if not, we are rushing to certain ruin. I beg you, I implore you, to inaugurate or invite proposals for peace forthwith."

Greeley informed newspaper readers that "Mr. Lincoln is already beaten. He cannot be elected." Hence the editor would have preferred to see a ticket headed by Grant, Benjamin Butler, or Sherman. In late August, staunch Lincoln supporter Thurlow Weed told Seward that he had earlier advised the president that re-election was an impossibility. "Nobody here doubts it," he added, "the people are wild for peace."

Lincoln had been adamant when his most intimate advisors urged him not to stand for re-election. He could cite the war emergency, they said, as causing such stress that he should step down, thereby avoiding certain defeat.

"No," said the president. "Unless the people have a chance to express their will, the purpose for which the war is being waged will be forfeited."

Determined to run against overwhelming odds and unyielding in his stance that the Union—the entire Union—must be preserved at any cost, the commander-in-chief hoped that men in uniform would rally to his support even if civilians deserted him.

Early in his administration, Republican leaders had opposed taking steps to give soldiers an opportunity to vote. After all, in 1861 the leading generals—McClellan, Halleck, and Don Carlos Buell—were all Democrats. But as the personnel of the military leadership changed and as White House pressure mounted, many leading Republicans changed their minds. By the summer of 1864, eleven out of the twenty-five states in the Union allowed soldiers in the field to participate in elections. Several of the crucial states still did not, however.

Informed that Pennsylvania hung in the balance because of strong loyalty to McClellan, the commander-in-chief pondered his options. Alexander K. McClure, who had his finger on the political pulse of the state, solemnly vowed that if 10,000 soldiers could be furloughed home for two weeks, Pennsylvania could be won. Surely U. S. Grant, all but idle before Petersburg, could spare 5,000 . . .

Lincoln hesitated. He was sure that Meade, now commanding the Army of the Potomac, would give no trouble. But Grant had been a nominee at the 1864 convention in Baltimore; even his elevation to the rank of three-star general did not entirely remove him from the political process.

Eventually the president acted in characteristic fashion. Instead of suggesting that Grant and Meade each furlough 5,000 Pennsylvanians, he decided to send personal messengers to Meade and Sheridan. Both men acted promptly, and the 10,000 votes garnered in this fashion were counted as "home vote" rather than as "soldier vote."

Far to the south in Georgia, heartland of the Confederacy, two bold and decisive strokes by William Tecumseh Sherman tipped the scales in favor of his commander-in-chief.

Sensing that Atlanta's fortifications were too strong to be penetrated and too vast to be surrounded, the Federal commander moved swiftly to the south and cut the city's last remaining railroad line. That forced Confederate defenders to pull out as soon as they had destroyed machine shops, rolling mills, railroad depots, and other facilities of military significance.

Sherman dispatched to Washington a brief but triumphant telegram: "Atlanta is ours, and fairly won." Lincoln telegraphed a reply in which he told the commander that the entire nation was in his debt; then he declared a day of thanksgiving for victory in Georgia.

Months earlier in a Nashville planning conference, Grant and Sherman had agreed that the former would strike at Richmond, the latter at Atlanta. When Sherman reached and seized his target, popular reaction in the North was far greater than either man had expected. At last, Federal troops had scored an impressive victory that also meant serious new problems for Lee's Army of Northern Virginia. Maybe the Union was worth fighting for, after all!

Only ballots cast in the field were counted in "the soldier vote." [HARPER'S WEEKLY]

With the ground swell of public opinion shifting in a fashion not realized by top political leaders of any party, Sherman began to implement a second plan of action. His men from Massachusetts, Illinois, Connecticut, New Jersey, and Indiana—Indiana, above all—were notified that they would be given furloughs to go home to vote. This action was taken on his own, without suggestion or direction from the White House.

Simultaneously, Sherman began making arrangements to set up polling places for those men in uniform whose state laws permitted them to vote in the field. At least one ballot box was improvised from an empty cartridge box. Other arrangements were equally crude, but effective. No one knows how many of the more than 70,000 men in Sherman's Western armies voted to return Lincoln to the White House, but their influence was undeniable.

On the evening of November 8, incredibly, the first complete returns came from Indianapolis, earlier considered sure to be lost because of widespread Copperhead influence. Twenty-nine regiments and two batteries furloughed home by Sherman must have delivered, for the president carried the state by 1,500 votes.

In the telegraph room of the war office, the president jotted down returns as they arrived. Three weeks earlier, on October 13, he had used a telegraph blank in the same room to pencil an estimate slightly more optimistic in tone than his August memorandum to cabinet members. According to his best guess three weeks before the election, it appeared that McClellan would win 114 electoral votes against his own 117.

But as the portent from Indiana suggested, the changing mood of voters combined with the impact of the soldier vote made all the pundits wrong. Although most of Lincoln's intimates had carefully stayed away from the White House during the day, they trooped to the war office that night to offer their congratulations. McClellan captured 1,805,237 popular votes, but won only twenty-one electoral votes from three states: Delaware, Kentucky, and New Jersey.

Sherman's great victory at Atlanta plus his delivery of the soldier vote were not the only important factors in the re-election of the man pledged to preserve the Union, no matter what. No one should ever underestimate the political acumen of the man in the White House whom the Richmond, Virginia, *Examiner* called "the obscene ape from Illinois." After all, Lincoln maneuvered Frémont out of the race and captured no-one-knows how many votes from weary secessionists who had to take iron-clad oaths in order to receive amnesty.

In distant Georgia, the triumph of Lincoln was also the triumph of Sherman who, earlier approached about becoming a candidate for the presidency, had snorted, "Only a fool would want the office!"

43

Black Soldiers Were Central to the War's Biggest Explosion

Before Petersburg, August 1864

Dear Wife:

. . . At first light, the 12th was ordered into the vast crater. Close to the outer ditch by which I entered stood a Negro soldier, begging for his life from two Confederates, who stood by him, one striking the poor wretch with a steel ramrod, the other holding a gun in his hand with which he seemed to be getting a shot at the Negro.

The man with the gun fired it at the Negro, but did not seem to injure him seriously. The man with the ramrod continued to strike the Negro therewith, whilst the fellow with the gun reloaded it, and, placing its muzzle close against the stomach of the Negro, fired, at which the latter fell limp.

The Southerners all seemed infuriated at the idea of having to fight Negroes. Soon so many of them lay dead that it was difficult to make one's way along the trench without stepping on them. . . .

Faithfully, George

Describing some of the events of July 31, George S. Bernard of the Twelfth Virginia did not go into detail about the immense hole soon to become famous as "The Crater." Except for those involved in creating it, the hole was still somewhat of a mystery among Federal units entrenched before Petersburg, Virginia.

Joseph J. Scroggs, who had begun to keep a diary in 1852, knew much more than did most fellow soldiers. A light-skinned black farmer of Columbiana County, Ohio, Scroggs managed to join the

Northern cartoonists poked fun at "the black dilemma" of the Confederacy, despite the fact that no one in the North knew what to do with contrabands. [HARPER'S WEEKLY CARTOON]

104th Ohio long before Federal authorities sanctioned the enlistment of blacks as soldiers. When the Union Infantry of African Descent was created in January 1864, Scroggs was made a second lieutenant.

Nearly a month before Abraham Lincoln forced cabinet members to sign a pledge they had not read, Scroggs got thrilling news. A secret operation, under way for some time, was nearing completion. Soon the black regiment in whch he served would have the honor of leading the first wave in a surprise assault upon Confederate defenses!

In early June, Grant had decided that Petersburg must be taken, regardless of the cost in lives. Once the key rail center was in Federal hands, he reasoned, Richmond could not hold out more than a week or two. It was ironic—even amusing—that the estimated 2,500 defenders of the Confederate city were commanded by the man who had led the assault against Fort Sumter, Pierre G. T. Beauregard.

Expecting a quick victory, Grant sent the Second Corps and the Eighteenth Corps against Petersburg's feeble defenses. But Federal leaders bungled their June 15 strike, and other commanders did no better during the next few days. Robert E. Lee sent an army on the double, arriving himself on the seventeenth, and rejoicing that during four days Grant lost nearly 12,000 men and in return gained only a few trenches well east of the city.

No longer regarded as easily stormed, Petersburg would have to be strangled! Grant launched a siege operation, not imagining that it would last for ten months and involve more than 100,000 Federal troops.

For the first time in a crucial operation of such magnitude, great numbers of soldiers wearing blue were men with black skins. Analyzing this radical change in Federal strategy, editors of the Richmond *Examiner* concluded that Grant wished to taunt and humiliate the defenders of Petersburg. In subsequent notices, the newspaper suggested that the policy of posting black attackers where they could be clearly seen was an affront to the African soldiers, who were picked off by sniper fire in great numbers.

As the siege dragged on and the summer days grew hotter, Federals were impatient for action. Nothing they tried seemed to bring results, however. In this dilemma, Colonel Henry Pleasants of the Forty-eighth Pennsylvania had an inspiration. Why not tunnel underneath a Confederate salient, set a big charge, and blow it sky high?

Meade, who had become the commander on the spot, vetoed the idea as foolhardy but reported about it to Grant. Grant, initially cool to the proposal, was persuaded by Burnside that Pleasants knew what he was talking about. An experienced civil engineer who could recruit ex-miners from the ranks of Pennsylvania units, Pleasants was persuasive.

His coal miners started their tunnel, a modified mine shaft that was designed to stretch more than 500 feet, on June 25. Earth was brought out in big baskets, carefully dumped at night to prevent Confederates from detecting what was happening.

Sounds beneath an artillery post raised suspicions among Lee's aides, however. They sank a few test holes in an effort to determine whether Federals were actually digging a tunnel, but found nothing. A London *Times* reporter, Lawley, happened to be at Confederate headquarters when staff members were suspicious of a possible tunnel. From his long experience with mines in Wales, their visitor told them, he knew positively that 400 feet was the absolute limit for a horizontal shaft, because of the problem of ventilation.

What Lawley didn't know was that Pleasants had devised a novel method of ventilation, crude, but effective. Working around the clock, his miners completed their tunnel in just under one month. It measured 586 feet in length and five feet in height. Almost as wide at the bottom as it was high, the shaft tapered toward the top. Men crawling through it pulled 320 kegs of powder—more than four tons—into position.

Black soldiers of the Fifth Colored Regiment helped to place the powder. Many were elated at the prospect of being the first to swarm through the hole that would be blasted in Confederate lines. Such an honor meant that their race had come a long way, indeed, in a very short time. In the early months of the conflict, northern leaders had shown little interest in blacks or sympathy for them. Washington insisted that in states that remained loyal to the Union, the Fugitive

Slave Law still required that military officers return runaway slaves to their masters.

Benjamin F. Butler, the first major general of volunteers named by Lincoln (possibly because of his well-known Democratic background) chafed at obeying an old congressional mandate during war. Placed in command of Fort Monroe on the Virginia peninsula, Butler gave an audience to three runaway slaves who reached the post May 23, 1861.

Lawyer-General Butler reasoned that to return them to owners would simply aid Confederates, so he worked out a way to evade the intent of Congress. He labeled the fugitives "contraband of war," placing them in the same category as smuggled goods or anything that neutrals were forbidden to supply to belligerents.

Editors of the northern press had a field day with Butler's ploy. It ripped the Fugitive Slave Law to shreds, they insisted. Lawmakers pondered the dilemma and initially ruled that the law must be upheld; later they passed a Confiscation Act. Under its terms, fighting forces in blue were authorized to seize and to use cotton, ships, slaves, and any other property of Rebels.

Cartoonists twitted the South about the dilemma presented by their black residents, but the problem was equally acute in the North. As the ranks of contrabands swelled, leaders argued about what to do with them. Abraham Lincoln remained deeply troubled; he wanted rights of "loyal masters to be respected by military and civil authorities alike." And he confessed that he was fearful of consequences if contrabands should be put in uniform and given rifles.

"Come, join us, brothers,"—recruitment poster showing a black unit with white officer at Camp William Penn, Philadelphia. [Chicago Historical Society]

On October 14, 1861, the chief executive signed a document that outlined a plan for use of contrabands as laborers at Port Royal, South Carolina. In his own hand, however, Lincoln added to the directive prepared by an assistant secretary of war: "This, however, not to mean a general arming of them for military service."

At Fort Monroe, where he boasted he was holding $60,000 worth of Rebel property in the form of ex-slaves, Butler gradually modified his practices. For practical purposes, he began setting runaway slaves free.

Other Union commanders took a different view. At Baltimore, Major General John A. Dix (another Democrat who got his commission from the commander-in-chief on the same day as Butler) announced: "We have nothing to do with slaves. We are neither negro stealers nor negro catchers; if they come to us, we will send them home."

An occasional ardent abolitionist called for permitting runaway slaves to enlist in the Union army. Most military leaders and top-rank civilian lawmakers were strongly opposed to such a course. Had it not been for his extremely light skin, Joseph Scroggs would have had to wait for months to enlist.

As late as August 1862, there had been no significant change in Union views concerning the increasing numbers of rootless blacks, now universally labeled as contraband of war. After paying several personal visits to contraband camps, on August 4, the president signed a draft order calling for an additional 300,000 militia. Men affected were to serve, not for ninety days, but for a full nine months. No doubt about it, Confederate victories in the field had made the Union desperate for manpower.

Yet on the very day the new draft order was signed, Lincoln made another decision. He met with what he termed "a delegation of Western men, including two congressmen." He listened politely to their offer to provide two Negro regiments from Indiana. Then he responded that he was not prepared to make soldiers of Negroes, but he thought it might be fruitful to use them as laborers.

July 1862 saw Congress go over the president's head by authorizing the use of blacks in the army, to be organized in black units led by white officers. Active recruitment of blacks as soldiers did not begin until after the Emancipation Proclamation was issued in January 1863. Even then, blacks were paid less than whites and had opportunity for advancement only in exceptional circumstances.

Hence the calculated use of black soldiers at Petersburg marked a turning point in Federal policy. It was the Twenty-second Colored Regiment of Duncan's brigade that was given the honor of assaulting the first line of Confederate works on June 16. Sketched by Edwin Forbes, the charge created a sensation when the artist's view of it was published in *Leslie's Weekly*.

Official Union records suggest that only hours before the powder set by Peterson's men was due to be fired, Grant changed his mind about permitting blacks to be first to enter the breach in Confederate lines. Joseph Scroggs's diary tells a different story.

According to it, the Fifth Colored got marching orders shortly before midnight on July 29. Brigadier General Edward Ferrero, in command of the black division that included Scroggs's regiment, was sitting in a bomb proof, roaring drunk.

At 4:45 A.M. on July 30, 8,000 pounds of powder produced the biggest explosion of the war. Onlookers glimpsed "the most awesome spectacle of the entire conflict." Nearly 300 Confederates, mostly from the Nineteenth and the Twenty-second South Carolina, were blown high into the air. When the dust settled, Petersburg had a hole 170 feet long, 30 feet deep, and 60 to 80 feet wide: The Crater.

Long before the dust settled, men of the Fifth Colored were in the vanguard of Federals who raced through the hole toward Confederate lines. According to the Richmond *Examiner*, these men shouted, "Remember Fort Pillow!" as they ran.

Attacking units, black and white alike, soon found themselves trapped in a thirty-foot hole. Thrown into hopeless confusion, dozens were picked off by Confederate marksmen who rimmed The Crater. Others, caught in the crossfire, died from Federal bullets.

New units of Federal troops, including most of Ferrero's black division, were thrown into the conflict. By the time the battle of The Crater ended about 1:00 P.M., the men in blue had suffered 3,798 casualties compared to just over 1,000 for the men in gray.

Grant angrily labeled the whole enterprise "a stupendous failure" and authorized a court of inquiry whose members assigned most of the blame to Burnside and Ferrero. Northern newspapers again charged that Confederates had shot down many blacks after they had surrendered; southern newspapers thundered that blacks had been brought to the siege and used in The Crater for propaganda purposes.

Whatever the motives that caused them to be used there, blacks performed valiantly at Petersburg. Their conspicuous role in the long siege spurred black enlistment and helped build momentum in the drive to give black soldiers the same pay as their white comrades.

After ten months, Petersburg fell on Sunday, April 2, 1865. Richmond was evacuated by Confederates the following day, and Robert E. Lee surrendered at Appomatox on April 9. Joseph E. Johnston still had a sizable Confederate army in the South, and scattered units were fighting in the far West. But on the day Petersburg was occupied, top leaders, in the South and in the North, knew that the war was settled.

CHAPTER
44

Sheridan's Ride Made the North Forget Sheridan's Raids

On a quick trip to Washington in mid-October 1864, the commander of the Army of the Shenandoah was made a brigadier general of regulars. Philip Henry Sheridan accepted congratulations for having soundly defeated C.S.A. Lieutenant General Jubal Early in the third battle at Winchester, Virginia. Privately, however, he wondered whether the big jump in rank was a way of saying "Thank you" for his zeal and efficiency in sending fighting men home to vote for the commander-in-chief who seemed to be on the verge of political defeat.

Half a day south of the Winchester battlefield, Sheridan reached one of his favorite units, the Seventeenth Pennsylvania cavalry, an hour before bedtime. As he ate with troopers the following morning, men frequently paused to listen. Sure enough, there was gunfire to the south, more than there should be from scouts who were out hunting the Confederates who were still led by Jubal Early.

As he rode out of the camp, the commander noticed that the pace of gunfire was picking up. Within a mile, he came upon a hopelessly tangled wagon train whose leader seemed to be both lost and frightened. They'd been headed for the front, he told Sheridan, when a rider warned them to turn around—the Confederates had decided to make a fight of it.

Behind the wagon train Sheridan soon spotted a ragged line of stragglers, headed north to get away from the action. Most were camp followers, but there was an occasional soldier in a blue uniform.

Widely known for impulsive actions that many in Washington called reckless, Philip Sheridan made an on-the-spot decision. He detailed most of his band to form a line across the path taken by those who were fleeing, to stop them and turn them around. Then, with forty or so of his best riders, he set out for the scene of action at a gallop.

His big black horse, named Rienzi for the town in Mississippi

Major General Philip H. Sheridan at field headquarters. [MATTHEW BRADY STUDIO, NATIONAL ARCHIVES]

where he had been captured, seemed almost to fly across the rolling countryside. Black-haired Sheridan soon outpaced his escorts and found himself riding furiously ahead of the column of dust made by their mounts.

To his amazement and disgust, the stream of stragglers grew larger as he rode. As he encountered them, he initially shouted encouragement and promised to send the enemy flying. After a few miles, Sheridan's manner changed. Suddenly he became the fierce-eyed leader later to shape his most famous quotation: "The only good Indian is a dead Indian." Almost as though he were fighting Comanches and Sioux on the western plains, the commander of the Army of the Cumberland began to wave his little flat hat as he approached new groups of men.

"Turn back!" he shouted over and over, gesturing to emphasize his words. "Turn back! Sheridan is here!"

Folklore has it that he made Rienzi gallop twenty miles without a stop, shouting and signaling with his hat as he went. Scornful Confederates later insisted that he did not ride more than a dozen miles and stopped several times to give his horse a breather. By the time the story of that ride became the subject of many a vivid tale, precise details made no difference. In the North and in the South alike, it was widely known that when Sheridan ended his famous ride he rallied his fleeing troops and stormed against the enemy at their head.

Shouting in jubilation that Sheridan was at their head, his veterans charged at such a pace that mounted men found it hard to stay ahead of the infantry. Brigadier General George A. Custer, who had been in the thick of the action at First Bull Run and almost every major engagement of the Army of the Potomac, had been picked by Sheridan for his Shenandoah Valley campaign.

At Cedar Creek on that October afternoon, Custer's riders smashed through the Confederate lines and made a hole through which other units poured. Custer admitted at the victory celebration that evening that he was a little disappointed; he had expected to have another horse shot from under him to make it an even dozen. But he rejoiced with Sheridan that Federal guns and wagons, which had been captured that morning, were all recovered, along with at least twenty-five Confederate guns and nobody knew how many dozens of Confederate supply wagons.

Cedar Creek, a disaster that turned into victory as a result of Philip Sheridan's ride, marked the end of the long struggle for control of the vital Shenandoah Valley. Confederates had no more resources with which to contest for the fertile farming region stretching for many miles between mountain ranges.

But if the enemies in gray were licked, their civilian supporters were not. For four solid years they had poured food and provisions into the Confederate cause. Grant decided it was time to teach them a lesson they would never forget, one even more memorable than that of the preceding August.

Grant wanted a decisive man in command at Monocacy, Maryland, to win and hold the Shenandoah Valley, a corridor through which Confederates had poured time and time again. Smarting over the debacle of The Crater at Petersburg, the supreme commander's own prestige was at a low level. He needed a dramatic signal that would show the entire North who was able to put fear into the hearts of every Confederate. So for the implementation of his plans for the Shenandoah, Grant picked the thirty-three-year-old son of Irish immigrants.

Secretary of War Stanton was opposed to the idea of giving Sheridan an independent command; he was far too young and was entirely too rash for such a post, Stanton argued. As outlined by Grant, the commander in the Shenandoah would be expected to slash his way south of the enemy and there fight off attacks while devastating the land.

Once again, the commander-in-chief had the final word. He bypassed the War Department and approved Grant's plans with a strongly worded warning that the general-in-chief should keep a vigilant eye on the action and force the Army of the Shenandoah to follow his instructions to the letter.

Grant's plan of action, revealed to his new commander, was bold. Once south of the Confederates, he was to "eat out Virginia clear and clean, so that crows flying over it for the balance of the season will have to carry their provender with them."

In the long corridor below the line of the Baltimore and Ohio Rail-

One of Sheridan's subordinates— George A. Custer. [LESLIE'S IL-LUSTRATED]

road, said Grant, he did not mean that troopers should burn houses. But he emphatically did mean that "all provisions and stock should be removed, and the people notified to get out."

Since there was no way for soldiers to determine loyalties of farmers, staunch Unionists would have to suffer along with ardent seces-sionists. At one little farm, a trooper of the Second Ohio Cavalry found it hard to keep his supper down. According to his diary, the owner—never a slave holder—had farmed poor soil for more than thirty years, barely scratching out a living. Yet he'd managed to put up a comfortable little log house and to care for an invalid son.

When Sheridan's men hit that farm, "it made him almost crazy to see all going to destruction in a single night—fences, barns, cattle, sheep, and even barnyard fowls."

Grim-faced Sheridan, whose 40,000 men were expected in Wash-ington to have their hands full as a result of frequent clashes with Early's Confederates, managed to ravage much of the valley during lulls in the fighting.

Once Early's forces had been smashed at Cedar Creek, Sheridan returned to the work of systematic destruction. His men burned bridges, barns, haystacks, fences, and even managed to fire a few fields of standing corn. Anything that could be eaten or otherwise used was carried off; everything else was destroyed.

Sheridan always insisted any farm houses that burned were casualties of the accidental spreading of fire. Long-time residents of the valley thought differently; one of them wrote that "from one end of the horizon to the other, the sky remains black with smoke." According to that account, streams of refugees forced out of their homes by starvation tried to make their way north. Describing his scorched-earth raid, Sheridan himself grimly reported that when he completed it, he expected "the Valley, from Winchester up to Staunton, 92 miles, will have but little in it for man or beast."

Turning his back upon the immense, devastated region and with the Virginia Central Railroad and the James River Canal destroyed beyond hope of repair, Sheridan told his commander that "I think the best policy will be to let the burning of the crops in the Valley be the end of this campaign, and let some of this army go elsewhere." Following his suggestion, some units were returned to the Army of the Potomac, and others were shipped by sea to join Sherman in Savannah, Georgia.

Federal leaders rewarded Sheridan with a promotion to major general of regulars in November, just sixty days after he had become a brigadier general of regulars.

Joyful civilians who heard of his October 19 ride, largely by word of mouth, painted his portrait, made imaginative sketches of the fearless rider, wrote editorials praising him, and made him the subject of hastily framed poems. Herman Melville, whose *Moby Dick* had not yet won critical acclaim, was among the dozens who turned their pens to the praise of Sheridan.

Thomas Buchanan Read, a portrait painter and dabbler in light verse, produced for elocutionist and actor James E. Murdock a lilting ballad that he called "Sheridan's Ride" while working on the painting "Sheridan and His Horse." Taken to the stage by Murdock, "Sheridan's Ride" stirred the blood of listeners so mightily that the second-rate poem became a part of American folklore. Generations of school children who never heard of Sheridan's Shenandoah Valley raids of destruction against civilians learned to recite the colorful lines of the poem that describes a history-making ride upon a great black horse by a soldier in blue.

45

What Happened
at Ebenezer Creek
Remains an Unsolved Puzzle

His hand trembling with anger, Major James A. Connolly of Sherman's Fourteenth Corps scrawled a detailed account of the day's events. Addressed to his Illinois congressman, it was penned with an accompanying note that urged "immediate publication, where as many readers as possible will know what has taken place."

December 8, 1864, started happily. Early in the morning, said Connolly, many men in blue insisted that for the first time they could smell the sea. They were now within easy striking distance of Savannah, where they expected to be placed on Federal ships to go north after many weary months of fighting and marching in Georgia.

Having passed the Ogeechee River with no major problems, it seemed unimportant that Ebenezer Creek soon barred the path of troops on the March to the Sea. But the name of the waterway was deceptive; it was broad as well as deep. With the temperature not far above freezing, a pontoon bridge had to be thrown up, stretching from marsh land on one side of the causeway to firm ground past swamps on the other.

As the last units in the command of Brigadier General Jefferson C. Davis surged toward the pontoon bridge, Major Connolly's suspicions were aroused. Squads of soldiers waved their bayonets menacingly at an immense horde of slaves crowding forward eagerly to continue their journey behind the Federal column.

"I knew it was the intention that when all of us had crossed the bridge, it would be burned," Connolly informed his congressman. "I inquired if the Negroes were not to be permitted to cross. I was told that Genl. Davis had ordered that they should not.

"This I knew, and Genl. Davis knew, must result in all the Negroes being captured or perhaps brutally shot down by the Rebel cavalry tomorrow morning."

In the long march from Atlanta to the sea, blacks became more numerous and more troublesome as days passed. At every opportunity, Sherman sent a strong message to leaders of escapees. Said the Federal commander, "Slaves are to remain where they were, and not load us down with useless mouths which would eat up the food needed for fighting men." His protestations were wasted. From nearly every plantation ransacked by civilian "treasure hunters" or "bummers" who concentrated upon seizing from civilians everything that could be eaten, field hands and household servants plus their children—a ragged army of contrabands that grew to half the size of Sherman's own force—followed the fighting men as closely as possible.

This fresh problem, mounting in size as the miles went by, demanded a firm hand to maintain some degree of control. So Sherman detailed his Fourteenth Corps as rear guard for Major General Henry W. Slocum's Army of Georgia. Brigadier General Jefferson C. Davis, at the head of the corps, was despised by many of his men, who ridiculed him behind his back. Some were sure that the report circulated by Connolly was the result of pent-up anger at Davis.

Because his name was so similar to that of the president of the C.S.A., some referred to Davis as "Gen'l Reb"—but never in his hearing. It was widely known that he had been quartermaster at Fort Sumter and had rashly agreed to yield the installation without orders from Major Anderson. Smarting, perhaps, from this early blunder, Davis had gained a reputation as a troublemaker and a killer.

In Cincinnati he quarreled with his commander, former naval officer William Nelson. Hoping to prod Nelson into a duel, Davis crumpled up a visiting card at the Galt House Hotel and threw it into his superior's face. When Nelson refused to fight him, Davis took out a hand gun and stalked his foe through the hotel before shooting him to death at point-blank range.

Regardless of what subordinates might think, it was precisely such a man as Davis who was needed to guard the rear of the fast-moving Army of Georgia. Encouraging bummers to range as far as possible in their foraging, Davis simultaneously managed to keep contrabands from becoming a serious nuisance. Their pursuit of the army ended at Ebenezer Creek, but questions concerning events of the day were never answered.

This much is beyond dispute. Union troops crossed the pontoon bridge without incident, but blacks were left stranded on the other side. Once they saw that they could no longer follow the army, scores of contrabands rushed into the icy water. A few soldiers of the engi-

Contrabands ask permission to enter Federal lines. [*ILLUSTRATED LONDON NEWS*]

neers' corps tried to rescue some of them. One reported that "as soon as the character of the unthinking rush and panic was seen, all was done that could be to save them from the water; but the loss of life was still great enough to prove that there were many ignorant, simple ones who preferred to die in freedom rather than to continue to live in slavery."

Connolly and others alleged that Davis put the pontoon bridge to the torch as soon as its usefulness to him had ended. Not so, the Federal commander insisted; he ordered the bridge broken down because he foresaw the possibility of needing it to cross some other stream.

No one had even an estimate of the number of black casualties, but a Federal spokesman denied that they had tried to cross the unbridged stream and had drowned. They died, according to this story, when Confederates under Major General Joseph Wheeler "charged on the poor affrighted darkies, driving them pellmell into the water so that mothers and children, old and young, perished alike."

At the time, Sherman knew nothing of the business. Riding in the vanguard of his armies, he came upon a group of medics trying to save a man whose foot had been blown off by a land mine. About the time that the bridge over Ebenezer Creek disappeared, Sherman selected Confederate prisoners for a special detail. Equipped with picks and

A pontoon bridge enabled Sherman's Seventeenth Corps to cross the Edisto River in South Carolina. [LESLIE'S ILLUSTRATED]

shovels and prodded forward at gunpoint, these men were told to discover and dig up Confederate torpedoes—or blow them up with their own feet.

Sherman's triumphant occupation of Savannah soon turned sour. From Henry W. Halleck he received a telegram telling him that the incident at Ebenezer Creek was getting wide publicity and warning him that "a certain class having now great influence with the President are disposed to make a point against you in regard to 'Inevitable Sambo.'"

Secretary of War Stanton visited the occupied city just before the beginning of the new year. He came, not so much to offer personal congratulations to Sherman for his glorious military achievements and for his role in the re-election of Lincoln, as to make a personal investigation of the way Sherman's men had treated contrabands.

Sherman supported Davis's contention that he had not burned his movable pontoon bridge but had taken it up to make use of it at some other point. Stanton interviewed Federal officers and a number of blacks, none of whom had been at Ebenezer Creek. In his lengthy formal report, he failed to say precisely what happened there. But he did note with pride that he had personally accepted, for the Union, $13,000,000 worth of Savannah cotton, also contraband of war.

Sherman discarded the idea of using ships to send his men to join the Army of the Potomac. Instead, he cut a fiery swath through South

Carolina and moved into North Carolina to accept the surrender of the last sizable Confederate military force on terms that brought him censure from Washington.

Somehow, the man who constantly irked many in the Washington establishment managed to escape censure over the events at Ebenezer Creek. But in his famous *Memoirs* he mused over the wholly unexpected turn of events precipitated by the war that a few in blue fought in the name of abolition, some fought for the preservation of the Union, and hosts fought simply because it was their duty to fight.

"The Negro question was beginning to loom among political eventualities of the day," Sherman wrote. "Many foresaw that not only would slaves gain freedom, but that they would also have votes. I did not dream of such a result then."

46

Mary Todd Lincoln
Shielded Her Son from Combat

January 19, 1865, saw Abraham Lincoln pen one of his strangest letters. Using firm words, but moving his pen in such hesitant fashion that his hand seemed almost to tremble, he addressed the man whom he had made general-in-chief. Would it be possible for Grant "without embarrassment to you or detriment to the service," he wondered, to arrange for Robert Todd Lincoln to "go into your military family with some nominal rank?"

Grant promptly suggested that the president's son, who had no military training or experience, should enter the army with the rank of captain, with the expectation that he would be made an assistant adjutant general on the headquarters staff.

That arrangement, which was finalized in February, occurred when the North had more than 620,000 combat-ready men compared to less than 130,000 Confederates still able to fight.

In spite of the size of the Union forces, the military leaders had an insatiable hunger for more and more manpower. That is the reason why, after months of furious debate, the decision was made to put blacks in uniform. Eventually more than 180,000 of them fought for the Union at one time or another. In distant Georgia, Sherman was a holdout against what had become established policy. When Grant suggested that he screen contrabands carefully, select able-bodied black males, and put them into his own ranks, Sherman simply failed to respond to his commander's memorandum.

Throughout the North, states and cities had boosted their bounty payments to men who enlisted as volunteers; still, the draft offices were busy everywhere. As a patriotic gesture, or in a bid to stifle growing criticism of his family, the president hired a substitute for himself in September 1864.

N. D. Larner of Washington's Fourth Ward acted as go-between for

the deal and found eighteen-year-old John S. Staples willing to be hired. With Staples in tow, Larner went to the White House on October 1. Money having already been paid, Lincoln just shook hands with his substitute. Then Larner handed the chief executive a framed official notice certifying that he had "put in a representative recruit." Lincoln shook hands with Staples a second time, and the boy was hurried off to war.

There is no record that Lincoln and Staples ever met again. But on October 12 the president was notified that the cost of his substitute was $750, an unusually high figure.

Robert Todd Lincoln, oldest son of the president, had been within a few months of Staples's age when war broke out. His home state, Illinois, was conspicuously eager to fill its quotas; hence, thousands much younger than Robert were among the early volunteers.

Dividing his time between Harvard University and the nation's capital, Robert never felt the impact of the conscription acts in Illinois. But he became the target of gossip and widespread criticism after the first Federal conscription act became law early in 1863.

Mary Todd Lincoln, the one-time Kentucky belle who was mistress of the White House, made no secret that she did not want her oldest son to fight. She remained inconsolable over the death of eleven-year-old Willie in 1862. That, plus the earlier loss in Springfield of six-year-old Eddie, and the possibility that Robert would be killed if he went into combat, was too much for Mary Lincoln, who retreated into a series of migraine headaches.

Visiting the White House with Daniel Sickles, Senator Ira Harris of New York did the unthinkable. He bluntly demanded of the president's wife, "Why isn't Robert in the army? He is old enough and strong enough to serve his country. He should have gone to the front some time ago."

Clutching her head that throbbed so violently she couldn't frame an intelligible answer, Mary Lincoln rushed from the room and took to her bed. She was adamant in insisting that, once Robert completed the undergraduate course, he should enter Harvard Law School and remain on campus.

It was Robert's father who could not resist responding to the emotional tug that came when news reached the White House that Mrs. Lydia Bixby, mother of five stalwart boys, had lost all five of them in battle. It made little difference that the report circulated by Massachusetts Governor John Andrew later proved erroneous; Abraham Lincoln personally penned a moving letter of sympathy to the bereaved mother.

As published in the Boston *Transcript* on November 21, 1864, the letter from the Executive Mansion to Mrs. Bixby read:

> *I have been shown that you are the mother of five sons who have died gloriously on the field of battle. I cannot refrain from tending to you the consolation that may be found in the thanks of the Republic they died to save.*
>
> *I pray that our heavenly Father may assuage the anguish of your bereavement, and leave you only the cherished memory of the loved and lost, and the solemn pride that must be yours to have laid so costly a sacrifice upon the altar of freedom.*
>
> *Yours very sincerely and respectfully,*
Abraham Lincoln

When news of the Bixby matter became public, with Robert Lincoln safe at Harvard, the Philadelphia *Age* published a stinging editorial that was reprinted in numerous other newspapers. In it Lincoln was castigated "for the hypocrisy of all this sympathy for poor bereaved Mrs. Bixby" while "keeping his own son at home in luxury."

Even the staunchly pro-Lincoln Indianapolis *Sentinel* could not refrain, in early December 1864, from calling attention to the fact that "Robert Lincoln is still not in uniform."

It was in this climate of growing public criticism that Mary Todd Lincoln reluctantly consented to allow her oldest son to put on a blue uniform, for a noncombat role.

Robert Todd Lincoln, wearing his brand-new captain's uniform, reported for duty on February 23, 1865, at Grant's headquarters in City Point, Virginia. He never went to the front, as Senator Harris had demanded. Instead, he served as official escort to commanders and notables, including his father.

Lincoln, who had been to City Point several times earlier, arrived on

Mary Todd, Kentucky belle.
[*GODEY'S LADY'S BOOK*]

the steamer *River Queen* on March 24. This time, much to the surprise
of staff members, Grant's visitor brought along Mrs. Lincoln and their
youngest son, Tad.

With the South all but out of the fighting, the commander-in-chief
told Grant that he wanted no more bloodshed, only submission by the
seceded states followed by return to the Union as quickly as possible.
Robert's mother, father, and brother told him goodbye and returned to
the capital. One month later, Robert Todd Lincoln resigned his commission after just sixty days of service and never a whiff of gunpowder.

Though documented in every detail, the stories of the short military
service of the president's son and of the chief executive's surrogate are
seldom told. The "totally inexcusable absence from the battlefield" of
Robert Lincoln is mentioned chiefly in newspapers of the era.
Stranger still, even the famous ten-volume biography of Abraham
Lincoln by his secretaries, Nicolay and Hay, does not include the
name of John S. Staples, who was paid $750 to fight as a substitute for
the commander-in-chief.

47

Desperate, Confederates Moved to Put Slaves into Uniform

For the first time since taking command of the Army of Northern Virginia, Robert E. Lee found himself under heavy criticism from fellow Confederates. A jubilant paragraph that first appeared in Washington and was widely reprinted exulted that Lee was reduced to a diet of cornpone and cabbage boiled in salt water, with a scanty serving of meat twice a week. Almost simultaneously, the Confederate commander went public with ideas he had been espousing in private for some time. With the flower of white southern manhood gone, said he, the Confederacy must adopt the course reluctantly accepted by the North: Put blacks in uniform.

"I think the measure is not only important," he said, "but also necessary. I do not think our white population can supply the necessities of a long war."

So far, he was voicing a point of view long expressed by Jefferson Davis and now supported by an increasing number of Confederate leaders. Then he went far beyond what most of them had said, "I think those who are employed should be freed. It would not be just or wise to require them to remain as slaves."

Early in the North/South struggle, a handful of blacks had volunteered to wear gray and had been accepted. When Louisiana's governor issued his first call for troops, nearly 1,000 men of the 13,000 or more free blacks in New Orleans, many of them descendants of men who had fought the Indians and the British under the leadership of Andrew Jackson, flocked to enlist. They formed the First Louisiana Volunteer Regiment, called the Native Guards, and drilled until they felt themselves ready to go into combat.

A handful of other men of African descent, perhaps 200 or 300 in all, made up more than a dozen black militia units that appeared on Confederate rosters very early. Like the Native Guards of Louisiana, these Confederate soldiers were free blacks, some of whom owned slaves themselves. But unlike the Native Guards, most such wearers of gray met the enemy in battle. In Louisiana, Benjamin Butler took control of New Orleans just four months after formation of the Native Guards and skillfully persuaded its members to exchange gray uniforms for blue ones.

It was the emphasis upon freeing those slaves who would fight for the C.S.A. that angered many of Lee's long-time followers. True, he argued against anything approaching a general conscription act to which manumission was tied; instead, he suggested that "the best class" of slaves would respond to a plea for volunteers. They, naturally, would have to have the consent of their owners.

Wealthy slave owners reacted with surprise and indignation, and their influence permeated state legislatures and the Confederate Congress. Some had come to the point where they were willing for their slaves to fight; but they were unwilling to promise them freedom, even at the conclusion of a war won with their help.

Irish-born and Arkansas-reared C.S.A. Brigadier General Patrick Cleburne earlier had discovered that it could be costly to advocate emancipation on any terms. In staff meetings of general officers, he repeatedly pointed out that the North was making good use of blacks. In addition to combat troops, an estimated 200,000 of them were employed in service units, an umbrella term for men working in support capacities as cooks, teamsters, and laborers.

It was Cleburne whom fellow Confederates credited with having rallied the brigade with which Federals were pushed all the way to the Tennessee River at Shiloh. That heroic leadership brought him a special vote of commendation from the Confederate Congress and his commission as a general officer.

There never was any doubt about the Irishman's courage; at Franklin, Tennessee, his division was in the forefront of the charge against Federal positions. When his horse was shot from under him, he mounted another and kept going. When the second animal was killed, Cleburne raised his forage cap on his sword and—on foot—urged his men forward until he took a fatal shot barely fifty yards from the enemy's line.

It was his judgment, not his leadership or courage, that many colleagues questioned. Never a slave owner, Cleburne had no personal experience with the South's "peculiar institution." So he was under the impression that a promise of freedom, preferably at once but possibly at the end of a successful war, would bring blacks to the Confederate colors by the thousands. He drafted and circulated a proposal to swell the ranks of fighting men in this fashion and managed to get a handful of fellow officers to sign it.

But when his suggestions reached the high command, its members were stunned. "I will not attempt to describe my feelings on being confronted with a proposal so startling in character, so revolting to Southern sentiment, Southern pride, and Southern honor," one statement read. "If this thing is openly proposed to the army, the total disintegration of that army will follow in a fortnight."

Not only was the proposal never openly presented, circulation of it in high circles put a stop to a strong movement to elevate Cleburne to the rank of lieutenant general.

Jefferson Davis, citing his experience in the Mexican War and his role as a former U.S. secretary of war, was an early advocate of the use of blacks, provided that they remain enslaved. However, as the Confederate manpower crisis grew increasingly severe, he began to soften in his opposition to emancipation in return for military service.

Unwilling personally to risk the loss of his supporters, Davis persuaded his secretary of state to go public with new support for the carefully controlled use of blacks as soldiers.

Judah P. Benjamin, the only Jew to serve in the cabinet of either warring government, had been attorney general and secretary of war before becoming secretary of state. As a loyal member of the inner circle of Davis's advisors, he was willing to risk personal loss to speak for his president.

According to his best estimate, said Benjamin, at least 700,000 slaves of military age remained in Confederate territory. Most of the great plantations on which many of them were held were idle, no longer productive because of the lack of seeds and tools. Would not common prudence suggest that an exchange of freedom for military service might yet tip the scales in favor of the beleaguered Confederacy?

Of course, Benjamin hastened to add, the issue of emancipation would be strictly up to member states of the Confederacy; that was made clear in the Confederate Constitution. But it was a matter that could be worked out, with patience and a little time.

Davis's proposal, coming from Benjamin, evoked a storm of fiery reaction. C.S.A. Senator R. M. T. Hunter of Virginia, who owned slaves worth at least $60,000, promised to fight enabling legislation to the end. The editors of the Charleston, South Carolina, *Mercury* cried that if any steps were taken to put arms in the hands of slaves, "South Carolina could no longer have any interest in prosecuting the war."

In spite of the opposition against it, the administration proceeded with plans to use black soldiers. Difficulties had begun to compound. In addition to its battlefield losses, the C.S.A. was weighted down with ever-increasing numbers of prisoners whose exchange had been halted by Grant.

The Fifty-fourth Massachusetts Colored Infantry charged Fort Wagner, South Carolina, on September 18, 1863. [HARPER'S WEEKLY]

High-placed Southerners, encouraged by proposals floated by influential Virginia editor Francis P. Blair (a thoroughgoing Unionist and a stalwart supporter of Abraham Lincoln) had briefly hoped for a negotiated settlement. Blair won permission from Washington to visit Davis in Richmond, where he suggested that Union and Confederate forces could forget their differences by joining together to drive the French from Mexico.

Though not attracted to the Mexican plan, top Confederate leaders took Blair's visit to mean that Federal leaders were ready to save face by working out some plan for peace. Led by C.S.A. Vice President Alexander H. Stephens, a band of commissioners went through Federal lines to Hampton Roads, Virginia, for negotiations with delegates selected by Washington.

From the start, Stephens realized that the mission was hopeless. Davis had ordered his representatives to enter into negotiations between two sovereign nations; Lincoln had instructed his commissioners to refuse even to discuss an armistice until Confederates agreed to reunion and gave up their arms. The abysmal failure of the Hampton Roads conference meant that the manpower crunch of the C.S.A. would be more severe than even pessimists had anticipated.

With Benjamin and Lee openly supporting drastic action and with Davis working for it behind the scenes, the Confederate Senate solemnly considered a bill designed to put 200,000 blacks into military service. The influence of Senator Hunter was enough to prevent the measure from having any chance of success.

Robert E. Lee urged that the sole hope of stopping the Federal advance lay in additional manpower, clearly not available from old men, boys, and political leaders still not wearing gray. Blacks must be employed at once, Lee urged, or the vast number of lives already lost, the millions of dollars spent, and the years devoted to battle would have been wasted.

Confederate lawmakers responded by drafting new legislation. Under its terms, blacks would be enlisted in the Confederate army and would get the same pay and rations as whites, a step not taken by the Union until thousands of blacks had died in combat.

No more than 25 percent of the male slaves of any state could become soldiers, under the proposed act. And the final clause stipulated, "Nothing in this act shall be construed to authorize a change in the relation between master and slave."

Jefferson Davis had finally gone public, saying, "The policy of engaging to liberate the negro on his discharge after service faithfully rendered seems to me preferable to that of granting immediate manumission." But his urge for "a policy of moderation" fell on deaf ears. By a margin of a single vote, a reluctant Confederate Congress took steps to put slaves in uniform, with no assurance of emancipation then or ever.

Lawmakers acted in early spring. Two days later, Richmond newspapers published accounts of the legislative action and announced that recruitment of slaves would begin at once. From that point, however, the pace of marching Federal troops accelerated.

April 4 saw Abraham Lincoln triumphantly riding through the streets of fallen Richmond. Four days later, the commander-in-chief toured Petersburg battlefields where many blacks had performed so well. Six days after having been in Petersburg, the man who had saved the Union was serenaded in Washington during most of the day. Once he asked a band to play for him a favorite tune, "Dixie."

One month and one day after the Confederacy agreed to fight the Union with black soldiers, the victorious General Grant attended a morning meeting of Lincoln's cabinet where the president spoke of a recurring dream about "a ship moving with great rapidity toward a dark and indefinite shore." Because Mrs. Grant and Mrs. Lincoln were continually at odds, the Grants declined an invitation to go with the Lincolns that evening to the Ford Theater to see the comedy *Our American Cousin*.

When John Wilkes Booth ended the life of Abraham Lincoln that evening (April 14, 1865), Lee had already surrendered at Appomatox, and Johnston was prepared to negotiate with Sherman for surrender of the last Confederate army.

Confederate lawmakers had taken what, for them, seemed drastic action. But it came too late to make any difference. Not one slave entered the Confederate army as a result of legislation that barely squeaked by the Congress on March 13, 1865.

Part Seven

Bittersweet Aftermath

48

Greed and Speed Proved to Be More Deadly Than Confederate Bullets

We're living once more
in the highest of clover,
For the shootin' an' stabbin'
an' killin' is over!
The dying is done,
my fine feathered friend;
The war has come
to a glorious end!

Shouting jubilantly, the chorus they had written in a prison stockade, men of the Ninth Indiana Cavalry and their comrades surged aboard the paddlewheel steamer *Sultana* at Vicksburg, Mississippi. "Full steam ahead for Cairo!" someone cried, confident that special trains would be waiting at the Illinois railhead.

Already, 1,300 happy veterans in remnants of blue uniforms had pushed and shoved to get aboard the *Henry Ames*. Much smaller, the *Olive Branch* had steamed upriver with 700 more. Still the wharf and streets leading to the river were jammed with men who were happy that "the dying is done" and who wanted nothing except a quick trip home.

Designed for the lower Mississippi cotton trade, the relatively new *Sultana* was equipped with four big tubular boilers and was rated for a passenger load of 376. With a crew of about 80 plus just under 100 civilian passengers, the big vessel had many tons of sugar in her hold when she reached Vicksburg. She also carried nearly 100 horses and mules as well as a few hogs and one alligator in a wooden crate. It looked as though 200 survivors of the Civil War might crowd aboard the speedy ship.

Suddenly there was an urgent cry, "Everybody aboard! Everybody aboard! *Everybody!*"

The men who happily surged forward did not know that the Federal officer in charge of transportation at Vicksburg had been charged with extorting one dollar a head from a steamship line to put returning veterans aboard its vessels. According to the story most widely told, the man charged with graft was so eager to demonstrate his innocence that he loaded the *Sultana* so heavily that she was low in the water before the last 500 or so crowded aboard.

The steamer had been packed with the largest passenger load since men began to travel up and down the Mississippi River: more than 2,000 persons. How many more, no one knew; one clerk thought there were 180 civilians and 2,400 soldiers for whom Washington was paying five dollars per enlisted man and twice that amount for each officer transported.

Meanwhile, back in Vicksburg, the steamers *Carroll* and *Gay*, were nearly empty. Their owners and captains fumed because they would be getting virtually no money from Washington.

At first, ship personnel tried to put Ohio veterans on the hurricane deck and Michigan troops on the main deck, with the promenade deck given over to veterans from Indiana. Long before the last man filed aboard, this pattern was broken, making an accurate head count impossible.

Moving at top speed, the *Sultana* was short of coal by the time she reached Memphis. While the vessel's bunkers were being refilled, two or three hundred passengers crowded into the fourteen saloons of Memphis's Whiskey Chute. A few of them gulped raw whiskey so rapidly that they passed out and were left behind; they proved to be the lucky ones.

At 2:00 A.M., while the *Sultana* was trying to make her way through a cluster of islands called Paddy's Hens and Chickens, a tremendous blast ripped a huge hole in the boat's side. An overheated boiler smashed upward through the hurricane deck, blowing timber, steel, and men high into the sky and leaving a gap so huge that a smokestack and the wheelhouse fell into it.

In the dark river, many who were thrown into the water could not swim. Those who could were seized by comrades; frequently they went down in clusters of three or four. On board, an estimated 200

The Sultana, *docked at Helena, Arkansas.*

veterans, injured only by falling metal, crowded together on the bow of the drifting hulk as a shift in the wind blew billowing flames directly toward them. Most jumped into the water, and a few managed to get off on an improvised raft.

Lieutenant George B. McCord somehow rode a four-foot plank to safety. Private Otto Bardon floated away in a trunk. Seaman William Lugenbeal snatched up a bayonet, killed the alligator, and drifted to shore clinging to the crate in which the animal had been kept.

Some men were saved by clinging to the tails of mules. A few drifted as far downriver as Memphis on bits of debris. Fifteen men in Union blue rode to the shore in a dug-out canoe brought to the scene by a former Confederate soldier.

No one knew the number or the names of the dead. Bodies continued to surface for more than a week. From the site of the explosion a death barge made daily trips to Memphis with a full cargo of burned, crushed, and drowned men who had spent months in prison and who had thought they were lucky to get a fast trip home.

According to the U.S. Customs Service in Memphis, 1,547 persons died. Combined Federal and Confederate deaths at First Bull Run were slightly over half the *Sultana*'s total: 845. No other marine disaster—not even the sinking of the *Titanic*—ever took so many American lives. At this time, too many other important events were more vital to the American people, taking up newspaper space (the New York *Times* ran the *Sultana* story two days later on page four and *Harper's Weekly* published a sketch a month later but gave no explanation of the tragedy). The same day, John Wilkes Booth, Lincoln's assassin, had been apprehended and killed. Within a week, the new president, Andrew Johnson of Tennessee, issued a proclamation naming Jefferson Davis and five others as having "incited, concerted, and procured" the murder of Lincoln. Above all, the long, bloody, fratricidal war was just over, and the nation was not in a mood to deal with another tragedy.

Attempts at investigation turned into a whitewash. Washington did revoke the license of second engineer Captain Nate Wintringer, but failed to notify St. Louis customs inspectors of the action. Therefore when Wintringer's license came up for renewal, he got it promptly, along with a newspaper account explaining that he was off watch when the explosion occurred.

Soldiers and sailors who survived the night of horror on the Mississippi held reunions for many years. In 1890 some of them had their pictures made. Sobered by his escape, Private Chester Berry had become a minister. William Fies was an undertaker. Former cavalryman Truman Smith was a member of the Grand Rapids, Michigan, fire department.

As for the *Sultana* herself, the Father of Waters soon erased all visible signs, and mud and silt completely covered the remains of the wreckage. Since then the river has changed its course, and whatever was left of the *Sultana* now lies under Arkansas soil.

49

Confederate Gold Was Scattered over Three Southern States

Any oldtimer in Wilkes County, Georgia, can spend an entire afternoon spinning tales of the lost gold of the Confederacy.

"Wilkes is the place to look for the metal," according to long-standing tradition. "Some folks believe it was scattered from South Carolina to Florida. Could be. But even after Lincoln County was set off—named for General Benjamin Lincoln, *not* for Abraham Lincoln—old Wilkes still had 470 square miles. That's enough swamp land and pine barrens to hide all the gold in Fort Knox for a hundred years—and Jefferson Davis didn't have Fort Knox; all he had was the Confederate treasury and what was left of the hard money in the Richmond banks."

The tale of the lost Confederate gold begins in Richmond, Virginia, on April 2, 1865. That is the day Jefferson Davis was interrupted during worship in St. Paul's church with an urgent dispatch saying that Grant and his men in blue had finally smashed through the lines at Petersburg.

Davis needed no detailed explanation. Once Petersburg went, Richmond would have to follow. Constance Gary, seated directly behind the president, later wrote, "With stern set lips and his usual quick military tread, he left the church. A number of other people rose in their seats and hastened after him. Those who were left were swept by a universal tremor of alarm."

Walking straight to the War Office to confer with John C. Breckinridge, Davis sent messengers to summon his cabinet members. Before they arrived, he got off a dispatch to General Robert E. Lee, urging him to hold out for one more day because a Sunday-night evacuation would threaten "the loss of many valuables, both for want of time to pack and of transportation."

Lee replied that the government should leave Richmond by 8:00

P.M. Then he added a long message in which he spelled out his plans for raising black recruits for his decimated regiments.

Since one railroad linking the capital with Danville was still in operation, the president had two special trains assembled. One was designed to transport key officials and members of their families to "a convenient point of safety." The other, assigned to Captain William H. Parker of the C.S.A. Navy, was designated as a special cargo train.

Parker, who knew that his freight would consist of double-eagle gold pieces, silver coins, gold ingots, silver bricks, and kegs of Mexican silver dollars from the Confederate treasury and the banks of Richmond, hastily assembled a special body of guards. Having no one else on whom he could call, he used midshipmen from a training vessel on the James River; some were as young as twelve.

Around midnight the two special trains left Richmond, unable to accommodate the scores of frightened civilians who begged to go along. Davis, his cabinet members, and his wife had started on what they at first expected would be a short journey that would take them safely behind Confederate lines. Instead, they were forced to extend their withdrawal, eventually splitting up and taking to horseback when the rail lines ended.

Following orders, Parker headed for Charlotte, North Carolina, and the old United States Mint building, which had been selected as a safe place in which to store millions in hard money. News that Union cavalry were on the march made Parker abandon the mint, first packing gold and silver into boxes, kegs, and bags that once held flour, coffee, sugar, and shot.

In a seesaw attempt to stay ahead of Federal forces, the treasure was sent through South Carolina and into Georgia, then recrossed the state line several times. Parker had turned the gold and silver over to John H. Reagan, C.S.A. acting secretary of the treasury. Reagan passed responsibility to Secretary of War Breckinridge, and Breckinridge immediately put Brigadier General Basil Duke in charge. Heading a body of less than one thousand men who constituted the only remaining Confederate force east of the Mississippi River, Duke put the treasure into six wagons and assigned eight veterans to guard each wagon.

Filing out of Abbeville, South Carolina, Davis and members of his cabinet, all on horseback, moved well ahead of the treasure-filled wagons. Their destination was Washington, Georgia, across the Savannah River and considered to be safely within Confederate control.

It was in the seat of justice of Wilkes County that the Confederate cabinet met for the last time. President Davis there signed his last official order, a document naming Captain Micajah Clark as acting treasurer of the Confederacy. Soon after having made that vital appointment, Davis rode south to escape the fast-closing Federal net. Six days later, on May 10, he was captured near Irwinville, Georgia. He still carried some of the gold set aside for him and his party in Washington, Georgia. Micajah Clark and others who had been present at the last cabinet meeting managed to reach Florida. Some of the gold they buried there was found years later.

Near Greensboro, North Carolina, each of Johnston's soldiers received transportation money after the surrender. From the money hauled south by train and then by wagon, veterans in gray each got $1.15 with which to get home. Parker's midshipmen and the men in Duke's tiny brigade fared better; each received $26.25 from the treasure train, with enlisted men treated the same as officers.

At Washington, Georgia, workmen hastily put a false bottom into a carriage to conceal a shipment of gold that was intended for Europe by way of Charleston, to establish a foreign bank account for the C.S.A. This money never reached its destination.

Bushwhackers, probably augmented by stragglers from the armies of Lee and Johnston, hit the Federal wagon train in which much confiscated Confederate treasure was being hauled from Washington, Georgia, to Washington, D.C., about the middle of May. Eliza Andrews, a Wilkes County resident who had firsthand knowledge of the incident, wrote that as bushwhackers left the scene of their strike, "they waded ankle-deep in gold and silver." According to her, many of the raiders "tied bags of gold to their saddles, riding away so heavily laden that they were compelled to discard much of their booty" in the swamps and forests of Wilkes and Lincoln counties.

Paper money that had been issued in Richmond was now worthless, and the debts of the C.S.A. and its member states would soon be repudiated. Slaves could no longer be counted as property, plantations everywhere were devastated, and the cities and towns were ruins of war. Hence those wagon loads of gold and silver constituted the only ready assets of the Confederacy.

Much of the treasure was buried or lost between Washington, Georgia, and the Savannah River, but some of it went into South Carolina and Florida. Even in 1865 the total was significant; today the precious metal that vanished in the storm created by the toppling of the Confederacy would be of immense value. That is the reason why the route of Jefferson Davis's flight constitutes a prime target for treasure hunters of the Space Age.

50

Ten Thousand Southern Leaders Went into Exile

Governor Charles S. Morehead of Kentucky was the first man into the water. July 4, 1865, had been selected for the dramatic crossing of the Rio Grande in the bid for personal independence on the part of one-time Confederate leaders.

Brigadier General Joseph O. Shelby, organizer of the band, solemnly took off the black plume that was his distinguishing mark and dropped it into the muddy water. As the leader of the Iron Brigade, he had made history by a forty-one-day raid of 1,500 miles in which property and supplies worth two million dollars were destroyed. Rebuffed when he offered his services to Mexico's Emperor Maximilian, soon to be deposed and executed, he accepted the ruler's invitation to establish a Confederate colony south of the U.S. border.

Shelby and Morehead were accompanied by Governor Pendleton Murrah of Texas, Governor Henry Allen of Louisiana, and Generals John B. Macgruder, Hamilton Bee, John B. Clark, Thomas Hindman, Sterling Price, Trusten Polk, William Hardeman, Danville Leadbetter, Monroe Parsons, and George Flournoy. Following the gesture of Shelby, other generals solemnly dropped battle flags into the water as they rode across the river that marked the beginning of a new kind of independence for them.

The flight of this band into Mexico was one of hundreds of postwar expeditions, mostly in groups of ten to fifty persons, that took a total of more than ten thousand southern leaders into foreign exile. The general amnesty proclaimed in Washington at the cessation of hostilities excluded "civil, diplomatic, and military leaders of the Confederacy."

Major Washington Goldsmith, veteran of several major engagements fought by his Georgia troops, teamed up with a Kentuckian and chose British Honduras as a haven. There they bought 150,000 acres at twenty-five cents an acre, developed splendid plantations, and attracted other refugees to the region. At its peak, this colony of expatriates numbered more than two hundred.

John Taylor Wood, grandson of President Zachary Taylor and nephew of Jefferson Davis, was aboard the C.S.A *Virginia* during its epic fight with the Union ironclad *Monitor*. He was made a captain in the Confederate navy as reward for his capture of the *Underwriter*, largest of all Union gunboats. Sitting with Davis in church when Lee's message came, he was with the presidential party in its flight and was captured with Davis. Wood bribed a guard to turn him loose and made his way through Florida to Cuba and then to Halifax, Nova Scotia, where he died in 1904, a self-described "loyal Confederate to the end."

Jefferson Davis, captured in May 1865, did not make it to Mexico or British Honduras, or anywhere else. Specifically excluded from any form of pardon or amnesty, he spent two years as a prisoner at Fort Monroe, Virginia, awaiting trial on a charge of treason. Eventually abolitionist Horace Greeley joined with other prominent northerners in signing a bail bond that set him free but stripped him of citizenship rights.

Jubal Early, so enraged at Washington's terms that he boasted that he could "scalp a Yankee woman and child without batting an eye," disguised himself as a farmer to make his escape to Mexico. He wandered through half a dozen countries before settling in Canada. At

Jubal Early, disguised as a farmer in order to make his escape from the United States. [LIEUTENANT GENERAL JUBAL EARLY, C.S.A. (1912)]

Niagara, Ontario, a colony of exiles was already flourishing. It included C.S.A. Commissioner to Britain James M. Mason, John B. Hood of Kentucky, and John S. Preston of Virginia, once a brigadier general. John C. Breckinridge, who had played the role of spoiler in the election of 1860 and who later became the Confederate secretary of war, chose the Niagara colony for what he called "personal reasons." Just across the border from New York, the site afforded easy viewing of the U.S. flag flying in the wind. A deeply emotional man who had opposed secession, Breckinridge said he got up early every morning to see Old Glory hoisted to the top of the flagpole.

Encouraged by Emperor Dom Pedro II of Brazil, Confederates established four large communities there. Collectively, they sheltered nearly four thousand political refugees. Villa Americana, about eighty miles north of São Paulo, eventually became just Americana, a haven that attracted a great-uncle of First Lady Rosalyn Carter.

Mexico's big Carlota colony, founded by the band of men who rode across the Rio Grande on July 4, failed to gain Matthew Fontaine Maury as a citizen refugee. His role as Confederate naval agent in Europe was not widely known; but throughout the scientific world he was honored as the founder of the science of meteorology and as the discoverer of the currents of the oceans. Instead of joining fellow exiles at Carlota or another of the half dozen flourishing Confederate centers in Mexico, Maury went to Mexico City where he was made director of the Imperial Observatory by Emperor Maximilian.

Only those Confederates who had managed to salvage part of their assets were welcomed in Great Britain, even though many Englishmen in high places had worked openly for Confederate interests and others were secret supporters of the C.S.A. Louis T. Wigfall, who tried to negotiate the surrender of Fort Sumter without authorization from Beauregard, fled to Texas and went into hiding upon the collapse of the Confederacy. Later the former brigadier general escaped to England for a six-year stay.

Judah P. Benjamin fled to England to escape arrest. It was not a quick and easy journey, however. Traveling initially with the party that left Washington, Georgia, for Florida, the fifty-four-year-old Benjamin arrived in the West Indies in disguise. Reaching London in 1866, he soon established himself as a barrister. Even when a new amnesty made it possible for most exiles to return to the United States, Benjamin stayed in his new home. As Queen's Counsel for Lancashire County, he had become so noted that he refused to accept any case for a fee of less than 300 guineas.

Brigadier General Robert Toombs was one of the few who fled into exile from his own home. He happened to be there when Jefferson Davis was captured at nearby Irwinville, Georgia. Union soldiers came

Some members of the family of C.S.A. Major General Sterling Price still wore life jackets from a shipwreck when photographed en route *to Mexico.* [MISSOURI HISTORICAL SOCIETY]

to his door, but Toombs managed to evade capture by pretending to help them hunt for General Toombs. Then he fled while his wife detained the search party.

Like Benjamin, Toombs made it to England by a roundabout journey. He stayed only two years, however, before deciding to risk a return to his Washington, Georgia, home to resume a once-thriving legal practice. As a regional celebrity, the former U.S. congressman, senator, and C.S.A. secretary of state was barred from again seeking a public office because he refused to take the required oath of loyalty to the United States. No other top leader who went into exile is known to have returned without taking that oath.

President Andrew Johnson lowered many barriers by his Christmas pardon in 1868. Under its terms, an unconditional pardon was granted to all war participants except "civil and military officials of high rank." These conditions persuaded an estimated 75 percent of the ex-Confederates to return to their homes. But the rest of them—perhaps 2,500 who had held high offices or military rank—never returned. Even in the half dozen bloodiest battles of the war, the South did not lose as many top leaders as it did in the departures that constituted the biggest wave of migration *from* the land of the free and the home of the brave the nation has ever seen.

CHAPTER

51

Staunch Unionist Andrew Johnson Was Labeled "Too Soft on the South"

With McClellan widely regarded as likely to defeat Lincoln in 1864, Republicans—briefly calling themselves Unionists—badly needed a vice presidential nominee who would strengthen the ticket. They settled upon staunch Unionist Andrew Johnson of Tennessee.

Radical Republicans, led by the Vermont-born chairman of the Ways and Means Committee of the House of Representatives, Thaddeus Stevens, had picked John C. Frémont as their own candidate. Stevens, who hoped that Frémont could siphon off enough votes to put McClellan in the White House, exploded when he heard that a Tennessean would run with Lincoln. "Couldn't the Republicans find a candidate without going down into one of those damned rebel provinces to pick one up?" he stormed.

Stevens—and most other national leaders—knew that Tennessee was no rebel province. When powerful men in the central and western parts of the state pushed through a secession resolution, many sections of East Tennessee, Johnson's home district, tried to secede from the state.

Whether or not Johnson's presence on the ticket helped Lincoln in his uphill battle for re-election is debatable. But Johnson's staunch pro-Union sympathies were not debatable; as a member of the U.S. Senate, he had refused to abide by his state's vote to pull out of the Union and remained in his senate seat until he was named military governor of Tennessee after Grant's early victories there.

With their state still a battleground, but no longer the focus of the fiercest fighting in the Western theater, Tennesseans complained bitterly about their military governor. Backed by Federal troops, he in-

A committee of seven prepared the indictment against Johnson. Its members included Thaddeus Stevens (third from left) *plus generals Benjamin Butler* (first), *James. F. Wilson* (second), *Thomas Williams* (fifth), *and "Blackjack" Logan* (sixth). [MATTHEW BRADY, LIBRARY OF CONGRESS]

stituted many measures that even some Unionists considered to be oppressive.

Controversial, he always was; soft, he never became. Yet he had hardly taken the oath of office as Lincoln's successor before Radical Republicans began castigating him as "too soft on the South." Paradoxically, his stance was sterner than the policies that Abraham Lincoln had announced for the postwar period.

Three weeks after entering the White House, the man who became president as a result of the bullet fired by John Wilkes Booth issued his first general proclamation. In it he announced that "armed resistance to the authority of the Government in the insurrectionary States may be regarded as at end." Then he named provisional governors as civil heads of seceded states. He also signed a special act giving financial relief to Mrs. Abraham Lincoln in the amount of $25,000.

Early in 1866, Johnson vetoed the Freedmen's Bureau bill even though he realized that it would bring new criticism. In a stinging message, the president charged that the Joint Committee on Reconstruction had been established by Congress to counter his own moderate views. He charged that a body of six senators and nine representatives, who were dominated by Thaddeus Stevens, was "an irresponsible central directory" that had seized "all the power of Congress."

The committee struck back. It issued a formal report laying out reasons why Congress, not the president, should shape the policies to be applied during "reconstruction" of seceded states.

Johnson was thunderstruck. As a senator, he had been one of the persons who drafted a congressional act in the aftermath of First Bull Run. With full support of Lincoln, lawmakers who backed military measures to suppress what they still called a "small rebellion" asserted that the purpose of Federal force was "to preserve the Union with all the dignity, equality, and rights of the several States unimpaired." Once these objects were accomplished, said Congress, hostilities should cease.

Johnson fumed that actions of the Thirty-seventh Congress were being ignored by the Thirty-ninth, whose members clearly had little or no interest in restoring a Union whose member states would have their "dignity, equality, and rights unimpaired."

With the president under increasing criticism from congressional leaders, lawmakers took matters into their own hands by means of a series of Reconstruction acts. Under their terms, the provisional civil governments established by Johnson in former Confederate states were dissolved and replaced by a system of military districts headed by federal generals. One by one, Johnson vetoed these acts; one by one, Congress overrode his veto. On March 2, 1867, the same day that the first Reconstruction Act was passed, Johnson vetoed a congressional measure entitled the Tenure of Office Act. Congress overrode the veto on the day it was issued.

Terms of the Tenure of Office Act prohibited the chief executive from removing civil officers without the consent of the Senate. Johnson saw in the act, which he held to be unconstitutional, a move to prevent him from removing Edwin M. Stanton, the president's thorn-in-the-flesh, as secretary of war.

It was Stanton who, following Lincoln's lead, had issued sweeping edicts under which Vallandigham and other opponents of the war were jailed without trial. Now Stanton was believed to be aligned with Stevens and his Radical Republicans who were seeking, not restoration of seceded states "with dignity," but revenge in every form. Stanton had first been seen to fume in public in December 1865 when Johnson issued a proclamation that revoked the long-standing suspension of *habeas corpus* in cases where persons were suspected of fomenting strife.

Preferring, if possible, not to trigger a confrontation with Congress, in early August Johnson asked Stanton to tender his resignation. A week later, when he refused to resign, Stanton was suspended from office by an executive order of August 1867. Johnson then named Ulysses S. Grant as the new secretary of state.

Congress seized upon what members termed a violation of their "wholly constitutional" Tenure of Office Act. As a result, the judiciary committee of the House of Representatives voted overwhelmingly in

The U.S. Senate, sitting as the court of impeachment [LIBRARY OF CONGRESS]

November to seek impeachment of the president "for high crimes and misdemeanors." Endorsement of that action by the full House followed immediately. Too feeble to walk into the chamber to cast his vote, Thaddeus Stevens was carried in upon a chair. Chief Justice Salmon P. Chase, whom many Republicans had wanted as their presidential nominee in 1864, presided over the trial by the U.S. Senate.

Ten specific charges were leveled at Johnson, plus an eleventh charge that summarized them all. When the crucial eleventh charge was put to vote, the prosecution fell one vote short of the number required for conviction. Strangely, though it was the Radical Republicans who led the fight against Johnson, it was the regular Republicans who saved him by consistently voting with the Democrats. Seven of them laid their political futures on the line by refusing to find the president guilty as charged. One of these Republicans, Edmund G. Ross of Kansas, held the swing vote. He was driven from public office because of his vote; much later he became a central figure in John F. Kennedy's famous book *Profiles in Courage*.

Once impeachment proceedings failed by a single vote, Johnson proceeded to remove Stanton from office and replace him with Brigadier General Lorenzo Thomas, an old foe of Stanton. Johnson's usefulness as chief executive was at an end, but the Roman circus of which he was the center persuaded lawmakers never again to consider impeachment proceedings except in the most extreme of cases.

Forty-nine years after the staunch Unionist, whom foes considered to be too easygoing during Reconstruction, was tried for having violated the Tenure of Office Act, the U.S. Supreme Court ruled the legislation unconstitutional.

52

Reconstruction Ended in Return for Yielding the White House to Hayes

T hough saved from conviction by a single vote when tried by the U.S. Senate, Andrew Johnson was helpless to prevent legislation that shaped Reconstruction in a fashion unlike that conceived by Abraham Lincoln. Federal troops were not fully withdrawn from former Confederate states until "the stolen election" was cinched two days before the inauguration of the nineteenth president of the United States.

Delighted to support Ulysses S. Grant in his bid for the White House, foes of Andrew Johnson rejoiced when the military leader won both the popular vote and that of the electoral college by a huge majority. Since returns from Arkansas and Louisiana were disputed in 1872, these were thrown out and not counted.

By 1876, the corruption of the Grant administration was enough to persuade Democrats that—for the first time since 1864—they had better than even odds to win the White House. On the eve of the election, it appeared clear that Republicans were, indeed, due to go down in defeat. "Tilden Is Elected," proclaimed a November 8 headline in the New York *Sun*. "Complete Democratic Victory," exulted the rival *Herald*. In Chicago the *Tribune* lamented that "Tilden, Tammany and the Solid South Are to Rule the Nation."

When votes cast on November 7 were counted, it was clear that the newspaper headlines had been accurate. New York's Samuel J. Tilden, the Democratic nominee, had 4,300,590 votes compared to 4,036,298 for Republican Rutherford B. Hayes of Ohio.

Hours before the popular vote totals were announced, Dan Sickles, who had lost a leg at Gettysburg, was returning home from the theater.

A fiercely Democratic cartoon derided the work of the Electoral Commission.

He stopped at Republican headquarters in New York City and found it deserted because Tilden supporters were already celebrating victory. Republican National Chairman Zach Chandler had gone home, leaving word not to disturb him.

Noted for quick decisions and rapid follow-up, Sickles briefly consulted Chester A. Arthur, who still used his Civil War title of Brigadier General of Volunteers. With the approval of Arthur, Sickles drafted telegrams to Republican governors of three southern states and sent them in Chandler's name. A few hours later, Chandler was persuaded to follow with a message of hope for the party: "Hayes is elected if we have carried South Carolina, Florida, and Louisiana. Can you hold your state? Answer immediately."

These messages went out because a careful count indicated that, although Tilden was nearly 300,000 votes ahead of Hayes, the Democrat had only 184 electoral votes solidly in his column, one short of the number required for victory. Before replies were received from the South, Chandler began assembling delegations to go to the three crucial states, with ample funds and code names under which to operate.

Already it was clear that tallies would be challenged in each of the three vital southern states. Hence President Grant entered the fray on November 10. He directed Sherman to use federal troops "to preserve peace and order during tabulation of votes."

South Carolina was already a battlefield. Governor Daniel H. Chamberlain, a carpetbagger who had come south to make his fortune, wanted more federal troops. Riots provided an excuse for using them. The worst of a series began in mid-September, spread over five counties, and saw 10,000 armed men roaming the countryside. In July 1875 South Carolina had been occupied by ten companies of infantry and two batteries of artillery; the size of the federal contingent was tripled by election day, 1876.

After the vote, both Chamberlain and his rival, Wade Hampton, claimed the State House. For a time, South Carolina not only had two governors but also two legislatures, one Republican and the other Democratic.

Florida saw less violence but at least as much manipulation of tallies as any other state. Manatee County went ten to one for Tilden and had its entire vote thrown out. Only twenty-six county returns went unchallenged. With two Republicans and one Democrat on the state canvassing board, that body eventually gave Hayes the state by a forty-five-vote margin.

Louisiana was, if possible, in even more confusion than Florida. A state-operated Returning Board accepted secret tabulations made by Republican clerks and held hearings from which local representatives were barred. All boxes from East Feliciana and Grant parishes were thrown out, along with sixty-nine boxes from twenty-two other parishes. That enabled the Republican-dominated body to report on December 6 that Hayes had carried the state.

Like South Carolina, Louisiana had two governors. One of them certified the count according to which Hayes was winner; the other, a Democrat, sent his own December 6 report in which he certified that Tilden was the winner.

Everywhere, there were rumors of resuming the Civil War. Federal troops were ordered to Washington from posts as distant as Leavenworth, Kansas. Units under Sherman's command drilled daily in public streets. A heavily armed warship was anchored within sight of the Capitol. Some members of Congress strapped on side arms before going to sessions.

Committees named by the two houses of Congress to deal with electoral challenges were hopelessly deadlocked from the start. With both Republicans and Democrats fearful that Grant might remain in office past the expiration of his term unless a successor was inaugurated, a compromise was hammered out in January 1877.

Under the terms of the compromise, the fate of the White House was placed in the hands of a special body created despite the lack of a constitutional provision for it. A special fifteen-member Electoral Commission would decide the disputed states. Five Democrats were solidly behind Tilden; five Republicans, including future President James A. Garfield, were united in support of Hayes; of the five members from the U.S. Supreme Court, two were Democrats, two were Republicans, and one was independent.

David Davis of Illinois, the independent on whom decisions of the special electoral commission were expected to hinge, was suddenly and strangely chosen by the legislature of his state to occupy a seat in

Dan Sickles, who lost a leg at Gettysburg, helped to make reunions popular.

the U.S. Senate on the very day that the Electoral Commission gained legal status. Since the high court had no other independent, Davis's empty spot was filled by Republican Joseph P. Bradley. As a result, every vote taken by the Electoral Commission was eight to seven in favor of Hayes.

Southerners used every possible delaying tactic and managed to prevent final action until Inauguration Day was imminent. Filibuster attempts remained alive until late February, when talk of a secret deal began to surface. Finally, on March 2 at 4:00 A.M., a joint session of Congress was informed that "Rutherford B. Hayes of Ohio, having received 185 electoral votes to Samuel J. Tilden's 184, is duly elected President of the United States for four years, commencing on the fourth day of March."

Few top-level southern political leaders protested at what later analysts almost always term "the stolen election," for their surrender of the White House carried with it compensation of a sort. When electoral votes of South Carolina, Florida, and Louisiana were thrown to Hayes, Republican leaders agreed to have federal troops withdrawn from these states.

A triumphant Hayes took the oath of office on March 4; twenty days later, federal troops moved out of their quarters adjacent to the Louisiana state house, the last capitol of the last carpetbag government. Twelve years after Lee had surrendered to Grant at Appomatox, the war was finally over.

Long before the military rule of the conquered South ended, many veterans of both the North and the South had buried old animosities. Soon after hostilities ended, men who had worn blue began to come together annually at Gettysburg, twice hallowed because of the enormous cemetery for Union dead and the unexpected impact of Abraham Lincoln's brief Gettysburg Address. Under the leadership of John A. Logan, reunions at Gettysburg helped to make the Grand Army of the Republic one of the most powerful political bodies ever.

By the time the war had been over for a decade, a few veterans who had worn gray began showing up for the Gettysburg reunions. Men from both sides felt that "the war ended when the last rifle was fired." Men who were earlier ready to kill one another camped together, ate together, and swapped stories together. An occasional black veteran was glad-handed by former Union and Confederate soldiers alike. Dan Sickles, who masterminded the stolen election, sat in his wheel chair surrounded by former comrades and former enemies who could be distinguished from one another only by shoulder patches and medals.

The aftermath of the war ended much earlier at Gettysburg than it did in Washington. There the strong hand of such long-time abolitionists as Thaddeus Stevens formed the Reconstruction Committee of Congress which oversaw the former Confederate states. A creation of the Radical Republicans, the Reconstruction Committee continued to rule the South until the election of 1876 provided these states with the opportunity to regain home rule in 1877.

With the subsequent return of the southern aristocracy to the position it enjoyed before the war, many of the old lines of authority and power were re-established, and those who had felt the oppressive yoke of slavery confronted new difficulties. An elaborate set of new laws, called Black Codes, was established, and ex-slaves were reduced to a new form of subjugation that went largely unchallenged until the emergence of the Civil Rights movement of the mid-twentieth century.

The Union had been preserved—at a terrible cost—but those who had seen the conflict through to its bitter conclusion soon turned to other interests. In retrospect it seems reasonable to ask why—*really why*—so great a price was paid for ideas that ultimately were set aside as men divided the spoils.

From Start to Finish,
It Really Was
Abraham Lincoln's War

Novelists frequently report that their chief character takes over and dictates the action. In this volume of non-fiction one person—Abraham Lincoln—did precisely that, in a fashion not planned or expected.

A Southerner by birth and a Unionist by conviction, Lincoln emerges as the larger-than-life central figure in the colossal drama of the North/South conflict. Clearly, Lincoln had no great interest in abolition, or even in the slavery question, as such. His one life-dominating goal, in which he succeeded against great odds, was the preservation of the Union, no matter what the cost to him personally, to the embattled sections, or to families and individuals caught up in a struggle that few fully understood.

It is not an exaggeration to label our nation's bloodiest conflict as "Abraham Lincoln's war." Had he not won the White House in 1860, events could not have taken the course they did.

Pledged to preserve the Union, the chief executive skillfully jockeyed secessionists into firing the first shots at Fort Sumter. Had he called Congress into session it would have been difficult or impossible to have gotten a declaration of war. So in order to wage undeclared war, he raised troops for his ninety-day militia, and when their terms were about to expire, he bulldozed reluctant military leaders into decisions that led to the fiasco at First Bull Run.

The nation teetered on the brink of military dictatorship during months in which Lincoln deliberately violated the Constitution for the sake of the war effort. His skillful selection of prominent Democrats for top military posts was part of the overall plan to win, regardless of what victory might require.

Now hailed as an epochal move toward a more equitable social order, Lincoln's Emancipation Proclamation was part of his war strategy, not a bid for social justice. It came only after he had twice countermanded emancipation edicts of his own generals, and only when he judged its timing psychologically right. Significantly, no slave owner in Union territory suffered financial losses as a result of the proclamation, and no slaves in areas not in rebellion gained their freedom. It was a superb thrust at the jugular of the Confederacy, but it clearly was not a carefully constructed move toward social justice for black Americans.

Finally, Lincoln barred the way to an earlier peace. His adamant refusal to discuss any terms less than absolute submission and return to the Union made peace movements—Northern as well as Southern—futile until the Confederacy was battered to its knees.

All this will lead many readers of this collection of tales to ponder a momentous question: "What would have taken place in the 1860s and thereafter had Lincoln not emerged as the dominant actor in the national drama?"

While any answer must include conjecture, clusters of well-established facts suggest a likely scenario. With no leader possessing the personal impact of Lincoln, the bitter conflict would have continued and eventually South Carolina and a handful of other hard-line pro-slavery, states' rights states would have seceded. Virginia (and hence Robert E. Lee) would have remained in the Union, and British success with cotton in India, leading to breakup of the southern cotton monopoly, would have created economic chaos in the already-faltering, one-crop economy of seceded states. Within a few decades—perhaps within a single generation—the cotton/slavery culture would have collapsed. Seceded states would have sued for readmission to the Union, perhaps under a plan of gradual emancipation with compensation of slave owners.

Such a train of developments would not have preserved the Union intact *at all times*, but even Lincoln failed at this objective. Had seceding states been permitted to go their own way, the Union would have been restored—bloodlessly—in relatively few years and at social and economic cost almost unbelievably low by comparison with that of the Civil War and Reconstruction.

Index

Numbers in *italic* refer to illustrations.